The Logic of Hindu Thought

Dr. Vilas D. Nene

To the countless Hindu thinkers of the past

Illustrations: Nandini Sathaye
Cover Design: Donna T. Campbell
Graphic Design: Communications by Design
© 2002, Dr. Vilas Nene
ISBN 0-9718927-0-9

Devan Publishing
2098 Robin Way Court
Vienna, VA 22182

Contents

Part II - The Art of Hindu Living
(The Rules of Ethical Behavior)

Part III – The Great Indian Epics
(Hindu Ethics by Example)

Preface

Indians, a majority of them Hindus, have been coming to the United States in large numbers since the late 1960's. Initial immigrants were mostly professionals, and after acquiring United States citizenship, they sponsored members of their immediate families who became the next wave of Indian immigrants. By the beginning of this millennium, there were over a few million Indian Hindus living in the United States, and now even the second-generation Hindu children are in their teens and twenties.

As a first order of business, these Hindu immigrants established themselves financially. Financial stability was achieved rather painlessly, mainly because of the professional background of the first wave of immigrants, and also because of the post-civil-rights liberal environment in the United States. Then, as a part of the effort in establishing their cultural identity in the United States, the Indian immigrants formed various local cultural organizations, usually based on their mother tongues: Marathi, Gujarati, Hindi, and others. These organizations provided a very useful and effective mechanism for satisfying the cultural needs of various groups. Consequently, these organizations have continued to flourish, although most of their yearly activities have become largely predictable. With the needs for fiscal stability and cultural identity satisfied, the

Hindu community is now focusing its attention on establishing a unique religious identity for itself. Several Hindu temples have been built within large metropolitan areas. New ones are also being built, although not in large numbers, simply because of the financial resources required to build and run a temple. Understandably, both the cultural organizations and the temples are serving the interests and the needs of primarily the first generation immigrants who felt the need to establish these. Unfortunately, most of the second generation does not really understand the cultural programs and the religious services offered by these organizations. Consequently, it has, more or less, kept its distance from the activities of these organizations.

It is inherently difficult for the second-generation Hindu children to establish their cultural and religious identities in such an environment. Presently, the temples simply attempt to recreate what goes on in temples in India, and routinely present a number of conventional rituals. The children simply do not understand any of these rituals and question their benefits, spiritual or otherwise. It is quite unrealistic to expect them to blindly participate in these activities. It is, therefore, necessary for all Indians to take a strategic view on the long-term survivability of the temples and various cultural organizations. The parents must boldly face this challenge and help the future generations in their quest for a Hindu identity.

The younger generation must also confront this challenge with courage. Clearly, they will face several major difficulties in their search for religious identity. Hindu way of life, as practiced today in India, in the United States, and in other countries is full of questionable rituals. Some Hindus in Malaysia, for example, torture themselves through bizarre body piercing in service to their God. This practice is no different than the self-whipping with heavy metal chains practiced by Shia Muslims, or self-whipping practiced in Spain by some Christians. One must search beyond these rituals to understand and enjoy the logic of Hindu Thought. Unfortunately, however, many parents have not searched this for themselves. Consequently, they are ill equipped to guide their children in understanding the lofty formulations of the Hindu Thought. They ask their children to *accept, not question.* Hindu Thought has always asked everyone to do just the opposite — *question, not accept.* Finally, there is really a lack of books in English on Hindu Thought that will hold the attention of the second and subsequent generations of Hindu children. There are hundreds of books on the subject, but the style, the language, and the vocabulary of these books are all outdated and quite alien to these children. These authors also use and simply transliterate hundreds of original Sanskrit words. Frankly, this is quite distracting for someone who has not grown up in India, and makes these books difficult to read.

I have always felt that we should not leave the upcoming generations of Hindu children ill equipped and helpless in facing the identity crisis that each of them will surely face someday. This problem is not of their making, and they should not have to face it alone. It is my sincere hope that we take this responsibility very seriously and help our children in this regard. This book is written expressly with that purpose in mind. More fundamentally, however, I want them to experience the ultimate reality — Brahman. Consequently, I have presented the Hindu Thought using contemporary style, language, and vocabulary that are consistent with the state of modern scientific knowledge. I have also attempted to establish a new paradigm in explaining the complex formulations of Hindu philosophy. Furthermore, I have used, excluding proper names, a very limited set of original Sanskrit words, most of which are already in use in English language.

Ancient Hindu thinkers developed various formulations of the Hindu Thought, some dating back several thousands of years. Some of these thinkers, unconstrained by the pride of authorship and copyrights, have not even left a trace of their names with their writings. I am greatly indebted to these uncountable heroes from the past. I must also thank all the students who have asked me questions during my lectures on

Hindu Thought at various American schools. These students have provided me with a window on the young American mind, and have helped me better understand their need for a spirituality that is consistent with modern science. I wish to thank Nandini Sathaye of Annandale, Virginia, a rare combination of artistic talent and spirituality, for all the excellent illustrations she prepared for this book. She is a close family friend and I am greatly indebted to her for her illustrations. Thanks are also due to Donna T. Campbell, a close friend and a colleague, for designing the beautiful cover for this book. She has truly captured the essence of Hindu Thought — individuals connecting with the universe and experiencing their identity with the ultimate reality of God. I also wish to thank a close friend, Carl Swanson of Vienna, Virginia, who read the manuscript carefully and made some very valuable suggestions.

1. Introduction

It is not easy to precisely define what we mean by the word *religion*. Broadly it refers to an institutionalized set of sacred beliefs related to God and other holy entities, observances, and individual as well as congregational practices in certain cultural context. Irrespective of how one chooses to define God, religion usually includes prayer and worship of God, and it is generally assumed that the religious beliefs are held with passion and faith. In addition, people have generally come to accept a certain hierarchical organization that oversees and regulates the religious activities of the congregation. An *ism*, on the other hand, does not necessarily relate to anything holy or sacred, although it is generally associated with doctrinaire, dogmatic, dictatorial, and cultish behavior. Considering all these various characteristics, one cannot really talk about a Hindu-religion or a Hindu-ism. Hindus are neither organized hierarchically nor do they exhibit any congregational behavior. They certainly are not doctrinaire or cultish. Precisely for these reasons, the title of this book contains the words Hindu Thought, and not Hindu Religion or Hinduism.

It is also almost taken for granted that various pronouncements by a religion do not have to be consistent with either logic or science. Religious leaders always remind the people that these pronouncements simply have to be taken on blind faith. If anyone commits the sin of independent thinking and points out that certain religious dictum is in complete contradiction with any known scientific fact, he is usually pushed back with anger and contempt. "Why are you asking such inconvenient questions? You know we are talking about religion here." is the usual reaction. Somehow, people do not see any problem in allowing religious books or leaders to make blatantly illogical or unscientific pronouncements. Such blind faith is usually based on the fear of God or eternal hellfire drilled into people's minds in their childhood, and the blind faith, in turn, appears to be encouraging religious zealots into making even more illogical and unscientific pronouncements. Religious leaders have somehow escaped accountability for anything related to religion. When they refer to God's word, no one stops them and asks how does one know it to be the God's word, or for that matter, if God exists in the suggested form. Moreover, with so many editions of God's word, how does one know who is right? Hindu Thought, however, does not differentiate between philosophical and scientific inquiries. It maintains that both should be based on logic, and any conclusions drawn by either of these inquiries must be consistent and in agreement with everyday experiences. One may scream at the top of his head and proclaim that you would not come down and hit the ground when you jump off the roof if you prayed long enough and with strong enough conviction. Anyone taking this pronouncement on faith will surely be seriously injured, and may even lose his life. Hindu thought never accepted *believe blindly, do not question* approach. It, in fact, insisted that one should *always question, and not believe blindly.*

Let me tell a short story here to illustrate a point. A blind man goes to his friend's house for dinner. After the dinner, the dessert, and a nice conversation, he decides to head back home. As he starts to leave, his host says that it is getting dark and gives him a lantern to carry. The blind man thinks that the host is playing a cruel trick and tells him so. The host then assures him that it is no joke, and that if he carried the lantern, others on the road will see him and not bump into him. The blind man understands the sincerity of the host and starts walking back home, confident that the lantern he was carrying will save him from the danger of collisions. After a few minutes on the road, however, a person bumps into the blind man. The blind man asks the stranger: "Are you blind? Can't you see me? I am even carrying a lantern in my hand." The stranger feels sorry for the blind man. He says: "I am sorry I bumped into you. I am not blind, but you must surely be blind. You are carrying your lantern without realizing that it is not burning. May be it has run out of fuel or the wind blew it out." Unfortunately, too many people following various organized religions are like that blind man. Every Hindu that practices only the ritualistic part of Hindu Thought is also like that blind man. They are all carrying the lantern of religion without realizing that it is not burning. Such lanterns are of no help, give a false sense of security, and are, in fact, a burden to carry.

Several of my colleagues including some from the National Aeronautics and Space Administration (NASA) have talked to me about a conflict of conscience they have had to face over the years. During the weekdays on their jobs, they designed space rockets, communications satellites, and interplanetary probes. On the weekends, however, they sat and listened to the religious babble that many considered being God's word. Clearly this was very stressful for them, and they asked me if I face any such problem. Fortunately, the core of Hindu Thought does not put faith ahead of logic or science. Hindu thinkers of the past have thought long and hard about the basic question every inquiry must face — *how do we know what we know?* This fundamental question has been debated extensively in the first few sections of this book.

Hindu Thought has also taken an integrated and holistic approach in debating and resolving various issues such as the nature of God and the Cosmos, faith, worship, prayer, right and wrong, individual and collective ethics, and salvation, if any. The Hindu Thought is essentially an inquiry into the nature and working of the Cosmos, into how and where we as individuals fit into this Cosmos, and ultimately it is an inquiry into how one should direct and conduct one's pursuit of happiness. We need to clearly understand the Cosmos so that this pursuit on our part is consistent with the cosmic rules of the game. Only then it could possibly be successful. This inquiry, like others, covered two basic directions: the science of Hindu Thought and the art of Hindu Thought. This dual approach is no different from, for example, the study of music or architecture. A professor of music is an expert in the science of music. He can talk about different standards of rhythm, melody, harmony, and notation. He can recite in detail the history of music. He surely can describe how an Indian musician and the accompanying instrumentalist carry on spontaneous imitation against the rhythms of the drums, and how this is possible only because they all adhere strictly to the rigid rules of melody. Just because he is a professor of music, however, he may not necessarily sing well. He may have studied the science of music, but may not have mastered the art of music. On the other hand, some other person may be a great singer, and may hold huge crowds spellbound for hours with his exciting music. He may thus have clearly mastered the art of music, but he may not necessarily know anything about an octave or about Pythagorean tuning.

The science of Hindu Thought presents various metaphysical formulations including Monism, the Law of Karma, and the concept of Liberation. Monism declares that there is no difference or duality between God and the universe. Every component of the universe including all animals and plants, and all non-living matter is just a projection of the ultimate reality that is God. Just as all golden ornaments such as necklaces or rings bear a monist relationship with a pot of gold, the universe has a monist relationship with God. A bale of cotton, a spool of thread, a piece of cloth, and a cotton shirt similarly bear a monist relationship among each other. The Law of Karma proclaims that each one of us is fully responsible for our own actions, and must bear the fruits of these actions. This causal relationship between our actions and their fruits extends well beyond just one life-and-death cycle; it spans the seemingly endless journey of each one of us towards our ultimate liberation from these life-and-death cycles. There is no confession behind a screen, and there certainly are no passes to the heaven. One simply cannot buy his way out of the clutches of this Law of Karma. The concept of liberation is the ultimate in simplicity. Liberation is nothing but waking up to the ultimate reality, the reality of God. Just as one wakes up from the dream world of sleep to the dualist reality of the day to day life, one simply wakes up from this dualist reality to the monist reality of God. All of these metaphysical formulations of Hindu Thought are expounded in great detail in the following chapters. The art of Hindu living, on the other hand, essentially addresses the rules of ethical behavior and provides a basis for conducting one's affairs in the day-to-day life. There are no edicts such as *thou shalt not do this or that.* The rules of ethical behavior are primarily based on the twin invariants of truth and non-violence with certain caveats. The rules are based on the phase of one's life as well as on one's profession. Clearly, the rules of behavior must be different for a six-year-old student than those for a three-star General trained to fight a war. These rules of behavior are also covered here in some detail in the following chapters.

Finally, short versions of the two lengthy Hindu epics of *Ramayan* and *Mahabharat* are presented. These epics are not history or biography. They are part of Hindu mythology. Persons and events portrayed in the literature are known to have an enormous influence on national character, sometimes more so than the actual historical heroes and events. Ramayan and Mahabharat are two such works that have continued to influence Indians, learned and illiterates alike, for several thousand years. Ramayan, written by Valmiki, is a story of the eldest prince of Ayodhya, Ram, the incarnation of Lord Vishnu. It describes Ram's childhood, his marriage to King Janak's daughter — Princess Sita, his long exile by a palace intrigue, his rescuing of Sita who is kidnapped by the demon king

Ravan, his triumphant return to Ayodhya, banishment of Sita, and final return of Sita to her heavenly abode. Its translations into other languages are also of great literary merit and are very popular all over India and Far East. Ramayan portrays Ram, Sita, Ram's three brothers, and several other characters as ideal role models who exhibit the best in humans, and who exhibit an unparalleled courage of conviction. Mahabharat, written by Vyas, is an intricate story of a family feud that ends up in a civil war between cousins. In addition, it is an exposition of Hindu code of conduct, covering from the proper conduct of a king to the proper conduct of ordinary people in times of calamity. Above all, it contains the Bhagawat Gita, one of the noblest of Hindu scriptures. Some of the characters of Mahabharat are portrayed as negative role models; they exhibit irresponsible behaviors that lead to unimaginable suffering to innumerable people. They let their ungodly emotions dictate their behaviors.

These epics are stories of heroic men and women, some of whom are divine. They describe a certain philosophy of human relationships, and handle varied subjects such as politics, diplomacy, diplomatic immunity, separation of state and religion, division of government powers, crime and punishment, medical ethics, war crimes, adoption, and women's rights. They teach ethics to the common man by presenting examples of how the different characters in these epics behaved in response to various situations facing them. These epics also illustrate that each one of us has choices to make, and there are always a number of good alternatives that will advance us on the path of liberation. We make wrong choices when we identify ourselves only with our bodies, we forget our essential monist identity, and we succumb to the ungodly qualities of anger, greed, jealousy, and others. I would urge the readers to quickly get to the heart of these epics and assess for themselves the experience of bliss that millions of Hindus continue to experience via these epics.

Part I – The Metaphysics of Hindu Thought

2. Process of Hindu Inquiry

The premise of Hindu Thought is incredibly simple: if we understand the Universe and the ultimate reality it represents, we all will be better equipped to pursue what is in our ultimate interest. The operative word here is *ultimate.* Our pursuit of happiness is really a tradeoff between a vast spectrum of alternatives, each consisting of varying levels of short- and long-term pain and happiness. This tradeoff is heavily influenced by a complex set of our social and cultural environment and experiences. On a very mundane level, we choose to suffer the short-term pain of surgical procedures so that we can be happy over a longer term. Given similar circumstances, different people make different choices depending on their concept of their ultimate interest. Some terminally ill patients who continually suffer extreme pain decide to bring an end to their life at a time of their choosing. Some others under exactly the same condition choose the life of pain; they believe that God must have willed it that way for a reason, and if they commit suicide, they will suffer eternally in hell. Here they are making a choice between short-term suffering and long-term suffering, based obviously on their conceptual model of a universe ruled by God's will. If the model is wrong to begin with, their choice of life with pain can hardly be justified as in their ultimate interest when they define their ultimate interest solely on the basis of this false model. On another level, freedom fighters from South Africa, China, and other dictatorial regimes have willingly suffered long intolerable imprisonment simply for asserting the concept of freedom and sovereignty of people. Under similar conditions, however, thousands of others have chosen life under the dictatorship attempting to make the best of a bad situation. Individuals like Mahatma Gandhi and Martin Luther King chose civil disobedience and non-violent struggle, whereas others chose armed struggle to achieve their goals. In recent times, hundreds of Christians and Buddhists have happily gone to communist jails instead of renouncing their faith. Over the past centuries, however, millions of people under the threat of death converted to Christianity and Islam. Clearly all these people acted in what they thought to be in their ultimate interest based on their specific concept of the universe. Reasonable people may, and in fact do, disagree on what is in their ultimate interest, and how valuable it is to them. However, they all generally agree with the concept of different levels of interests, and possibly the notion of an ultimate interest.

People generally have a notion of multiple levels of reality. When young children get all excited about making hundreds of thousands of dollars in a game of *Monopoly,* the adults do not share that excitement, but they continue to play along anyway. Some children, for example, want to have all their money in high denomination notes; the adults, of course, promptly exchange their high-dollar bills for the children's loose change. For adults, it is not real money; real money is something we can use to buy things. Even with real money, we make distinctions based on the source of the money. When someone makes money by selling drugs or by cheating old retirees of their hard-earned pension funds, not only do we not value that person, but we do not value that money as well. That money can buy things just as well as the money earned by honest people. But somehow, the money earned by cheating others does not seem to be right. Its level of reality is, for some, not at par with that of money honestly earned. Here we are imposing levels of reality on money. We also come across several other examples of levels of reality. Children drive fast cars in video parlors, and airline pilots fly simulators to train for abnormal flight scenarios. Both are not real, although all will agree that flight simulators are much closer to the reality than the video parlor cars. These and other systems are a growing part of a brand new scientific discipline of Virtual Reality, or simply VR. One criterion of evaluating a VR is *participant immersion;* it is the level of immersion it offers the user or the viewer. In the video parlor example, the driver of the car is the participant. In older versions, a video screen placed in front of the driver showed a car moving on a winding road. The driver used a steering wheel, the brakes, an accelerator, and the transmission gears to drive the car on the screen. Since the children really do not feel that they are driving actual cars, the participant immersion provided by these electronic games is quite poor. The flight simulators are much better in that sense. The pilots sit in a cockpit similar to that in the real plane, and see recorded scenes representing what they would actually see while landing at different airports. In newer VR systems, the participant can use a head-mounted display, and feel as if he is experiencing the real world. For example, he can conduct a walk-through in a VR building and evaluate the building design; the participant can move from room to room by simply moving a joystick back and forth. In a VR living room, for example, he can see where the furniture is placed by just turning his head from left to right. He can also use force-sensitive data gloves, and pick up objects within the VR and move them around to assess alternative arrangements. With the availability of fast computers with large memory, the VR technology is advancing very fast and now even some sense of smell immersion is possible. The participant may be able to smell different foods in the VR kitchen or different after-shaves in the VR bathroom. Of course, he can exit the VR world by simply removing the head-mounted display. The participant immersion provided by these systems is of a very high quality when compared even to the flight simulators. We all thus experience various levels of reality. Who is then to say that the reality of our day to day life is the ultimate reality, simply because it seems to offer an apparently full participant immersion?

We are, of course, free to have our own separate concepts of ultimate reality. A significant majority, however, will at least agree on the notion of an ultimate reality.

Cosmos or Chaos?

Any inquiry must necessarily begin with the most important question: "Is there anything to inquire about?" Is the universe around us an orderly, harmonious, holistic, synergistic, and a systematic entity, that is, is it a Cosmos? Or is it just a disorderly, unorganized, and confused entity where everything is left to chance, that is, is it simply a Chaos? Chaotic does not imply statistical or probabilistic in nature. Although they are not individually deterministic, the statistical systems are quite orderly. They are predictable in a statistical sense, and every prediction can be associated with a specific confidence level. In a chaotic universe, on the other hand, chance is supreme, and one cannot then associate any level of confidence to any prediction related to the behavior of the universe. If the universe is a Cosmos, then one could possibly examine it and discover how it operates. If, however, it is a Chaos, it will be a tragic waste of time to look for some law governing the universe — a law that does not exist to begin with. It would be like someone who searches in the living room for something he has lost in the family room simply because there is light in the living room and the family room is dark.

When all the scientific evidence is evaluated, as the early Hindu philosophers demonstrably did, it is quite clear, except possibly to the present members of the Flat Earth Society, that there is order and harmony in the universe. The natural satellites orbit around their parent planets. Moon orbits around the Earth. Io, Europa, Ganymede, Callisto, and its fourteen other known satellites orbit around Jupiter. Triton orbits around Neptune, and Saturn's twenty moons similarly orbit around Saturn. The planets of our solar system, in turn, orbit around the Sun in elliptic orbits. The orbital periods of the planets vary from 88 Earth-days for the closest planet Mercury to 248.5 Earth-years for the farthest planet Pluto. These cyclical periods are very small when compared to the orbit of the Sun around the center of our Milky Way galaxy. The Sun completes one orbit in about 250 million years at a speed of about 500,000 miles per hour. There are, in addition, several other cyclical motions such as, for example, the wobble of Earth's axis over 26,000 years, the Sun's crossing the mid plane of Milky Way once every 30 million years, and the Sun's crossing of spiral arms of Milky Way once every 100 million years. The stars and the galaxies in this universe appear to be following specific laws of motion for the past billions of years. Various phenomena across the universe also appear to be governed by known laws of physics and chemistry. Clearly, the universe is a cosmos and not a chaos.

Scientific Approach

Once the Hindu thinkers decided that the universe was a cosmos, they then proceeded to examine and understand it. First, they took a scientific approach as they proceeded with this inquiry. One of the most important characteristics of a scientific approach is to go from *the known to the unknown.* We begin by examining that part of the universe that is observable to us. We make use of all our senses and any tools and instruments we may have, and collect as much data as possible about what is observable. As our tools and instruments improve, more and more portions of the universe become observable to us. We then examine the collected data and make a hypothesis that will tentatively explain all the available data. A hypothesis tacitly implies that the data available for analysis may very well be insufficient, and the hypothesis may have to be radically modified or occasionally may even have to be discarded, as additional data becomes available. A real scientist proposing a hypothesis does not exhibit a *know-it-all* arrogance; he only has an honest desire to learn the truth. A hypothesis proposes laws that govern the behavior of different components of the universe. In addition to explaining the observations, it allows us to derive certain logical as well as empirical consequences of the hypothesis; that is, it allows us to predict the behavior of different components of the universe under certain conditions. We then conduct controlled experiments and gather additional data that will help us verify these predictions. If this additional data is consistent with the predictions, our confidence in the hypothesis increases, and we then know a little more about the universe than before. If, however, the additional data is inconsistent with the predicted behavior, we first repeat the experiment and make sure that our data is correct. If the data is found to be correct and still inconsistent with the predictions, we do not punish or hang the person who collected the data. We conclude that the hypothesis is flawed, step back, and develop a modified or a completely new hypothesis that is consistent with all the old data as well as with the new data that was inconsistent with the old hypothesis. Every time a hypothesis is proposed, it must explain all the data available up to that point in time. All it takes to disprove any hypothesis is one single valid data point that is inconsistent with the hypothesis. This is how we proceed, step-by-step, and incrementally go from the known to the unknown.

Consider, for example, the scientific developments related to the effect of gravity on light rays. Isaac Newton proposed that light rays consisted of minute particles called *corpuscles* and that these particles had a finite mass. He predicted that light rays will bend in the vicinity of massive bodies such as stars, and he also estimated the expected amount of deflection of these rays. Since this deflection was too small to be measured with the then available instruments, this prediction by Newton could not be verified at the time. Einstein's theory of light was, however, vastly different from that of Newton. He said that light was massless, and the light rays bend in the vicinity of massive objects such as stars because the spacetime itself gets distorted around these objects. In the early 1900's, accurate astronomical telescopes were available and scientific measurements were made to distinguish between the two models of light by Newton and Einstein. Unfortunately, observations made by Eddington in 1919 were not precise enough due to adverse weather conditions. Three years later, however, the staff at the Lick Observatory in Australia made accurate observations during the solar eclipse; these observations conclusively proved that Einstein's hypothesis was right. This is precisely how sciences like physics, chemistry, and others progress, and there is no reason why philosophical inquiry into the Cosmos should not follow the same path.

Let us now examine what happens when we go from *the unknown to the known*. Here we put the cart before the horse, and let the tail wag the dog. We first make, without any basis in reality, certain pronouncements describing the unknown. Next, we try to fit the known into this absurd model. When someone makes observations that are contrary to our model, we get angry, and if we are in power, we may even hang the observer. Our arrogance of power, our conviction that we are the chosen few, and more importantly, our stupidity keeps us from accepting the inevitable, and the truth is sacrificed.

In the *geocentric* model of the universe, the Sun, the planets, and the stars all moved around the Earth while the Earth stayed still in space. This model is pretty simple and appears to be consistent with the daily experience of the millions of people that the Earth seems stationary while the Sun and the stars in the sky are seen to be rising and setting each day. This model existed long before a sacred scripture included a statement that "Joshua commanded the Sun to stand still." Since the Sun, and not the Earth, was commanded to stand still, Sun must be moving, and not the Earth. Well, that was enough for some to verify that the universe is Earth-centered. There is nothing wrong with anyone proposing this geocentric model as an initial hypothesis. What is not acceptable, however, is for some church to declare, based on a scripture, that God had confirmed the geocentric model, and that geocentrism was God's law.

Once the Church got involved, no one could, without seriously endangering one's life, question the Earth-centered model developed by Ptolemy in the second century. What was common knowledge in India at the time now became blasphemy in Europe. This state of affairs continued for over a thousand years when, in 1543, Copernicus proposed a *heliocentric* model for the Solar system. In this model, the Sun was at the center of the solar system, and the Earth was just another planet like Mars, Jupiter, and others orbiting around the Sun. This, however, was not what the Catholic Church wanted to hear. It declared that Copernicus' work was forbidden and would stay that way until corrected. The *reformer* Martin Luther called Copernicus a fool. Some even suggested that Copernicus did not really believe in the heliocentric model, but had proposed it to simplify calculations related to the planetary motions. The Catholic and the Protestant Churches continued to insist on a geocentric model, and continued to harass the supporters of the heliocentric model. Kepler for example, who introduced the concept of elliptic orbits, was in 1598 exiled forever from Graz. Galileo, who was the first one to use an optical telescope for studying planetary motion, spent years in gathering data that supported the heliocentric Keplerian model. The Catholic Church still remained unconvinced; it insisted that God was on its side. It again declared that heliocentrism explicitly contradicted the sense of Holy Scripture, and consequently, was heretical. The Church brought Galileo to trial in 1633 for suspicion of heresy and put him under house arrest outside Florence, Italy. It took almost 350 years before Pope John Paul appointed a commission in 1981 to review the Galileo case. The commission took over a decade to come to a conclusion in 1992. Their conclusion was even more revealing than the original action against Galileo. They concluded that the Vatican or the Church did not make any mistake; apparently there was some misunderstanding on the part of the majority of theologians at that time. The commission completely ignored the fact that Pope Paul V had approved the condemnation of Copernicanism and that Pope

Urban VIII had approved the verdict against Galileo. Popes, in the Commission's mind, are infallible and do not make mistakes.

The same story was essentially repeated with scientific theories related to the age of the universe, evolution of life, and innumerable other profound subjects. When millions of people readily surrender their rationality and logic to anyone who professes to be the one and only messenger of God, the truth is a sure casualty.

The development of Hindu Thought has meticulously avoided such a dangerous path. The metaphysical formulations proposed over time by various thinkers cover a very wide spectrum. Early formulations were modified when necessary, without any protestation either by their authors or their supporters. Even today, anyone is free to suggest alternative formulations without the fear of having a price put on his head by some fundamentalist Hindu fanatic.

Internal Consistency and Universal Application

The Hindu thinkers also insisted on internal consistency and universal applicability of their propositions. Internal consistency requires that different propositions be not in conflict with each other. As an example, we should not say that God is all merciful, and at the same time say that he sends people to eternal hellfire with no way out. We should not say that God is all-powerful, and at the same time say that he is powerless against Satan and cannot simply ask him to cease his activities. These statements are not internally consistent with each other. Universal applicability implies that all laws of physics, chemistry, and other sciences are valid across the entire universe and for all times, that is, across the entire spacetime of our relativistic universe. There is no Confucian physics or Buddhist chemistry; philosophical propositions should be no different and should be as universal as electromagnetism and thermodynamics. Physicists are attempting to develop a unified field theory that would be valid for all times beginning with the Big

Bang itself. A stone has always fallen to earth whether it is dropped from the Tower of London or from the Tower of Pisa, and it will fall to the Earth for all times to come. Similarly, the causal relationship between the probability of a man going to the heaven, if one exists in the proposed model of the universe, and his actions should be independent of external factors such as, for example, if he was born in the Vatican on Ash Wednesday, or if he had bought a ticket to the heaven from a local priest. The proposed metaphysics of the universe, in other words, must be spacetime invariant.

Let us, for example, examine a proposition that one cannot go to heaven (whatever and wherever it is) unless one is blessed personally, either by a messenger of God that lived over 2000 years ago or by his designated representative(s) living today. With such a proposition, it is obvious that all those who lived and died before the above messenger was even born are condemned forever to hellfire, with nowhere else to go. Apart from this basic problem, there are several other possible problems with this proposition. For example, it will clearly be inconsistent with a proposition, if one such exists, that one cannot be sent to hell (whatever and wherever that is) if one did not commit any sin (whatever it is). Now if a baby died within minutes after birth, something that happens not very infrequently, the baby cannot be sent to hell because he did not commit any sin; and he would not qualify for heaven either since the baby was not blessed by the proper authority. This difficulty will force us to define some third entity other than heaven and hell, or to send the child to hell by proposing that just being born is sinful. We will, of course, have to forget about fairness in all of this, but then who said God has to be fair? If we do not start with a consistent set of propositions, we will always get into trouble like this.

Dynamic Development

The other most important characteristic of the Hindu inquiry is its dynamic development. The human civilizations have experienced enormous changes over the past several millennia. In the past hundred years or more, we have witnessed industrial and agricultural revolutions, space exploration, nuclear development, and more recently, genetic engineering. Philosophical and metaphysical constructs as well as ethical guidelines must keep pace with such revolutionary changes in these other fields.

Thousands of years ago, Hindus lived along the banks of rivers. There was no electrical generation and distribution, and there was no indoor plumbing. People essentially worked on farms, raised animals, and used hand tools to make some useful products. People were therefore asked to wake up before sunrise and to take a bath in the river. Subsequently, they moved inland away from the rivers and dug wells for drinking water. Then they were asked to go to the well and take a bath by dumping well water over themselves. Now if someone would ask the Hindus in Washington, D.C. to wake up before sunrise and go to the Potomac River for a bath, he would be laughed out of the room. Except for a few die-hards, most of the people ignore such commands anyway. Furthermore, when organized religions refuse to reconsider their age-old positions that are obviously out of place, it leads to a crisis of confidence in the religious authorities, and no one benefits.

Consider, for example, the way Catholic Church refuses to reconsider its positions on the issues of sexuality, birth control, artificial insemination, in-vitro fertilization, priesthood for women, celibacy for priests, and right to die. The world population was around 2.5 billion in early 1950's, and it is presently over 6 billion. The world has already witnessed the horror of hunger in a number of countries on the African Continent, and many people, including a significant majority of Catholics think that the Church's position on birth control is patently unreasonable. The Church steadfastly holds that *every marital act must remain open to the transmission of life.* Consequently, it is against all forms of birth control, except the highly unreliable and ineffective rhythm method. This method requires a woman to follow the complex ritual of charting her body temperature to determine her ovulation period so that she can avoid sexual intimacy during that fertile period. Imagine teaching this method to countless illiterates around the world! This method is popularly known as *Vatican roulette or voodoo birth control.* Many believe that this policy of the Church is inherently immoral, and a vast majority of Catholics around the world simply ignore this teaching of the Church. As one Catholic obstetrician-gynecologist put it, it is difficult to imagine that salvation is based on contraception by temperature and damnation is based on the use of rubber. It is also important to note here that the whole Catholic debate on this issue is not whether the policy makes sense, but whether the Pope spoke *ex cathedra* (infallibly) when he banned artificial birth control. According to Catholic theology, when the Pope speaks like that, *he does it with the assistance of Holy Spirit,* and hence he is then errorless and virtually divine. A woman may have had one or more C-section deliveries or she may be suffering from renal or cardiac disease, and the doctors may conclude that another pregnancy could be fatal for her. Even under these conditions, however, the Church forbids sterilization or contraception.

The lack of dynamism on the part of many organized religions is clearly evident if one examines their treatment of women. The whole concept of God creating man in his own image has already delegated all women to a second class citizenship under many religions. The basic premise of God having a gender is questionable. We do not ask if an electron or a proton is male or female. We do not ask if a camera is male or female. We all know that the gender is associated only with plants and animals that exhibit sexual reproduction. Then why should God have a gender? Similarly, we should not ask if God is black or white or any other color. Until recently, women were not allowed to be priests in many religious congregations. Some believe that the sacrament of priesthood is denied to Christian women on the grounds that Jesus did not have any women at the table when the sacrament of Holy Orders was instituted at the Last Supper. Other religions may have similar other reasons for denying women their rightful place side by side with men.

There is no doubt that, over the years, the old stereotypes of women as baby machines and cake bakers have broken down. It is, however, still true that some of the organized religions simply do not take women seriously. Consider the issue of abortion. An overwhelming majority of people would basically agree that:

i) within certain period of time after conception, a woman should be free to end her pregnancy, if she so chooses, without any interference from anyone;

ii) within certain period of time prior to the expected time of delivery, a woman should not be allowed to end her pregnancy, even if she so chooses; and

iii) between these two time periods, a woman's right to end her pregnancy should not be hers alone.

What the above two time periods should be is, of course, eminently debatable. Some may think it should be only a matter of days while some others may think it should be on the order of weeks or more. Most believe that these two time periods are clearly linked to the survivability of the fetus outside the womb and how dangerous it would be for the woman to continue her pregnancy. Consequently, these time periods will change as the medical technology progresses.

Religious fundamentalists, however, do not agree to any such granting of a choice to women. Their idea is to force women to complete their pregnancies under any and all circumstances. Furthermore, they want to do this in the name of God. Some theologians have, of course, proposed a ridiculous theory that the human life begins at the time of *individuation,* sometime between the fourteenth and twenty-first days. This way, they can support early abortion and still consider themselves to be pro-life.

With spectacular advances in science and technology, people's life experiences today are fundamentally different than those of the past. Under these rapidly changing conditions, people expect some guidance from philosophers on how to reconcile the complex issues of faith and reality. The leaders of the organized religions, however, are essentially abandoning the roles they have chosen for themselves and the people have come to expect from them. These leaders are doing a disservice to the people they profess to lead. They still ask their followers to wrap this or that over their heads, cover their hair, grow their hair, believe that the Earth is only several thousand years old, use rhythm method of birth control, and do other meaningless things that have absolutely nothing to do with human spirituality.

The Hindu inquiry, however, has exhibited, from its very beginning, a level of maturity that is hard to imagine. It began with the early simplistic speculation that the forces of nature such as the wind, the fire, the earthquakes, the volcanoes, and others were controlled by individual gods, and that these gods could be appeased by means of animal sacrifices and other offerings. As the Hindus studied and understood sciences such as astronomy, mathematics, medicine, chemistry, metallurgy, and others, they developed new philosophical formulations that were consistent with the scientific knowledge of the times. Social sciences such as politics, governance, economics, ethics, and others were also dynamically progressing along with the philosophy. Together, the Hindu thinkers presented a holistic view of life. Concepts of separation of the church and the state, ethics of behavior during war, and ideas of medical ethics were developed and practiced at the time. By insisting on a scientific approach of going from the known to the unknown, they always maintained internal consistency and universal application for their philosophy, dynamically keeping it in step with the scientific progress.

3. Criteria of Knowledge

Before starting any inquiry, it is of utmost importance to decide what is the criterion of knowledge for that inquiry. In other words, we must answer the question: *how do we know what we know?* What is the basis of what we know? In some fields of inquiry, this question is not all that difficult to answer. For example, if someone asks us how we know that *one plus one is two,* we can prove to him that it is so. We would take one penny and put it in an empty bottle, and then we would take another penny and put it in the same bottle. Now we would empty the bottle and count the pennies in it: one and two. This way we can prove that *one plus one is two.* Even in mathematics, however, other proofs are not that simple. The entire structure of geometry is based on certain axioms such as the definitions of a point, a line, a plane, and space. A *point* is an entity that has no linear dimension; it has no length, no width, and no height. Once we accept the notion of a *point,* it is then natural to extend the argument to one or more dimensions. We can then define a line as having only one dimension of length, a *plane* as having two dimensions of length and width, and *space* as having three dimensions of length, width, and height. However, it must be understood that it is impossible to offer, in any sense of the word, a proof of existence of a *point.*

In other fields of investigations as well, we first decide on a certain criterion of success. If we want to examine if a certain medicine is effective against a specific infection, the current practice is to conduct double-blind studies. In such a study, a number of subjects participating in the study are divided into two groups A and B. Two sets of pills, tablets, or doses of liquid medicines are then prepared: for example, tablets M containing the recommended dose of the medicine under test, and tablets P containing just a placebo and no medicine. The members of group A are given one type of tablets, and those of group B are given the other type. The subjects, that is the people taking the tablets, as well as the scientists conducting the study are not told what group is being given the medicine. The response of the subjects to the tablets is carefully monitored over a certain period of time. The data is then analyzed for statistical differences in the responses of the two groups. The results of this analysis are then used to determine if the medicine is effective or not. Since no one connected with the experiment knows who was given what, the results are clearly very objective and believable. Such a double-blind study directly answers the question: "How do we know that a medicine is effective?"

In the scientific world, there are several generally accepted criteria of knowledge such as, for example, repeatable experiments, mathematical proofs, and logical inferences. In the United States criminal law, on the other hand, the criterion is a unanimous verdict by a jury of one's peers.

In some fields, a criterion may be different in different parts of the world. Such a difference results from differences in the psyche of the people or from certain values and/or behavior patterns established over hundreds or thousands of years. A school teacher, for example, is still highly respected in the Indian society. This respect has, of course, been earned collectively by the profession over the past centuries. In any dispute between a teacher and a student, the criterion there is to accept the teacher's word. Even the student's family will accept the teacher's word over their child's word.

As another example, consider the relationship between the United States Government as the buyer of some service or commodity, and an American industrial organization as the supplier of these services or commodities. When the government buys certain equipment from industry, it first develops performance requirements for such equipment. If the government were to buy a rocket, these requirements will cover topics such as its thrust, payload capacity, size, fuel consumption, orbital height of payload delivery, etc. The government then requests proposals from industry for supplying the rocket to the government. The industrial organization that wins the contract then designs and manufactures the hardware and the software related to the rocket. It also has to develop and deliver to the government a *verification plan*. Generally, such a plan describes the various tests to be conducted and various criteria to be followed for verifying that the equipment meets the requirements. Once this is done to its satisfaction, the government accepts the equipment and pays the company as required by the contract. Now, this process of the buyer testing the equipment before paying for it is clearly based on the concept of *caveat emptor*, that is, *buyer beware*. This concept is at the heart of the laissez-faire or the Western capitalist economies, and is deeply rooted in the Western psyche.

In the Japanese society, however, the government, industry, and the people have not had an adversarial relationship like that in the West; instead, they all maintain a symbiotic relationship. Also, Japanese companies, not unlike the people, value and honor their word as a tradition. The companies, therefore, conduct extensive in-house verification before delivering the equipment to the Japanese government or to any other customer. The concept of *government testing before accepting* is kind of alien to them. According to them, when a company such as Fuji or Toshiba assures that the equipment meets the requirements, the *company's word* should be enough of a criterion for the government to accept the equipment. For a typical Japanese company, its honor is more important than making profits. Consequently, the criteria there are different than those in the West. The importance of family honor, for example, also explains why the rate of personal bankruptcies is very low in Japan. The Japanese would rather commit hara-kiri than declare bankruptcy.

Every field of inquiry thus has clearly defined criteria of knowledge. Such criteria establish a common ground for all working in the field of inquiry — every field, except in the field of religion. Here, it does not appear that there are any criteria. Anyone can say that he is one of the God's chosen few, or that he knows and is the sole keeper of God's word. Anyone can say that Satan made him do this or that, or that Angels roam the Earth and take care of us or for that matter anything one may choose to say.

The Hindu Thought, however, unlike the organized religions, has devoted a significant effort in determining a valid criterion of knowledge. How should one distinguish between the real knowledge and non-real, virtual, or false knowledge? When someone says, *I know such and such,* several problems arise in attempting to interpret such a statement. It presupposes that *such and such* exists; does this mean that one needs to prove that *such and such* exists before asserting its knowledge? Next, who exactly is this *I* who is professing to know *such and such?* Thirdly, is a simple declaration of knowledge enough of a criterion for accepting the *fact* of knowledge? The individual professing the knowledge may, in fact, be in error, or he may be dishonestly saying something he knows to be untrue. Clearly, these problems are very generic, and will arise at every declaration of knowledge. These profound topics of the nature of *I,* validity of knowledge, and the reality of *such and such,* however, have been completely ignored by every religion, except by the Hindu thinkers. Presently, we will only examine the validity and the criteria of validation of knowledge, and discuss the nature of I only as it relates to the Hindu criterion of knowledge. The other aspects of the nature of *I* and the reality of *such and such* will be examined in depth in later Chapters.

Direct Personal Observation

Direct observation is essentially sense perception with or without the help of different types of tools or instruments. The universe is perceived here as a collection of material objects that continue to occupy space over a length of time. Human senses, with or without the help of instruments, are capable of responding to various emissions from these objects if these emissions are above certain thresholds. Consequently, these objects are potentially observable by people. A man becomes aware of the existence of any particular object when one or more of his senses register the emissions from that object. For example, when the light rays reflected off a dog enter a man's eye, the eye registers their effect on the retina and his brain interprets these effects. The man then becomes aware of the presence of the dog. In a similar fashion, other senses — touch, hearing, taste, and smell — make him aware of specific objects in the universe. If there is not enough visible light, he may be able to use an infrared (IR) device for assisting the eye to register the effect of IR radiation reflected off an object. He could also use other devices such as a microscope, a telescope, or an amplifier.

Direct observation, at first glance, inherently appears to be one of the best, and possibly, the ultimate criterion of knowledge. When you see something or hear something yourself, who would doubt its validity? When one examines this in depth, however, one quickly realizes several important limitations of direct observation. An observer, for example, may lack, partially or totally, capability of certain senses. A person may be colorblind, and consequently unable to distinguish between shades of color or between colors themselves. All colors will then appear to him as various shades of gray. A person blind since birth will find it almost impossible to understand what sight is. He will wonder how anyone can know the size and shape of anything at a distance without touching and feeling the object. We would not be able to describe to him how much we enjoy watching someone act or dance on stage. A person deaf since birth, on the other hand, will not understand speech or music. The scope of direct observation is thus clearly limited by the capability of the senses. There is a classical story of five blind men who were led to an elephant and were asked to describe the animal. One gets hold of the elephant's tail and describes the elephant to be like a small piece of rope. Similarly, other blind men, who happen to get hold of various parts of the elephant, describe the animal differently to be like a hollow cylinder, a tree trunk, etc. The scope of each blind man's observation was thus limited, although the observation itself was truthful within that scope.

Now, even if one is fully endowed with all five senses, the very nature of the phenomenon of observation limits itself in several ways. An act of knowing something via direct observation has three distinct components to it: a piece of information entering the body via one or more senses; the information being transmitted to the brain via one or more transmission media; and the brain interpreting the information by comparison with earlier experiences and storing it for future comparison. Any one of the three components could be corrupted for one reason or another. An out-of-focus lens, for example, would ruin the visual signal entering the eye directly or through a telescope or a microscope. A multi-billion dollar Hubble Telescope orbiting the Earth had a similar problem that was corrected by NASA in 1993 by a special unprecedented Shuttle mission. The hearing, touch, and smell can similarly be corrupted. Assuming that the information entered the body uncorrupted, the transmission media, if not fully functional, can corrupt the signal, and may even prohibit the signal transmission itself. Any malfunction in one or more parts of the nervous system of a human body could thus change the signal received by the brain or even eliminate it. Finally, assuming that the senses and the transmission media are perfect, the interpretation of the data by the brain may itself be faulty. A person entering a semi-dark room may look at a piece of rope on the floor and be scared, thinking that to be a snake. In this case, the senses are registering the signal right, and the transmission medium is transmitting the signal correctly to the brain. The brain, however, is misinterpreting the data. Similarly, several children are unfortunately shot dead by the police every year, simply because a police officer's brain mistakenly identifies the child's toy gun to be a real one.

When we analyze the use of direct observation, we must conclude that what we discern by direct observation may be quite different from the truth. Consequently, we need some other criteria to validate direct observation. If, for example, a man sticks his finger in luke warm water, he may sense it to be very hot if his finger had earlier been in icy water. On the other hand, if his finger had earlier been in very hot water, he may sense the same lukewarm water to be very cold. One may then use a thermometer as an independent criterion for deciding the water temperature. Such a use of a thermometer is still a direct observation and would raise another question: "How do we know that the thermometer is without any error?"

Because direct observation can lead to misleading or incorrect *knowledge,* it clearly cannot be accepted as the *ultimate* criterion of knowledge, although direct observation is one of the most important tools of scientific research. If several observations are made and they validate each other, the confidence level of the observer goes up in proportion to this validation. What we are seeking with the ultimate criterion, however, is one hundred percent confidence level, that is, the certainty of knowledge. This is precisely why direct observation cannot be accepted as the ultimate criterion of knowledge.

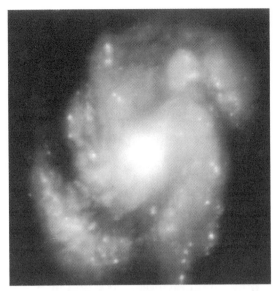

Before Lens Correction

After Lens Correction

Hubble Telescope Pictures of M100 Galaxy (Courtesy NASA)

Logical Inference

Logical inference essentially involves the process of drawing a conclusion from a set of propositions or statements known to be true. There are basically two branches of inference: inductive inference, and deductive inference.

Inductive inference begins with individual observations or facts and draws a conclusion covering a group or a class of individuals. As an example, we observe the facts that *Crow A lays an egg, Sparrow B lays an egg, ...,* and *Eagle M lays an egg,* and then draw a conclusion that *All birds lay eggs.* Here, the scope or the coverage of the proposition goes from one to many. The proposition, *Crow A lays an egg,* covers only one individual, Crow A. Similarly, the proposition, E*agle M lays an egg,* covers only one individual, Eagle M. On the other hand, the proposition, *All birds lay eggs,* has the scope of an entire class of individuals, the birds. The scope of inductive inference thus increases successively at every step of induction. A series of inductive inferences can be drawn to cover widening class of individuals such as *all crows, all birds, and all animals.*

Now let us examine if inductive inference can be an ultimate criterion of knowledge. For this, let us define a ratio R as the ratio of the number of individual observations to the scope of the inference arrived. As an example, let us suppose that a certain football team has 50 members. If we make observations relating to randomly selected 10 members and arrive at an inductive inference relating to the whole team, the ratio R is 10/50 = 0.2. If we measure the weight of every team member, find it to be over 200 lb., and then infer that *all team members weigh over 200 lb.,* the ratio R for this inference is unity. Clearly, when R is unity, the inference is a certainty. If we measure the weight of only 10 members, however, and finding them to be over 200 lb., make the same inference that *all team members weigh over 200 lb.,* then the inference is not a certainty. Thus whenever the ratio R is less than unity, the confidence level associated with the inference is clearly less than

100 percent. If we want certainty, that is 100 percent confidence level, we must know every team member's weight, and that may not be always possible. The world of scientific research is full of examples where researchers jumped to wrong inductive inferences with a limited knowledge of individual cases. Also, people's prejudices are essentially the result of broad generalizations (inductive inferences) based on limited individual experiences. With such an approach, no wonder that people are still judged not by the content of their characters, but by the color of their skin, size of their noses, opening of their eyes, and many other irrelevant factors. Observations related to *a few* should not lead to an inference for *all*. Consequently, inductive inference, although a very valuable tool for developing hypotheses, cannot be accepted as the ultimate criterion of knowledge.

Deductive inference goes from a proposition with global or large scope to an individual case with singular scope. It starts with a conditional in the form of an if-then statement such as *if it is a dog, then it is an animal (if p then q)*. This conditional is then examined with an additional observation such as *A is, or is not, a dog (p or not-p), or B is, or is not, an animal (q or not-q)*, for arriving at a deductive inference. For example, consider

Original conditional: If it is a dog, then it is an animal.

Observation: A is a dog.

Inference: A is an animal.

It is quite clear here that the original conditional is true and final inference is valid. It is not always possible however to draw an inference from a given conditional and an observation. In the above example, consider an observation that *A is not a dog*. With such an observation, since A may or may not be an animal, a valid inference is not possible. Similarly, a valid inference is not possible for an observation that *B is an animal*, because B may or may not be a dog.

It can be seen that valid inference is possible with an observation *A is a dog* (inference: A is an animal), or with an observation *B is not an animal* (inference: B is not a dog). A whole branch of science, called mathematical logic, examines various ways of combining conditionals and observations, and identifies situations where deductive inference is possible.

It will, however, be at once clear that the entire validity of any deductive inference depends on whether the original conditional is true. As an example, let us consider a faulty inference. Let us begin with the following conditional: "If a girl eats normally recommended meals everyday and is losing weight, then she must be bulimic. The conditional would seem to be quite reasonable to most of us. Everyone eating a recommended diet is supposed to stay healthy, and most do. If a girl is eating regular meals with her family and is getting thinner everyday, it would seem reasonable to think that she is deliberately purging after her meals. Now if we observe that Ann eats normally recommended meals everyday and is losing weight, then we will infer that Ann is bulimic. Everyone in the medical field however knows that the original conditional is patently false. Bulimia is just one of the many possible explanations of Ann losing weight. She may have some serious medical problem that causes her to lose weight while eating normal meals. As a result, the inference regarding Ann may be completely wrong. Ann may not be bulimic at all. The process of deductive logic is valid only if the original conditional is true. In other words, the deductive inference needs additional criteria of validity, that is, the validity of the original conditional. A close examination of the original conditional will reveal that such a proposition is usually the result of an inductive inference based on a limited number of observations (ratio R less than unity). The basis of a deductive inference is thus some process of an inductive inference. Since the inductive inference itself does not qualify for being the ultimate criterion of knowledge, neither would the deductive inference. Faulty deductive inference is a classic case of *blind leading the blind.* In fact, if the original conditional is false, all sorts of contradicting inferences can be drawn; books on logic are full of such examples.

Others' Revelations

Revelation, as is commonly understood, is the phenomenon wherein a person believes or claims that God has revealed Himself to him and has told him His will. He then further believes that God has chosen him to be His (God's) Prophet, and has asked him to pass His will on to others.

Clearly, revelation presupposes a God that is distinctly different from the universe around us. It also presupposes that God, for reasons known only to Him and by using one or more criteria known only to Him, selects a person for revealing His will, and does so at a time and space of His choosing. If this premise is not true, then revelation cannot be true. Consequently, this premise needs an independent verification. The act of God revealing the truth individually to a prophet has always been reported to have happened in private. There is no circumstantial or other evidence that will remotely stand any scrutiny. People are simply supposed to accept the prophet's word that he has been visited by God in private and that he has been the recipient of the word of God. When God's revelation was reported to have been witnessed by a group of people, these reports have been made not by those present, but as hearsay by others.

Now let us examine whether revelation, reportedly experienced by others, can be the ultimate criterion of our knowledge. It must be noted that we are not examining here the verification of a first-hand revelation experienced individually by us. We will examine only if *another's* revelation experience can be the basis of our knowledge. First, there is really no basis for the presupposition that God is distinctly different from the universe. This presupposition is the ultimate in going from the unknown to the known as discussed earlier. The basis given by the prophetic religions for this presupposition is the prophecy

If Mario can go up the mountain, so can Luigi

itself. God told the prophet that He exists, that He created the universe, that He created Man in His own image, etc., etc. Why should we believe it to be the God's word? There is the classic circular argument between faith and belief. You must have faith in order to believe; and you must believe in order to have faith. It is somewhat like the story of someone who said that he saw a UFO, and when asked how he knew it to be a UFO, said that it was clearly written on the vehicle U-F-O. The vehicle identified itself as an unidentified flying object.

Even if one gets past this hurdle of God being different from the universe, there is never any valid evidence for revelation. For example, the founder of Mormonism, Joseph Smith, claimed to have been directed by an angel to some buried golden plates describing the American Indians to be the descendants of Hebrews who had sailed to the United States several centuries earlier. These gold tablets, of course, are nowhere to be found today. The whole story of the angel and the gold plates must, therefore, be taken on faith. The revelations received by some prophets are reported to have been collected shortly after their death. We thus need separate criteria to confirm that the memory of the writers was perfect. The other problem is that if Mario can receive revelation, so can Luigi. Anyone can say that he has received revelation and that we all should accept him as a prophet. In fact, several prophets have been acknowledged in Judaism, Christianity, Islam, and Zorostrianism. Each religion says that its prophet's word is the final version of God's word. There is, for example, no problem in accepting the prophetic status of anyone who came earlier than your prophet as long as your prophet's revelation is accepted to be the *final and perfect* revelation — a sort of a mid-course correction by God to earlier revelations. If two prophetic revelations are inconsistent with each other, as they usually are, how does one decide who is right? One, therefore, needs other independent criteria to verify prophetic vision of others. Consequently, prophetic vision of others must be rejected as the ultimate criterion of our knowledge.

Hindu Criterion – Atman's Mystical Awakening (AMA)

The Hindu thinkers of the past have paid an incredible amount of attention to this issue of the ultimate criterion of knowledge. As suggested earlier, the statement *I know such and such* raises some very fundamental questions: who is this *I* that is professing the knowledge of *such and such;* and does *such and such* exist, and if so, is it real? It is quite possible that *such and such* may not pass the test for ultimate reality, but one may still be able to associate a certain level of reality to it. The first question about the meaning of *I,* however, will still remain irrespective of the level of reality of *such and such.* Consequently, Hindu thought confronts the question of *I* first, and this then forms the essential basis for further development of the ultimate criterion of knowledge.

Atman, the essence of each of us, is that *I* that *knows such and such.* It has self-awareness, and is a portion of the ultimate reality that identifies itself with only one individual living (possibly even non-living) entity within the virtual reality of the universe. Each living entity, in turn, consists of a body-mind-intellect (BMI) complex that has Pran (life force) and experiences an I-awareness.

The BMI Complex

Earlier, we have discussed how the five senses of sight, smell, touch, taste, and hearing register the effect or impact of the external universe on our body, and how the nerves act like transmission media between the senses and the brain, and how the brain interprets the received data. These senses are thus the five gateways through which the surrounding universe interacts with our body. In common scientific terms, the eyes, nose, skin, tongue, and ears are the *sensors* of our body. Similarly, there are five *actuators* through which the body acts on the surrounding universe. These actuators are — arms and hands, legs and feet, mouth, anus, and the urination and sexual apparatus. Both the sensors and the actuators are connected to the brain via a network of nerves. All actions by the body are on a *physical* level.

The sensors register the raw data from the universe. The data becomes useful information only when interpreted by the brain. This information is then used to control the actuators and other elements within the body. Some of the actions are purely involuntary, and certain stimuli will always result in a unique bodily action. When, for example, a doctor taps you with his little mallet at certain location on your elbow or below your knee, the arm or the leg quickly moves as a reflexive involuntary action. Similarly, eyes close in a reflexive reaction to a clap of hands in front of the eyes. These actions are quite similar to the deterministic reactions of any industrial control equipment. To that extent, our body acts like a cyber-netic organism, *cyborg* for short. Several other actions are, however, voluntary, and a closer examination of these volun-tary actions helps us understand who we are and how we operate beyond our material body.

When a person speaks, he generates air pressure waves that travel outward with a certain emission pattern. These sound waves fall on our ear sensor, and it responds with varying sen-sitivity to the different frequency components of these waves. The ear is generally sensitive to frequencies below 20 kHz, although it is more sensitive in the frequency range 10 Hz to 5 kHz. In technical terms then, the diaphragm of the ear converts the pressure changes into specific movements of the footplate of the stapes. These movements, in turn, set up waves in the fluid of the inner ear. The action of these waves on the organ of Corti generates action potentials in the nerve fibers. The neural messages are then transmitted via auditory nerves to the region of the brain that is responsible for interpreting these messages. Finally, the brain compares this information with information from other senses and with past experi-ences, and correlates the air pressure waves experienced by

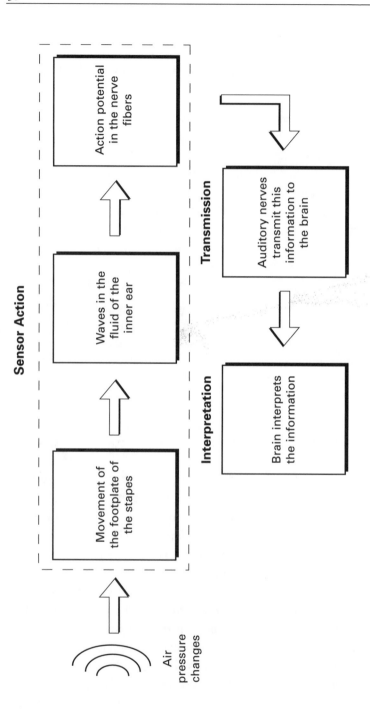

Elements of Hearing Action

the ear to useful pieces of information. For example, an air pressure wave $P_1(t)$ may be interpreted as "Roger said the words: Let us go to Lunch," and the air pressure wave $P_2(t)$ may be interpreted as "Boss said the words: You get a raise."

Similarly, all the raw data collected by the five sensors is correlated and converted into different pieces of useful information. These pieces of information could be any one of the different types illustrated here:

The clock shows it is 8:00 AM.

The alarm on the clock is ringing.

The coffee in the mug is very hot.

The milk in the carton has a disagreeable odor.

The candy is very sweet.

All the sensors are thus constantly gathering raw data, which is being continually transformed by the brain into pieces of useful information. Some of the above information leads to involuntary response. Quick retraction of hand when touching a hot surface, blinking of eyes and many such actions fall under this category. But voluntary responses to other pieces of information involve several distinct functions. The information is first *organized for collective evaluation.* As an example, the computer clock showing 11:30 AM, two friends showing up at your door, someone calling you on the phone and reminding you of your lunch appointment, and your eyes looking at your brown bag, all have to be evaluated collectively to mean it is time to go for lunch. Usually, of course, we are dealing with a number of more complex sets of information. Clearly there are several alternative ways in which one may respond to the organized information. Consequently, after the information is organized, these possible alternative responses are developed, evaluated, and ranked. These evaluations are prepared as illustrated below:

Alternative A: If you go to lunch now, your body will get nourishment, you will be able to meet with a friend who is also going to the same place for lunch, and you can come back in time for a meeting at work. But then, either you will have to throw away the lunch you brought, or eat it next day, and your mother who wanted you to visit her during lunch time will be disappointed.

Alternative B: If you go to your mother, you would get a good meal and your mother will be happy; but then your wife will be angry because you went to your mother.

It would at once be clear that this is really an intellectual and analytical exercise. After these alternatives are developed and evaluated, *one response is selected* for execution. The selected alternative is then simply executed by the physical body. The brain generates the necessary commands, the appropriate nerves transmit the commands to the appropriate actuators, and the actuators carry out the commanded action. You will either join your friend for lunch or go to your mother. It must be remembered here that there may be many more alternatives in other complex situations, and that the above scenario is just an illustration.

A close examination of these three functions — organizing the information for collective evaluation, developing and evaluating alternative responses, and selecting a response — shows that, qualitatively, these three can be grouped in only two distinct types:

Type 1: Organizing information and selecting a response: These functions are governed by various emotions such as fear, anger, love, hate, pity, jealousy, and many others. Emotions, however, come and go, and as a result, our response to any given information may be, and in fact is, different at different times.

Type 2: Developing, evaluating, and ranking of alternatives: These functions essentially represent an intellectual exercise. These are governed, not by the emotions of the time, but by the quality of our intellect. Consequently, the quality of the result of this exercise is largely time invariant.

The Hindu Thought has assigned the Type 1 functions to an entity called *mind*. The *mind* operates on an *emotional level*. The Type 2 function is assigned to an entity called *intellect or reason*. It operates on an *intellectual or rational level*. This entity, the intellect, is quite different from the intelligence, or the intelligence quotient (IQ) exhibited by an individual. The body-mind-intellect (BMI) complex operates in a variety of pathways. The sensors gather data from their interactions with the external universe. Some data causes an immediate involuntary response by the actuators, and all the processes related to this response take place on the *physical* level. The mind processes other types of data in useful packages. Some of these packages sometimes cause a quick *emotional* response and the mind quickly orders the actuators to carry out the necessary actions. A woman, for example, may see the automobile of her husband's mistress parked on the road, and may immediately let the air out of all the tires. This instantaneous response is purely emotional. The mind does not involve the intellect in such responses. In absence of such a purely emotional response, the mind presents the organized data packages to the intellect for analysis, evaluation, discrimination, and ranking of possible alternative responses. Under the preferred mode of behavior, the mind then selects the first-ranked response and gets the actuators to act accordingly. More often, however, the mind corrupts this decision process. In spite of knowing the rank-ordered responses, it lets emotions take over and selects an alternative identified by the intellect as less than desirable. Then when the emotions subside and we rethink our responses, we may regret our actions and feel sorry for the pain we may have caused others by our actions. If, however, we listen to our intellect, and always do the best under the circumstances, we do not have to feel sorry. Our best may not have been good enough, but we could not have done better. Whether our mind routinely corrupts the decisions of our intellect, or whether the intellect takes the right decision, depends on the qualities and characteristics of our mind and our intellect.

The Fundamental Qualities – S, R, and T

The mind and the intellect are characterized by the three very fundamental qualities — s, r, and t — defined by the early Hindu thinkers. The *s-quality* is primarily defined as the ability to identify what is in our *ultimate best interest* and to strive to achieve it. The *t-quality* is just the opposite; it misidentifies what is in our worst ultimate interest as to be in our best ultimate interest, and does everything to execute it. The *r-quality* signifies a desire to do something even if it is in our interest to do nothing; it signifies an intense desire for activity whether it helps or hurts anyone including us. In most individuals, the mind and the intellect are endowed primarily with one of these three qualities, although other two are also present to a varying degree and for varying periods of time. The life of people like Mahatma Gandhi or Mother Teresa is full of noble deeds because their minds and intellects are endowed primarily with the s-quality. The life of a repeat criminal, however, is full of horrible deeds because his mind and intellect are endowed primarily with the t-quality. Such predominance of t-quality is also precisely why, except in a very few cases, in spite of great efforts, jails do not appear to rehabilitate criminals.

At this time we are simply introducing various entities that together form this multi-dimensional complex called *I* that professes to know *such and such*. We will address in later chapters other related issues such as "How does one acquire the s-, r-, and t-qualities?" The three entities — body, mind, and intellect — can now be characterized as follows:

Entity	Plane of action	What governs the actions
Body	Physical	Material things such as food, exercise, and environment.
Mind	Emotional	Emotions, both noble and ignoble; and inherent mix of s-, r-, and t qualities of the mind
Intellect	Intellectual	Inherent mix of s-, r-, and t qualities of the intellect

Our involuntary responses are essentially of two kinds: natural and learned. The natural responses come from deep within us; these are inherited by us over hundreds of thousands of years via the process of natural selection as suggested by Darwin. Consider, for example, the fact that our eyes are rolled up when we sleep. This way, our lenses retain their moisture and the quality of our eyesight is maintained. Through the years of human evolution via gene mutation, some humans (or possibly even some of our mammal ancestors) must have developed this response quite accidentally. Those without this response surely could not maintain the quality of their eyesight for long. Consequently, a significant number of those humans without this response did not live long enough to procreate, and did not pass those undesirable characteristics on to the next generation. Those humans that developed this preferential response, protected their lenses, retained their eyesight, and lived longer to have more children, thus passing the genes responsible for this response to a larger portion of the next generation. Now we all have these genes and this very valuable response. Similarly, when we sleep, the threshold of our synapses is automatically reset so that the nominal sounds received by our ears are not passed on to our brain. Otherwise we would not be able to sleep. Only when the sound level exceeds this threshold, the auditory nerves activate the brain, and we wake up. Again, we all acquired this preferred response via the mechanism of natural selection. Other type of involuntary

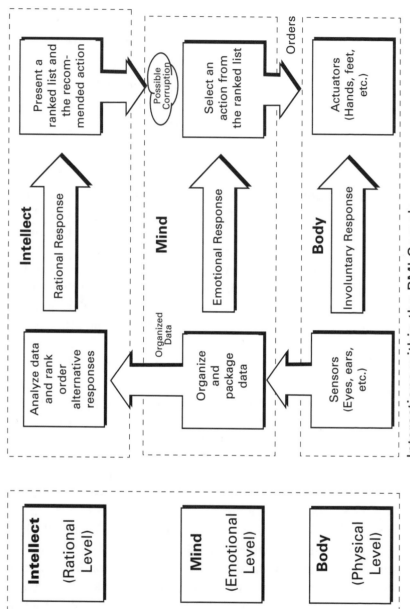

Interactions within the BMI Complex

response is *learned*. Such learned involuntary responses could be caused by, addiction to alcohol, drugs, gambling, shopping, or even to a person; here we are not talking about chemical dependency resulting from some genetic disposition. With such an addiction, the realm of voluntary responses is reduced, and more of one's responses become obsessive, automatic, and involuntary. One should, of course, distinguish between this type of learned involuntary response and the earlier one resulting from the natural selection. It is involuntary only to the extent that it is automatic. The path of decision-making here does not involve the mind and the intellect. Since anything learned can be unlearned, it is possible to bring the mind and intellect back into the loop and essentially get off these types of addictions.

Our response to the data gathered may actually have two components: a quick involuntary reaction (natural or learned), followed by a more deliberate voluntary response resulting from the actions of the mind and the intellect. We should not fight to control the initial involuntary reactions; we should only attempt to surpass them as fast as possible. As an example, a young, male emergency medical technician may be called in to help a young, buxom, gorgeous woman who has fainted. Seeing this young woman on the floor, the technician may for a split second get sexually excited. This reaction is from what the animal in him has acquired over millions of years. But then, the human in him, that is his mind and his intellect, would take over and remind him of his civic and professional duty. Most of the technicians would then help her recover. In an extremely rare case, however, a technician may act merely like an animal and may rape her instead.

It must also be understood here that the physical, emotional, and intellectual planes of activity are essentially mutually exclusive. For example, if one uses a wrong aftershave, the skin could react to it only on the physical plane, that is, it may become dry, a rash may breakout, or it may just be itchy. The skin, however, does not exhibit an emotional response. We would never say, "My chin is kind of feeling emotional today because I used a wrong aftershave." The body acts exclusively on the physical plane, the mind on the emotional plane, and the intellect acts only on the intellectual plane.

Pran

Pran, sometimes referred to as the life force or the life energy, is what distinguishes the living from the non-living. An automobile, a satellite, and any complex hardware/software system also use fuel or energy, and interact with the external universe via their sensors and actuators. Everyone would agree however, that they all are non-living entities. Setting aside these clear distinctions, let us examine Pran as it relates to living entities. A man's body, for example, is an intricate, integrated, interdependent collection of respiratory, nervous, reproductive, digestive, and other subsystems. When a man dies, all the matter that formed the body is still there, although the atomic and the molecular arrangements are not working together as intended. The atomic and the molecular motions as defined under the classical or quantum mechanics are still present. These motions can be easily confirmed with the use of appropriate instruments; but something is missing. Or is it simply similar to an automobile engine that is out of tune? Most of us will agree that the two situations are not quite equivalent. However, it is also equally true that when it comes to human life, it is not all that easy to define death. Doctors have kept brain-dead pregnant women hooked on to machines for several months to keep the fetuses growing in their wombs. Now are these women dead or alive during this period? Some systems or mechanisms are clearly working, at least partially, although surely not as an integrated whole. On the other hand, the fetus is undoubtedly interacting as a holistic entity with its own external universe. So it is generally agreed that the woman does not have Pran, but the fetus has. One can similarly construct other difficult scenarios where it is equally difficult to clearly define when a person has Pran or when a person is dead.

It is, however, somewhat easier to examine this issue at a cellular level. Consider, for example, any single-cell bacteria. There are some universally accepted laboratory techniques to determine if the cell is alive or dead. These techniques are based on specific transport phenomena that govern the flow of matter in and out of a living cell. These bacteria can be frozen and kept at -70 degrees Celsius or so for a long time. When the frozen cells are then defrosted at a later date, only some of them continue to function normally, and some others are found to be dead. In the frozen state, the usual thermody-namic motions of the electrons, atoms, and molecules exist as they would in any non-living matter so frozen. However, there is no known method today for differentiating between cells and for telling if such a frozen cell is alive or dead. But clearly, at some point between the time they are frozen and they are defrosted, some cells do lose this vital entity Pran. The Pran, just like the mind and the intellect, exists outside the physical, or the material plane. Our inability to differentiate between a living and a dead frozen cell certainly gives credence to this Hindu concept of Pran being outside the physical plane.

I-awareness

I-awareness is simply the feeling of being different from the others. Sometimes this is wrongly identified as the ego in all of us. Ego is the feeling of being *superior* to others or being better than others are. Philosophically, whether you feel being superior or inferior is quite irrelevant. It is the awareness of just being *separate and different* from everything else that is of significance here. This awareness of separateness naturally leads to the feeling that our interests differ from those of others, and every action of ours then perpetuates this I-aware-ness further.

A BMI complex acts on behalf of the Atman associated with it; the Atman only acts as an observer or as a witness of what goes on. Whatever Atman knows via the BMI complex therefore results from BMI interactions on physical, emotional, and intellectual planes. Hindu Thought maintains that these interactions alone are not enough to verify the certainty of knowledge. It also maintains that Atman is fortunately capable of *mystical* interaction that occurs beyond the physical, emotional, and intellectual planes, and that a mystical component, howsoever minimal, is necessary for verifying the certainty of knowledge. Mystical does not mean mysterious and there is certainly nothing magical about it. It simply means *beyond physical, emotional, and intellectual planes.* Furthermore, Hindu Thought calls the process of acquiring the knowledge of truth an *awakening* since the truth exists whether anyone knows it or not. One only awakens to the truth because it exists after all.

The process of knowledge, and hence the criterion of knowledge is, therefore, termed as the Atman's Mystical Awakening (AMA). It is *mystical* because it has a component that is beyond the physical, emotional, and intellectual planes, and it is *awakening* because the truth exists irrespective of its knowledge. The AMA is the ultimate criterion that does not need additional verification.

In common terminology, one can describe AMA as the first-hand, *hyper-sensory apprehension of reality.* It is *first-hand* because it is not someone else's apprehension. It is hyper-sensory because it has a *mystical component* beyond the physical, emotional and intellectual planes. Here one does not take a parent's word, or anyone else's word. One does not accept anything written in any book as the basis of knowledge. One only accepts one's first-hand apprehension as the basis of one's knowledge, and one certainly does not accept someone else's revelation, howsoever sincere it may appear. As an example, when one wakes up in the morning, he knows that he is awake. He, that is, the Atman knows via every sense, every limb, and every cell in the body that he is awake. He does not ask his wife or his girlfriend, his parents, his children, or his pastor, and he certainly does not consult any book to find out if he is awake. Even if dozens of his friends tell him he is still asleep, the Atman knows! This is what we call the Atman's mystical awakening or the first-hand, hyper-sensory apprehension of reality.

4. Hindu Concept of Monism
— The Nature of God and the Universe —

Any serious metaphysical inquiry must address the following fundamental issues:

1. Does God exist as an entity, and if so, what is the nature of this entity?

2. What is the nature of the universe and of the individuals such as us? and

3. What is the relationship between God and the universe?

All of these issues have been addressed very logically by the concept of Monism.

The development of the Hindu concept of God follows the earlier approach of going from the known to the unknown. We are surrounded by the universe at all times, and we have a first hand experience of interfacing with the universe. The universe to us is, therefore, an entity that is known, at least partly, although the level of reality of the universe may be debatable. Consequently, it is quite natural for us to start with the universe, before speculating on the existence and the nature of God. In examining the nature of the universe, one can use time regression and ask if our universe had a *beginning* and if so, when and where it began. Such regression leads to only two possibilities:

    i) the universe had a beginning, that is, it is possible to define an instant of time when the universe was born; or

    ii) the universe has no beginning, that is, it has existed forever in the past.

The first possibility would most certainly raise the question of what was *before* the birth of the universe.

Any examination into the future of the universe would similarly lead to two possibilities:

    i) the universe will have an end, that is, it will cease to exist at some point in time in the future; or

    ii) it will continue to exist endlessly into the future.

Here, the first possibility would immediately raise the question of what will come after the end of the universe.

There are, therefore, the following four distinct possibilities with respect to the nature of the universe:

    i) it has a beginning as well as an end;

    ii) it has a beginning but no end;

    iii) it has no beginning but has an end; and

    iv) it has neither a beginning nor an end.

The words *beginning* and *end* are used here in the context of time as we understand it today.

The Hindu view of the universe is that our universe has a beginning, will have an end, and such a life cycle of the universe will repeat endlessly. Our universe began at some point in time in the past, it will grow and expand for some period of time, then it will shrink and contract for some period of time, and will cease to exist at some point in time in the future. The notion of time, as we understand and use it today, is valid only in the context of events happening in one life cycle of our universe. Consequently, once the universe ceases to exist, we really cannot use words such as *later* and *then.* In the most generic sense of time, however, this expansion and contraction cycle of the universe will repeat itself endlessly. For this expanded sense of time, one may have to define a higher dimensional time, *supertime,* that is different from the time we now experience. This supertime will extend infinitely, both *before* the birth of the universe and *after* the end of the universe. Our time within our current cycle of expansion and contraction is expressed with reference to the beginning of this cycle. It is somewhat similar to continuously cyclic trigonometric functions of *sine* and *cosine,* where angles are referenced to the beginning of the cycle.

The Hindu concept of God is quite simple and may be stated as follows. Our universe had a beginning. In the beginning, there was an entity from which this universe began. We may call this entity X, Y, or Z; we may even call it ABC, PQR, or STP. We just happen to call it G-O-D. Whatever existed *before* the beginning of our universe is what Hindus call Brahman, the Sanskrit language word for God.

Let us first examine the concept of dimensionality and the nature of God in terms of dimensionality. Imagine a small ant moving along a long thin thread. The ant thus moves back and forth along a straight line. The position of the ant at any time is fully described by just one parameter — its distance from any point of reference on that line. If the reference point is changed, the value of the parameter will be changed; but even then, just one parameter will define its position. This is precisely why the universe of this ant is considered to be one-dimensional (1-D). Furthermore, this ant would simply not understand any higher dimensional universe; it could not possibly imagine what the words up, down, and sideways mean. If, however, the ant is allowed to move on a large sheet of paper placed flat on the floor, the ant's universe would become two-dimensional (2-D). One now needs two parameters to define the position of the ant: for example, a certain distance North or South, and a certain distance East or West from a given point of reference. Even if some other coordinate system were used, one would still need only two parameters; in polar system, for example, one would need a radius and an angle as the two parameters. Also, this ant would not be able to imagine any universe having more than two dimensions; it would, however, understand the predicament of the 1-D ant. The same concept of dimensionality can be easily extended to 3, 4, or more dimensions. The universe we move in was considered to be three-dimensional (3-D) because we can also move up or down, in addition to north or south, and east or west with reference to any reference point. This Newtonian way of thinking presupposed that *time* is absolute, although *space* is relative. At the beginning of the twentieth century, however, Albert Einstein introduced a relativistic universe where even time is not absolute; he defined the spacetime as a four-dimensional (4-D) reality that includes both space and time. Other scientists have found it necessary to define an even higher-dimensional universe so that certain physical interactions that occurred between various sub-atomic particles immediately after the Big Bang can be explained. Just as the above 1-D ant cannot imagine any 2-D or higher dimensional universe, we cannot imagine any of these higher dimensional universes; they can only be understood with the help of advanced mathematics.

God is beyond the 4-D spacetime as we know it. It is also beyond the higher dimensional universes defined by some scientists. In terms of dimensionality, God is infinite dimensional continuum. At the time of the beginning of the universe, God transformed self into the universe. The universe is then the four-dimensional projection of God. Every element of the universe such as non-living matter and living matter including each one of us humans is a 4-D projection of God. God continues to exist as the ultimate reality (UR) before, during, and after each cycle of expansion and contraction of the universe. The universe is then a virtual reality (VR). In the most technical sense of the VR paradigm, this VR environment offers a total, real time, four dimensional, stereoscopic, auditory, and force-sensitive touch immersion for the participant. It feels so real that we do not even attempt to seek any reality beyond the reality of this universe. God is the only and eternal ultimate reality. Universe is a transitory, 4-D projection of God and presents itself to the participant as a virtual reality (VR) environment with almost perfect immersion.

Let us now explore the unique relationship between God (UR) and the universe (VR). According to the Hindu Concept of Monism, both are one and the same, but in different form; one is UR and the other is VR. God is not the creator of the universe; God *is* the universe. When a creator creates something, his creation is distinctly different from himself. After the act of creation, one can point to the creator as well as to his creation. There is a duality between the two. This is a *dualist* relationship. When a sculptor creates a piece of art, we have two separate entities: the sculptor and the sculpture. God-universe relationship is not like a creator-creation or a sculptor-sculpture relationship. It is not a dualist relationship. Now imagine a goldsmith working in his shop making gold ornaments. Let us suppose he makes a set of earrings, a necklace, and a ring. The goldsmith, with the use of his instruments and his labor, has essentially transformed the piece of gold into different shapes and sizes. In the VR world, we see the ring, the necklace, and the earrings, as three separate entities. However, on a higher level of reality, all these three are pure gold. The goldsmith and the necklace have a dualist relationship. The gold, on the other hand, has a monist relationship between itself and the necklace or the ring. The two — gold and the necklace — are identical, and there is ultimately no difference between the two. If the necklace is melted into a liquid form, it ceases to be a necklace, but it is still pure gold. The gold and the necklace can be transformed back and forth from one form into another. Gold is eternal whereas the necklace is transitory. The gold (UR) continues to exist whether or not it is transformed into an ornament (VR).

A bail of cotton similarly gets transformed successively into thread, cloth, and clothing. The cotton, the thread, the cloth,

A monist relation between presidents' heads and Mount Rushmore

and the clothing have a monist relationship among themselves. They are one and the same. After spinning a thread and weaving a cloth, we really should not ask where the cotton and the thread are. Cotton is the ultimate reality; it continues to exist before and after its successive transformations into thread and cloth. Mount Rushmore and the four Presidents carved in it have a monist relationship. Imagine an ice sculpture showing a bride and the groom cutting the wedding cake. The bride, the groom, their clothes, the cake, the knife, and every component of the sculpture have a monist relationship with the water used to make the block of ice used for the sculpture. The difference between all these components is virtual, not real. They are different in the VR world; they are, however, identical in the UR world. God and the universe have precisely this kind of monist relationship.

God-universe relationship is also not causal in nature. They are not a cause-and-effect pair. Cause and effect bear only a unidirectional relationship. Cause precedes the effect. It is a time-dependent relationship. Also, the two are identifiably different and real. The Hindu concept of monism is that only God is the ultimate reality and the universe is only a virtual environment. At the time of the birth of the universe in each cycle, God transforms self into the universe. When the universe ends, the VR environment collapses, and God, the UR continues to exist as an entity beyond the spacetime we experience. It is as if the cause is real but the effect is unreal and virtual. If both were real, then the cause-effect relationship would have to be bi-directional — both causing each other at some point in time.

Let us now examine some of the characteristics that logically must be associated as well as those that cannot possibly be associated with this entity we call God. First, God cannot be a man, or for that matter, a woman. The genders of male and female are defined only in the context of sexual reproduction of life forms. Consequently, the terms male and female have no meaning and are irrelevant outside this context. We do not ask if a chair, or an automobile, or sugar is male or female. If someone raised the issue of gender of these things, we would immediately question his sanity. We routinely tolerate such debates about God however. The entire issue of a woman's place in the church is settled by some on the basis of a notion that God is male. It is quite obvious why God is assumed to be a male. If a committee of cows and birds were to describe God, it would be a flying cow. The concept of God as a man or a woman really insults human intelligence. If God were to be a 4-D life form made of physical matter, additional questions arise: where does God live now? where did God live before the universe was created? and most importantly, who created the matter that forms God? Also, one cannot associate human-like feelings of likes and dislikes, love and hate, rewards and revenge and others with God. Association of such feelings would immediately raise more questions: if God created the universe, then out of its own creation, why would God like or love someone and dislike and hate someone else? what is the basis of his likes and dislikes?

We cannot also associate material qualities such as long or short, hot or cold, heavy or light and others with God. The fundamental problem with these qualities is that they are all comparative in nature. When we say something is long, the inherent question is *long compared to what.* When we say that a picture frame is half a meter long, we really mean that the length of the picture frame is one-half of the distance between two points marked on a particular platinum bar that is kept at a constant temperature at a certain place in Paris, France; the distance between these two points is defined as one meter. Similarly when we say that two certain events are one minute apart, we really mean that the time between the two events is a certain multiple of the period of atomic oscillation of Cesium or of some such element. The point to be made is that the space and time components of our spacetime are *relative,* and are defined in relation to something. Since God exists before and after the life cycle of the universe, there is no spacetime or anything else to compare God with. Simply put, any quality defined in a dualist reality cannot be associated with God.

Clearly only those qualities that stand the test of a monist reality could possibly be associated with God. The first and the foremost of these is of *existence*. In our language of duality, it is eternal existence without a beginning or an end. We must really resist the temptation of adding adjectives before the word existence; these are defined in the context of our dualist reality. It is all right to use these terms to help us understand or explain to others the monist concepts we are attempting to establish. But at some point we must throw away our crutches of duality and firmly enter the monist reality. In the monist reality, we should only say that God exists. The other quality that one can associate with God is that of *self-awareness*. At some point, God transformed self into the universe we know and experience, and set in motion certain phenomena that will surely lead to the inevitable end of the universe. Consequently, God must be aware of its ability to transform back and forth between itself and the universe.

No other quality can be logically associated with God because it will not pass the test of monist reality. Some thinkers have associated God with the quality of *blissfulness*. Happiness and unhappiness, however, can be understood only in the context of a dualist reality; consequently, blissfulness does not pass the monist test. Clearly, if it must be one or the other, we would rather like God to be blissful than hateful. Hindu thinkers have attempted to explain this blissfulness in the context of personal experiences of the mystics. All mystics have experienced bliss when they have awakened to the ulti-mate reality, and they have attached to God this quality of bliss. However, this leads to the question of what is God happy for? There is nothing left outside the reality of God for God to be happy for. The mystics have, therefore, compared this with an infant that sometimes smiles and is happy simply lying on its back. The infant is apparently quite unaware of all cosmic activ-ities except possibly in its close proximity. It does not recog-nize its parents, or other relatives, or for that matter, anything around itself. It smiles and is happy with *itself.* It is in this sense that God is blissful.

The nature of the universe now becomes quite clear. It is dualist for sure; that is, all of its elements or components can be described only in relation to each other. An elephant is *bigger* than an ant, and a human being, on an average, lives *longer* than a dog. The universe is not the ultimate reality because it has a finite life cycle. It only presents itself as very real, simply because it is a virtual reality with the fullest known participant immersion. It is only a 4-D projection or manifestation of the ultimate infinite dimensional reality we call God.

The universe consists of animal life forms, plant life forms, and non-living material. It is not necessary to define these and other elements such that the boundaries between the groups are sharp and non-overlapping. Any taxonomy one suggests may be questioned by others, and such taxonomies are not really necessary to understand the philosophical formulations presented by the Hindu Thought. For example, it is not necessary to understand if a virus represents a life form or not. In the context of Hindu philosophy, either possibility can be accommodated. It is also not necessary to argue if non-humans are or can be *rational* beings. If any other element of the universe is found to be rational, it can be grouped with humans in the context of Hindu Thought. There is also no clear-cut dichotomy of *rational* and *non-rational* species of life forms. A monkey, for example, exhibits a number of behaviors that would have to be called partly rational. When a certain type of monkey wants to eat ants, it selects a twig of certain length, shape, and stiffness, and cuts that twig from a tree. It then goes to an anthill, wets the twig by licking it, and selects a spot on the anthill to insert the twig. It then pushes the twig into the anthill, moves it back and forth, and guides it into the chamber where the ants are. A number of ants get stuck to the wet twig. The monkey then pulls the twig out and eats the ants that are sticking to the twig. Many researchers have tried to do this themselves and have found it impossible to do what these monkeys have been routinely doing for generations. Many other animals also exhibit a limited number of such behaviors that can be termed partially rational.

Clearly, humans exhibit mostly rational behaviors and non-humans exhibit mostly instinctive behaviors. Furthermore, the quality of rational behavior of humans is far more superior to that of other animals. Consequently, Hindu Thought accepts that, in this dualist world, human life is more valuable and more important when compared to non-humans. It does not accept, as many other religions do however, that in a cosmic sense human life is so important that other forms of life are there simply for its enjoyment and benefit.

Let us now examine if these Hindu concepts about the cyclical nature of the universe are in agreement with the generally accepted scientific theories of the universe. The current theories of cosmos have been developed only during the past 70 years or so, and the developments still continue. The cosmologists and astronomers do not yet have a consistent theory that explains all observed phenomena. However, they are fairly certain that the universe had a beginning at what we call the Big Bang. Many scientists also believe that it will have an end in what they call the Big Crunch. There is yet no conclusive evidence for the expected crunch and, without such a proof, we cannot rule out the possibility that, although unlikely, the universe may exist endlessly.

The stars in the sky are far away from the Earth and they all look like point sources of light to us. The only way then to differentiate between the stars is to examine the spectrum of electromagnetic waves emitted by them. If we limit ourselves to the visible spectrum (light waves), we can identify the specific frequencies that are absent from the spectrum, relate those to the specific chemical elements, and thus determine the chemical composition of a star's atmosphere. When we examine these spectra received from different stars, we find that most of the frequency distributions are similar, except that the frequencies are all shifted by various amounts towards the red (low frequency) end of the spectrum. To understand the profound meaning of this *red shift,* we need first to discuss what is known as the Doppler effect. If we stand near a railway crossing and listen to the whistle of a train as the train passes by, we find that the whistle appears to be blowing at higher pitch (high frequency) when the train is approaching the crossing. The same whistle then appears to be blowing at lower pitch as the train goes away from us. The larger the speed of the train, the higher the difference in frequencies. This is the classical Doppler effect where the frequency of a signal received by a stationary observer depends on the velocity of the source relative to the observer. The frequency of the received signal is higher than the source frequency if the source is approaching the observer, and is lower when the source is moving away from the observer. The Doppler effect in the visible spectrum means that a red shift (to lower frequencies) indicates a light source moving away from us; a blue shift (to higher frequencies) on the other hand would indicate a source moving towards us.

The profound meaning of the above red shift is then at once clear — all stars are moving away from us. We also know that the red shift is directly proportional to the distance of the star from us; that is, the more distant the star, faster it is moving away from us. This means that our universe is expanding and the distances between the galaxies are increasing.

If the universe is expanding now, it means, ipso facto, that the universe was smaller in size in the past, and that if we go sufficiently back in time, the universe must have had a beginning. The commonly accepted beginning of our universe is the Big Bang, when the universe began with a big explosion and started to expand. Physicists have developed mathematical models that explain the behavior of the universe from a time very close (10^{35} second or less) to the Big Bang. As we get closer and closer to the Big Bang, the present concepts of quantum mechanics and relativistic mechanics fail, and one needs higher dimensional models to explain the behavior of the universe. The instant of the Big Bang is presently considered to be a mathematical singularity.

It is also generally accepted that the temperature of the matter created at the Big Bang was infinitely high (singularity) and that immediately the temperature began to drop at an exponential rate. The temperature is estimated to have dropped to 10 billion Kelvin (10^{10} K) within the first second after the Big Bang. It continued to drop fast and was estimated to be one billion Kelvin at three minutes after the Big Bang. As the universe continued to cool, elementary particles such as electrons and protons, chemical elements such as hydrogen and helium, galaxies, stars, and planets were formed in succession. The present temperature of the universe is about 3 Kelvin, and the cooling continues even today.

Cosmologists around the world unanimously agree today that our universe had a beginning in such a Big Bang. The next obvious question is when did this Big Bang occur, that is, how old is our universe? The scientists predict the age of the universe on the basis of a constant called the Hubble constant. The Hubble constant essentially gives the rate of expansion of the universe. It is estimated to be 15–30 km/s per million light years. This means that if a galaxy is 100 million light years away from us, it is moving away from us at a speed of 1500–3000 km/s. The same constant is also expressed as 50–100 km/s per megaparsec; a *megaparsec* is equal to 3.26 million light years. The second way is used more often, and the units are usually not written explicitly. The estimated value of the Hubble constant is simply given to be between 50 and 100, and the units, although unwritten, are assumed to be km/s/megaparsec.

If the rate of expansion of the universe is higher, clearly it must have taken a shorter time for the universe to grow to its present size. The age of the universe is, therefore, inversely proportional to the Hubble constant. The larger the constant, smaller is the age of the universe. Until 1994, the age of the universe had been estimated to be 15–20 billion years. In 1994, however, new observations taken with the help of Hubble telescope suggested that the Hubble constant might be higher than the generally accepted value of 50-100. This would correspond to a much younger universe. More recent observations however indicate the value of the Hubble Constant is 70 ± 7, corresponding to a universe that is 12-13.5 billion years old. It should be noted here that the Hindu thinkers of the past had estimated the age of the universe to be 5-6 billion years. Since the margin of error in all these estimations is quite large, it is remarkable that the estimation made by Hindu thinkers of the distant past is so close to the present estimations.

Let us now examine what scientists know about the future of the universe. It is generally agreed that the fate of our universe depends on its average mass density (kg/m^3). The attraction of gravity tends to bring masses together. Consequently, the gravitational attraction between bodies in the universe is opposing the presently ongoing expansion of the universe. This gravitational force depends on the total mass or the mass density of the universe. If this density is less than a specific value, called the *critical mass density,* the gravitational forces will be unable to stop the expansion of the universe, and the universe will then continue to expand forever without a limit. If the mass density is equal to the critical density, the universe will continue to expand, although at continually decreasing rate, and will asymptotically reach a finite size. If, however, the mass density of the universe is higher than the critical density, the universe will at some future time stop expanding, and will begin to contract due to the gravitational forces. This contraction will eventually lead to the Big Crunch as predicted by the ancient Hindu thinkers. This concept is quite similar to the concept of escape velocity for Earth-orbiting satellites. If a satellite is thrown upwards with a velocity lower than the escape velocity, the satellite will reach a maximum height (depending on the initial velocity) and fall back to Earth. If the initial velocity is equal to the escape velocity, it will orbit the Earth at some distance from the center of the Earth. If, however, the initial velocity is higher than the escape velocity, it will move away from the Earth endlessly and escape to infinity.

The critical mass density of the universe is also related to the Hubble constant; it is proportional to the square of the Hubble constant. For a Hubble constant of 50–100, the critical mass density is estimated to be $4.5–18.0 \times 10^{-27}$ kg/m^3; this is about 3–12 hydrogen atoms per cubic meter of space.

The present estimates of the mass density based on the known matter in the universe are between 10 to 20 percent of the critical density. However, these estimates may turn out to be highly inaccurate because of two factors. First, the scientists believe that there is a large amount of matter in the known galaxies and in the intergalactic space that has yet not been observed by us because it does not emit any type of radiation. Such matter is referred to as the *dark matter;* its presence has to be inferred by observing other phenomena caused by its presence. Secondly, there is some recent evidence that the elementary particle *neutrino* may not be massless as had been assumed earlier. An international team of physicists, using the underground Super-Kamiokande neutrino detector, has estimated the mass of this subatomic particle to be about one ten-millionth the mass of an electron. That may not sound like much, but some scientists believe that the estimated number of neutrinos present in the universe is sufficiently large such that this infinitesimally small mass, if confirmed by other experiments, may be enough to make the density of the universe more than the critical density. In addition to neutrinos, there is another potential candidate particle for the dark matter. These weakly interacting massive particles (WIMPs) are predicted to exist and to be ten to hundred times heavier than protons. If these particles are found to exist, there are a lot of them in the universe. By one estimate, about ten trillion of them shoot through every kilogram of matter every second. An Italian-Chinese research team, using a detector made of about 100 kg of sodium iodide buried under about one-and-a-half kilometer of rock, has recently reported to have detected these most fervently sought WIMPs. Other teams have not yet repeated these experiments, and these preliminary results must therefore be considered unverified. Scientists expect to come to a decisive conclusion regarding the existence of WIMPs within the next several years. There is also another way to examine if the mass density of the universe is larger than the critical density. It is to determine if the rate of expansion of the universe is slowing down, and by how much. Although there are a lot of uncertainties in these kinds of measurements and calculations, a recent examination of distant galaxies has shown that the expansion of the universe is indeed slowing down. The rate of slowing down is also close to the rate that would be expected if the universe does have critical mass density. The question whether the universe is closed or open has yet not been conclusively resolved. In fact, some scientists have recently proposed that the universe may continue to expand forever even if the mass density was found to be higher than the critical value. This, they believe, is due to the presence of an entity called the *vacuum energy*. Clearly, there is no consensus within the scientific community if the data presently supports an ever expanding universe or a universe that will end up in a big crunch in the future. If conclusive evidence is found in the future for a closed universe, the universe will certainly be stuck forever in endless cycles of expansion and contraction as predicted by the early Hindu thinkers.

The concept of monism does not recognize but one entity God as the ultimate reality. Everything else exists only in lower levels of reality. The universe we experience every day is a virtual reality environment, one level below the ultimate reality. We should not find it difficult to understand and accept this formulation because we do recognize lower levels of reality such as seeing a mirage and experiencing one or more levels of dreams. While driving on a highway, many times we think we see a wet road ahead and wonder if the road will be slippery. As we keep driving, the wet spot keeps moving ahead of us, and then we realize that it is just a mirage. Thirsty camel riders crossing the hot sandy deserts are often fooled by a mirage and go after a non-existent oasis in search of water. At

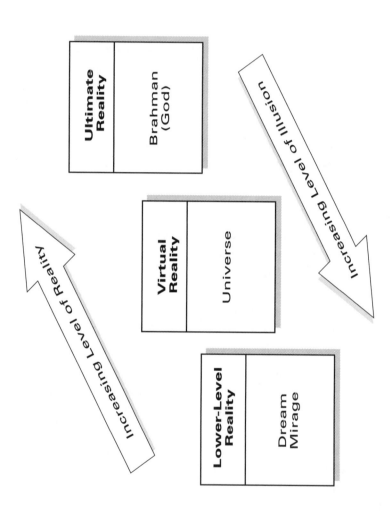

Levels of Reality

the time, the wet spots on the road and the oasis look very much real until we go closer and see the higher level of reality. Similarly, when we dream in our sleep, we travel to distant places, win lotteries, and we are attacked by snakes and ghosts. Sometimes, we even go to sleep in the dream and start dreaming within the dream. Then when we wake up from the second dream, we still continue to experience the first dream. So we do experience lower levels of reality, although we take for granted that the universe we live in is the highest level of reality. The Hindu Thought takes us one step further, and defines the ultimate reality to be one level higher than the virtual reality of the universe.

5. Law of Karma and Liberation

In Chapter 3, we saw that each one of us human beings is the Atman associated with a body, a mind, an intellect, an I-awareness, and Pran (a BMI^2P complex). Atman is a portion of the ultimate reality that identifies itself with an individual BMI^2P rather than with the ultimate reality (Brahman or God). It acts as a separate entity via the BMI^2P of the host complex. The ability of the Atman to interact with other complexes is, therefore, clearly constrained by the BMI^2P limitations of the host complex. Atman, for example, may wish to see flowers bloom in the spring season. If, however, the host body is blind, this will not be possible. Atman may want to go up in space and walk on the Moon without wearing a space suit, or may want to land on the planet Mercury where the daytime temperature is over 900 degrees Celsius. These desires are, however, simply not going to happen with any host human body. Wishes of Atman can be extended to the animal world as well. Atman associated with an ant, for example, may wish to eat an elephant; clearly this is not possible because of the size constraint of the ant. In short, an Atman and the associated BMI^2P complex interacts with the universe within the inherent constraints of the individual BMI^2P complex. *The Law of Karma,* an important element of Hindu Thought, provides a causal basis for these interactions that appear to be going on endlessly in the universe.

The word *Karma,* used both as singular and plural, means one or more such interactions between an individual BMI²P and its surrounding universe. Karma may occur on any level — physical, emotional, and intellectual. On the physical level, when we talk, eat, see, or sleep, we do Karma. When we feed the hungry, treat the sick, or read a story to a child, we do Karma because we interact with the universe. When we hate or love someone, when we feel compassion or anger, and when we forgive someone, we do Karma on the emotional level. Similarly, when we analyze the data from our sensors presented to the intellect by our mind, or when we advise someone about what is in their interest, we are doing Karma on the intellectual level. Since Karma is defined as an interaction between one BMI²P complex and other components of the universe, ipso facto, it can exist or can be defined only within a dualist reality; it does not exist within the monist UR.

It should be noted here that what we are seeking is an internally consistent, universally applicable and logical causal basis for what we daily observe in the universe. At the very beginning of this inquiry, we have ruled out a chaotic universe; consequently, we must rule out *luck or chance* as a possible basis. As we begin to examine the Law of Karma as a causal basis, it helps to understand the concept of *degrees of freedom* (DOF) and examine how scientific investigations usually proceed. When we examine a deterministic system, its condition, or its state can be completely defined in terms of a finite number of independent variables. One may choose to use different variables such as position, velocity, momentum, kinetic energy, electric field intensity, magnetic flux density, or others to define the state of a system at any instant. However, the number of independent variables necessary to completely define the state of a given system is constant. This number is called the degrees of freedom (DOF) of the system. Consider, for example, a simple pendulum formed by attaching a mass to a string of some length. The stable or the rest position of this pendulum occurs when the string is vertical, and the mass will not move from this position unless some external force disturbs it. The swinging motion of the mass, that is, the *state* of the pendulum at any time can be completely defined in terms of two independent variables, for example, the angular position of the mass from the vertical, and its angular velocity. One could use some other two variables if one so chooses. Since two variables completely define the system, a simple pendulum is a 2-DOF system. Such a pendulum describes the classical Simple Harmonic Motion (SHM). Foucault, however, found that the plane of oscillation of the pendulum rotates around the vertical axis, and that it completes one full cycle over a period of one day. He also found that the simple 2-DOF model does not explain this behavior. One must use a >2-DOF model to describe the motion of a pendulum caused by the Earth's rotation. An example of Foucault's Pendulum that illustrates this motion is on display at the world famous Smithsonian Institute in Washington, D.C. Now consider a pendulum with a magnetic mass attached to a string. A student places this pendulum on a table, and proceeds to do certain experiments. Unbeknownst to him however, one of his friends places a strong magnet under the table, and uses a mechanism to move this magnet at will. The pendulum on the table exhibits erratic behavior, and does not follow SHM. The motion of the mass is no longer cyclic, and is really under the control of the friend who is moving the magnet under the table. The student conducting the experiments concludes that a 2-DOF model can no longer describe the motion of the pendulum as he had imagined. Faced with this situation, the student can either immediately declare it to be a God's miracle, or examine if a more complex higher-DOF model would explain the behavior of the pendulum. Scientists have traditionally taken the approach of using higher-DOF models to explain apparently abnormal system behavior.

Let us now attempt to take a similar approach in the time dimension. Imagine what would happen if our memory was limited only to one single day. Under this scenario, when we get up every morning, we would not have any memory of anything that may have happened prior to that morning.

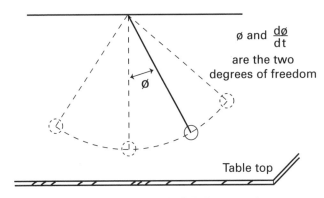

$\varnothing$ and $\dfrac{d\varnothing}{dt}$

are the two
degrees of freedom

$\varnothing$

Table top

A simple pendulum (2 DOF System)

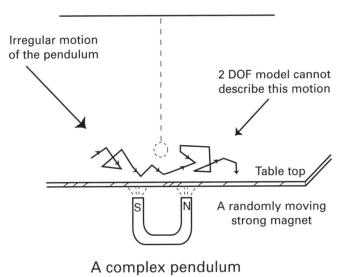

Irregular motion
of the pendulum

2 DOF model cannot
describe this motion

Table top

S   N   A randomly moving
strong magnet

A complex pendulum

Pendulums and Degrees of Freedom

We would see small babies, young adults, old people, sick people, pregnant women, small trees, large trees with flowers and fruits, small and large animals, and many other things. During the day, we would see children being born and people die with high fever; we would see some riverbeds dry and some overflowing with water. We would probably not know the reasons for any of these things, and would wonder if God had a master plan governing all of this. If we had longer memory, we would know that a person had died that day because he was bitten a day earlier by a poisonous snake, or that a person's health improved that day because he was treated earlier by a physician. Many things happening in the world today may thus have perfectly valid reasons that are completely unknown to us because of our limited memory.

In an effort to establish a causal basis for different happenings in the universe, the Law of Karma extends the scope of cause-and-effect beyond our specific life cycle. Since a cause must precede its effects, if we are examining why someone is born blind to poor parents in Mogadishu, Somalia, we must seek this cause prior to the baby's birth. When we see bad things happen to good people, we always wonder if there is justice in the universe. It is not uncommon to see idiots enjoying all the pleasures of life while nice people are facing incredible horrors. What purpose could God possibly have in making humans commit vicious violent acts against other humans, or for that matter, against animals? A few years ago, a California mother shot a suspect with a long criminal record during his trial for raping her daughter. The mother was afraid that the lenient justice system would give him a very short sentence and that he would be free in a few years to rape again. If someone who did not know this background had seen the mother shoot the suspect, he would naturally think that the mother was insane in shooting someone assumed to be innocent until proven guilty. The knowledge of the past would, however, help us understand the behavior of the mother, although we would certainly not be able to justify her taking the law into her own hands. We would, of course, clearly justify any punishment the suspect may receive if he is declared to be guilty in a fair trial. Even today, we see 85-year old Nazis being prosecuted for what they did over 55 years ago. Several of these Nazi criminals have been living in the United States, Canada, Argentina, and other countries as ordinary human beings, and their neighbors are shocked when these criminals are arrested. Everyone at least understood the action however, when their past deeds were revealed. Not everyone agreed with or justified these trials. Some thought that these matters are best forgotten because these Nazis are now too old to stand trial and their actions were too far in the past.

The Law of Karma says that we do not understand many things in this universe because we do not have a long enough memory. Also, just as a cause may have occurred prior to birth, an effect may occur after death. The Law of Karma therefore introduces the concept of endless life cycles. Some of the fundamental elements of this Law of Karma can be expressed as follows:

1. Every karma bears fruit when it matures at some time in the future after it is performed. The time of fruition may extend over many life cycles.

2. In general, a good karma bears good fruit and a bad karma bears bad fruit. A good karma is one that moves us towards our ultimate interest and a bad karma is one that takes us away from it.

3. An Atman is held accountable for and is bound by every karma done during all the life cycles by all the individual BMI^{2}P complexes associated with it.

4. Each one of us is on a potentially endless journey of life and death, driven cumulatively by karma done by all BMI^{2}P complexes associated with our Atman.

5. A life cycle is just a management of our assets and liabilities; the currency here is karma. Obviously, the good karma is an asset whereas the bad karma is a liability.

74

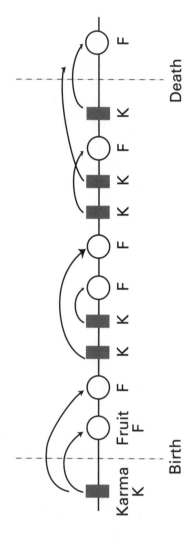

Relationship between Karma and its Fruit

6. No karma can be destroyed by any means. Every accountable karma must be retired, that is, must be checked off by Atman accepting and experiencing its fruit.

7. The karma account is automatically and fully retired when the Atman achieves liberation (explained later in this section) from the life-and-death cycle.

Clearly the Law of Karma is the ultimate in accountability and individual responsibility. Here there is no insanity defense, no plea bargaining, no plea for mercy of the court, and no parole. There is no blaming of others, no *society made me do it* or *the devil made me do it* defense, and there is no *I will not do it again* plea. No one can take up suffering on our behalf for our Karma, and no one else can die for our sins. Each one of us is fully accountable for all our actions, but only for our actions. Each one of us is, of course, free to change the patterns of our behavior and change the course at any time we choose. Clearly this is possible only during a human life when most of our actions are voluntary and we have more control of our actions.

The karma account can generally be considered as follows:

$K_0(n)$ — The total karma that an Atman is responsible for and accountable to at the beginning of any specific life cycle;

K_p — A portion of the $K_0(n)$ karma whose fruit the Atman has chosen to accept during the current life. It is a kind of a karma checking account that Atman opens at the beginning of a particular life.

ΔK_p — A collection of new karma performed during the current life and that is yet to bear fruit.

At the end of any given life, the total accumulated karma that is yet to bear fruit can be written as

$$K_0(n+1) = K_0(n) - K_p + \Delta K_p$$

The Atman is now responsible for, and accountable to, this totality of karma. The Atman will open a new karma checking account at the beginning of a new life, and the cycle will repeat.

The karma K_p, the portion of the total karma that Atman chooses to accept during a life, essentially determines the type of life one is born into. In members of human race, it explains why someone is born a blind beggar on the streets of Calcutta, and someone else is born into a royal family in Europe. It explains why someone is born a slave and someone a slave owner, why someone is born to a poor teen-age gang member in an American inner-city and someone is born into a wealthy Wall Street family. It explains why some mother from an upper class American family turns into a drug addict, and why apparently innocent thousands perish in severe earthquakes. It also explains why smart people sometimes take wrong decisions leading to their own ruin. Why did President Nixon not destroy the Watergate tapes? Why do some people go out skiing when they know a winter storm is approaching, and why do some people smoke in bed when they know it can cause a deadly fire? It is as if their Karma drags them and forces them into these actions.

The karma K_p also determines if one is born as an animal or as a plant. It must be remembered that an individual Atman is associated with every life form, and could also associate itself, for a finite period of time, with any non-living matter. If the fruit of any karma is to experience death by suffocation, it is certainly possible for one to be born a fish only to be pulled out of water suffocating in a fisherman's net. As another example, consider Hamadryas baboon monkeys. The baboon males are usually twice as large as their females, and they keep their harems in complete bondage with no hope of escape. If a female shows some reluctance when the male wants to have sex, she is quickly bitten in the neck, and may even have her skull crushed by the biting male. Is it not possible to imagine a serial rapist from the human race being born a Hamadryas

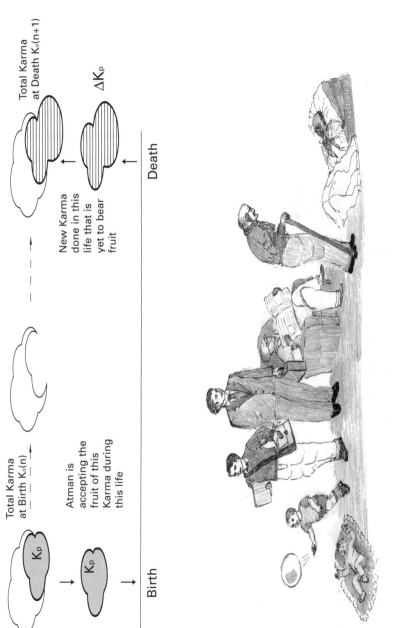

The notion of Karmic Cycle

female baboon to answer for his crimes against human females? Clearly this does not mean that we should not feel any compassion for all these baboon females or for any other animal or human victims. It does not justify the behavior of the oppressor; it only explains it. One can think of the Law of Karma as the universal reward and punishment system with no statute of limitation.

The karma K_p and $K_o(n)$ are clearly a *fait accompli* for us at the time of our birth. This karma has already occurred in the past and we cannot change it *post facto*. We can, however, control the type of, or the quality of karma ΔK_p that we add to $K_o(n)$ during our present life. The quality of ΔK_p does not obviously change the totality or the quality of the old karma that we are accountable to. It will, however, determine the quality of the fruits resulting in the future from this karma. The karma ΔK_p also has the potential of advancing our progress towards liberation from the life-and-death cycle itself. It is, therefore, necessary to understand the criteria for determining the quality of karma.

S-, R-, and T-type Karma

Each one of us performs karma with a desire for certain beneficial fruit. Many times however, our actions result in unintended undesirable consequences to us and to others. When we initiate any karma, our intention is to pursue happiness on a physical, or an emotional, or an intellectual level, or on a combination of these levels. Sometimes, we may be forced to trade off happiness on one level for some unhappiness on another level. For example, if there is not enough food for the entire family, a mother may choose to go to bed hungry so that her children may eat that night. Here she is accepting unhappiness on a physical level in order to receive emotional pleasure of seeing her children eat. Another mother may choose to deny her children food so that she can buy a pack of cigarettes for herself. In both these cases, the mothers are pursuing their happiness as they see fit at the time. Our intention to seek fruits of our karma establishes an adversarial relationship between us and other members of the universe — both humans and other kinds. Consequently, our decisions regarding the performance of karma are influenced by love, hate, jealousy, and other emotions, and our karma may directly or indirectly hurt others. It is this aspect of karma that makes it *binding* to our Atman. The Atman is accountable to this type of binding karma. Any karma done without an accompanying desire for its fruit is *s-type* karma. Such karma is not binding and should be pursued. It is not based on our physical or emotional needs but purely on reason. When our intelligence, acting without a conflict of interest, that is, without thinking *what is in it for me,* tells us what action or karma is appropriate at any time, we call it an s-type karma. This karma is determined on the basis of pure reason and should be pursued with uninterested activism. One should be enthusiastic in doing that karma, but at the same time be uninterested in its results.

There is some karma that we pursue simply for its fruit, and some we pursue to prove to ourselves and to others how great we are. Sometimes we climb mountains just to impress others for a moment. Also we do not like to stay quiet and work endless hours in search of real or perceived happiness. This karma is *r-type* karma.

We do some other karma without giving any thought to our capacity to do it, or to the effect it may have on us or on others. Knowingly or unknowingly, we put others in harms way simply because of our attraction to, or our desire for, the alleged fruit of our karma. Buying a lottery ticket when your children are starving at home, getting drunk knowing fully well that you abuse your wife and children when you are drunk, cheating vulnerable retirees by selling them worthless insurance policies, and many other similar karma fall into this category. This karma is *t-type* karma.

The karma type (s, r, and t) essentially depends upon the intention of the doer. Every karma can be basically identified as one of these types. It must be noted here that just because one is willing to give up the fruits of one's action, karma done recklessly without giving a thought to its consequences does not become s-type karma; it is still t-type karma.

Clearly both r- and t-type karma should be avoided, and one should pursue only s-type karma. This way, as we retire our karma from our past by accepting its fruit, we do not pile up any binding karma that will surely force some unwelcome fruits on us in the future. The pursuit of s-type karma, while avoiding r-, and t-type karma, then essentially means that one must perform karma based only on pure reason while renouncing its fruit forever. In general, one does not have to be a rocket scientist to be able to define such karma. A father must look after his children, a doctor must take care of his patients, and a teacher must educate his students. Because of the total associated past karma, however, such a pursuit of s-type karma alone will not immediately take us out of the life-and-death cycle. Such non-binding karma does not add to the total karma account that must be retired. As a result, it will bring our liberation a little closer.

Predetermination or Free Will

If most of our karma essentially binds us with its fruit, and if there is really no escape from the results of our karma, it raises a very serious philosophical question. Is everything in our life *predetermined*, or do we have any *free will* to act? In a clock mechanism, there are several wheels geared together, and each wheel has a fixed number of teeth. Each wheel, therefore, rotates at a fixed speed determined by the number of its own teeth, the number of teeth on the driving wheel, and the speed of the driving wheel. No tooth or wheel is free to rotate at a speed of its choice; each must rotate at a predetermined speed. Are we such teeth in a giant cosmic clock mechanism, or do we have freedom of will at every step of the way?

According to the Hindu Thought, there is predetermination at a *macro* level and there is free will at a *micro* level. The macro level here implies really a large scale. For example, on the largest level, it is predetermined that each of us is going to die some day. When a child dies in an accident, whether it is an automobile accident, or a hurricane or a tornado, the timing of such a death is also predetermined by karma. After almost every aircraft accident we hear stories about how someone fought hard to buy a ticket on that flight or how someone really rushed to make that flight. Some others get into minor traffic accidents along the way to the airport and miss the doomed flight. Some person who missed the flight was probably constantly blaming the guy who caused that minor accident for his missing the flight. It is predetermination when people rush to get on such flights, or when people are saved in spite of themselves. On the day of the 1995 bombing of the Federal Building in Oklahoma City in the United States, one child who usually went to the day care center in the building fell sick and had to stay home. I believe the child's mother stayed home as well. She was probably angry at the time because she had to use her valuable vacation time that day to care for her child. Clearly, the survival of this child was predetermination on the basis of karma. As another example, we sometimes find that normally cautious folks, without a moments thought, invest their life savings into some questionable stock they buy over the phone and lose everything on the deal. All these events represent predetermination at a macro level. Imagine an ordinary person playing a game of chess against a grand master. It is quite predetermined that the person would lose, but he is free to make any move he wants. The only thing left undetermined is the number of moves it will take for him to lose the game.

We, however, have tremendous freedom of action at a *micro* level. Every day we make hundreds of decisions exhibiting free will. When we show up late at a party, when we blame others for no fault of theirs, when we choose to get drunk and embarrass ourselves at a party, when we steal or lie, we show free will. Our life is full of choices we make every step of the way.

Liberation

If even s-type karma does not take us out of the life-and-death cycle, how does one get out of it? How does one then liberate oneself from the clutches of the Law of Karma? One must first examine the Hindu concept of liberation to be able to answer this question.

What do we really mean by the word *liberation?* Liberation *of whom and from what?* Let us quickly recap the nature of various components of living as well as non-living elements of the universe. A human being is a combination of a BMI^2P complex and the Atman associated with it. An Atman is a portion of the UR that wrongly identifies itself with just one BMI^2P complex, individually separate and different from the other portions of the UR. When a human being dies, the body, the mind, and the intellect (BMI) stop operating as a cybernetic organization because it no more has Pran, the life force. After some finite time period, the Atman, as governed by the Law of Karma, associates its I-awareness with some other BMI (human or otherwise) with Pran, and the new incarnation begins. It must be noted here that animals are also BMI^2P complexes with varying degrees of development of the mind and the intellect. A one-cell amoeba, for example, has a body and Pran because it operates as a cybernetic organization. It has no mind or intellect but has I-awareness that comes from the Atman associated with it. Similarly, other animal life forms may have extremely limited mind and intellect, and their bodies may also have severe limitations. But they all have I-awareness and Pran. Plant life, on the other hand, has a body, I-awareness, and Pran, but no mind or intellect.

In short, it is the Atman who needs to be liberated, and it needs to be liberated from its notion of separateness from the UR. With this liberation comes its liberation from the Law of Karma and from the life-and-death cycle.

Now let us examine the basic concept of liberation. We have earlier discussed the multiple levels of realities. As long as we are in one level of reality, we only experience that reality, and we think that is the ultimate level of reality. Only when we wake up from sleep we realize that our dream was just an illusion. We can also examine the qualities of the dream world. We know that in our dreams we cannot run when attacked, we cannot scream when we are scared, and we debate endlessly if we see colors in our dreams. With such poor levels of participant immersion, we wonder why it all seems so real during the dream. Clearly, when we wake up to some higher level of reality, the lower levels of reality appear to be so unreal and illusory.

The universe also similarly seems so real! We can see and touch things, hear wonderful music, cook and eat a variety of foods, and travel around the world. We can see the Taj Mahal of India, the Iguasu Falls of Brazil, the Statue of Liberty in the United States, and we can see the Leaning Tower of Pisa. How can these things be unreal? In the paradigm of virtual reality, this universe offers the best imaginable participant immersion. In spite of all this, however, it is still not the ultimate reality. It is a dualist reality and not the ultimate monist reality. In this virtual reality, we have pleasure and pain, love and hate, success and failure, conflict of interest between parties, and we have saints and villains. Only when we wake up to the ultimate monist reality, this universe seems so unreal. If the waves on an ocean beach develop an I-consciousness, they may begin to think that they are individually separate from the ocean. However, for someone standing on the beach, this dualism between the waves and the ocean is meaningless and ridiculously unreal; for him, they are all an integral part of the higher reality of ocean.

Individuality of ocean waves is a virtual reality

The liberation of the Atman is simply its waking up to the ultimate monist reality. In this state, the Atman then lets go of its I-awareness and realizes its monist relationship with the one and the only reality. In absence of duality, there is no inter-action and there is no karma, and one is fully liberated from the clutches of the Law of Karma. There is no reincarnation because there is no separate identity.

There is a wonderful story in the classical Hindu literature that explains this concept of liberation. Thousands of years ago, Indian hunters and trappers used to catch parrots and other birds with the help of a simple apparatus. They made a hollow tube from a piece of bamboo. They then put a solid axle bar through this tube so that the tube was free to rotate around the central axle bar. They hung this device from some branch of a tree by means of two threads at the two ends of the axle bar. While flying around from tree to tree, a parrot or some other bird would come there and land on the tube. The tube, being free to rotate, would quickly swing the bird around and the bird would then hang upside down. With this unex-pected turn of events, the bird was usually scared thinking that it was somehow trapped, and would hold on even more tightly to the tube. The trapper would then go up the tree and simply grab the bird, bring it down, and wait for the next bird to land on this special swing

No one has really trapped the bird. Nothing could be farther from the truth. The trap is just a figment of the bird's imagina-tion, an illusion, and a virtual reality. Out of fear of the unknown, the bird thinks the illusion to be a reality, and traps itself. No one can free the bird from this non-existent trap. How do you kill a son of a barren woman? How do you reduce the emissions from a black hole? How do you destroy the ghost of someone who is still living? As long as the bird does not wake up to the reality that it is not trapped to begin with, it will continue to tightly hold on to the tube and will stay there in fear. A few birds however used to figure this out, just let go of the tube, and would fly away. They regained their

A bird arrives at the swing

THe bird hangs upside down

A bird wakes up to reality and lets go

freedom that they had never lost to begin with. Similarly, imagine a person entering a darkened room. He sees a snake on the floor near the bookcase. He is scared and stands there transfixed, completely motionless. He tries to call others for help, but cannot get a word out of his mouth. His wife, wondering what he is doing there in the dark standing at the door, comes and switches the light on. The man then realizes that it is just a piece of a rope that looked like a snake in the dark. He now does not need any additional efforts to free himself from the fear of the snake. The instant he wakes up to reality, the fear is gone.

This is the Hindu concept of liberation. None of us is trapped needing liberation. Trapping and liberation are terms that can exist only in a dualist reality. In the ultimate monist reality, who would trap whom, and whom would we liberate ourselves from? The instant we realize our monist identity, we do not need to make additional efforts to liberate ourselves from the non-existent trap.

Part II – The Art of Hindu Living (The Rules of Ethical Behavior)

6. The Concept of Dharma

Each one of us is individually pursuing, some of us totally unknowingly, a journey towards our liberation. This life is just one segment of this apparently endless journey. We also struggle to be happy in life. We live here as members of our respective communities and develop a certain culture. A culture is a complex collection of knowledge, beliefs, morals, laws, and customs that we acquire as a member of a society. Culture helps to control animal urges in humans and modifies human behavior from powerful urges such as sex and hunger. Uncontrolled human behavior based solely on animal urges leads to the demise of the society. Similarly, if the society is not functioning well, we as individuals cannot pursue our happiness. Consequently, we must make sure that our pursuit of happiness is consistent with the well being of the society. A robber, for example, can profit from robbery only when robbery is not common. Even a robber does not like to get robbed. A society of robbers would not work very well. Similarly, we would not be able to pursue our happiness in a society that is based only on *might is right.* Some things that may outwardly appear to benefit someone thus may be quite detrimental to the well being of the society. Consequently, the Hindu thinkers developed the concept of *Dharma* for guiding one's journey towards liberation in a way that is equally beneficial to the well being of the society.

The concept of dharma is quite simple as well as complex at the same time. In simple terms, dharma specifies the kind of karma that is the *right thing to do under given circumstances*. Irrespective of the intention of the doer, this karma contributes towards the well being of the society as a whole. In its simplest form, it is, for example, a doctor's dharma to treat patients, it is a teacher's dharma to teach his students, and it is a parent's dharma to take care of his or her children. The concept of dharma, however, is also complex because it is not always easy to decide the course of action when multiple dharmas come in potential conflict with each other. Sometimes, it is easy to determine which of the conflicting dharmas should take precedence. For example, it is a judge's dharma to punish the guilty. Now if a judge's own son is tried and found guilty in his court, there is a conflict between the judge's dharma to punish the criminal and his dharma as a father to protect his son. If the judge's criminal son is freed unpunished, he will get a wrong message and will continue to commit crimes, adversely affecting the lives of innumerable innocent members of the society. Considering the interest of the society, one would clearly expect the judge's dharma to take precedence over the parent's dharma. Sometimes, however, there is no such clear distinction between the alternatives. Everyone would agree that it is our dharma to make our friends happy, but what is one to do when in making one friend happy, some other friend becomes unhappy? Or, what if the parent's dharma towards one child comes in conflict with that towards another child?

The principal objective of dharma is to establish a wholesome, healthy, holistic, stable, nurturing, and integrated society in which individuals may flourish and be all they can be. Without such a framework of a society, an individual does not stand a chance to progress spiritually or otherwise. Consider, for example, the urban ghettos of Washington, Detroit, South Central Los Angeles, and other such downtowns in the United States. When babies are born with AIDS, eight year olds sell drugs at the street corners, twelve year olds get pregnant, fifteen year old boys and girls sell their bodies for drugs, eighteen year olds join street gangs and carry out drive-by shootings, and twenty year olds are sent to jail for life, can one realistically expect the children and adults there to quietly pursue spirituality? Such a situation is hardly an environment for developing a culture of monism. It is instead a classical recipe for the law of the jungle where everyone is for himself. In fact, it seems that humans have sunk lower than animals where mothers starve their babies to buy drugs, fathers rape their own daughters, adults abuse children, husbands beat their wives up, and older parents are ignored and left to fend for themselves.

Hindu thinkers of the past developed several ideas based on the need for a society that would support an individual's quest for his ultimate liberation. They understood that a society fundamentally needs four distinct types of contributions from its members. It needs intellectual leadership for guiding the progress of the society in fundamental human rights, education, and spirituality; a role assigned to the *Brahmins*. A society needs military skills for ensuring the safety and security of all its members; a role assigned to the *Kshatriyas*. A society also needs skilled labor and business expertise of the *Vaishyas* to provide agricultural products and industrial commerce. Finally a society needs unskilled labor of the *Shudras* for performing the necessary service-oriented tasks.

Under this concept of the original caste system, the four castes —*brahmin, kshatriya, vaishya, and shudra* — are of equal importance to the well being of the society as a whole. This system provided in those days the needed structure for the society. A person's caste was decided not on the basis of his birth, but on the basis of his actual contributions to the society. A brahmin's son could very well be a kshatriya, or a vaishya, or a shudra, and so on. The king was usually a kshatriya with great military skills. His governance was, however, guided by his brahmin guru. Guru's word was final, and the king would abide by the rulings of his guru. The king served his people as if he were their father, and people's interests would take precedence over any personal interests of the king. The concepts of *public service free of any conflicts of interest* and of *separation of powers* (between a king and his guru) were the basis of governance at the time.

Clearly, this original Hindu concept of castes has nothing in common with the present system in India that has been practiced for the past thousand years or more. The present cast system of India is a complete fraud. Just as one is born a Hindu if one's parents are Hindu, one is now born into the caste of one's parents. The present system is fundamentally flawed, corrupt, unjust, and immoral. It is an anachronism, and as men and women marry out of their castes, the system will eventually collapse and fall into the ash heap of history. Unfortunately, the mankind is condemned to be associated with such atrocities as religious persecutions of anti-Semitism and inquisitions, tribal warfare, genocide, slavery, and the present caste system.

Every caste has a distinct and essential role to play for the survival of the society. A society made up entirely of doctors, for example, cannot survive. It needs teachers, mechanics, cooks, baby-sitters, and hundreds of other specialties in addition to doctors. Each is equally important. Depending on the role, certain qualities are clearly more important than others for various individual castes. For example, unquestioned compassion is a great quality to have, except for a kshatriya. It may, in fact, be suicidal for a kshatriya to have this quality. Consider for example a story from the life of the great King Shivaji (1630–80 A.D.) of Maharashtra in India. One of his Generals, Pratap Gujar, was fighting a battle against Muslim forces. Gujar eventually encircled the enemy, and cut the supply of food and water to the thousands of Muslim soldiers. The Muslim army was then ready to surrender, and sent a peace envoy to Gujar. The envoy described how innocent soldiers were dying of thirst and hunger. He told Gujar that the Muslim General was sorry for invading Shivaji's territory, and that he would simply walk away if Gujar lifted his siege. The envoy then appealed to Gujar's compassion, and assured him that the Muslim forces would never invade again, now that they had learned their lesson. Unbelievable as it may seem, Gujar let the Muslim army go back. Shivaji was shocked to hear what his General of the Army had just done. He wrote to Gujar: "Compassion is a Godly virtue, but not for an Army General. I can understand showing compassion towards civilians, and towards sick and injured soldiers. However, you should have arrested as prisoners of war at least the Muslim General and his staff, if not his entire army. Now I do not know what price we will have to pay for this foolishness on your part." Needless to say that the Muslim army was back later and Gujar was killed in action.

Similarly, forgiveness is a great personal quality to have, except for a King or his Officers of the Law. Fair and speedy justice is important for the betterment of the society, and undeserved or unqualified forgiveness will be detrimental to this goal. Nonviolence is no doubt valuable; however, a kshatriya is obliged to fight the evil at any cost. Hindu thinkers thus recognized the need for recommending and encouraging certain special qualities for members of different castes. Consequently, dharma of different castes stressed different qualities and different karma.

Hindu thinkers also understood that every person, irrespective of caste or gender, goes through four distinct phases in life. First phase is the learning phase or the developmental phase. During this phase, a baby grows up to be a young child, goes to school, and learns the fundamental tenets of dharma and certain skills appropriate for one's caste. He finishes his training, and as a young adult, he is now ready to enter the next phase of life. During the second phase of life, he gets married, works and earns a living, raises his children, is a productive member of the society, follows the dharma that he learned in school, and takes care of his parents and other elders at home.

Sometime after his children grow up and start their own second phase, he enters the third phase of life. He retires from active life, travels and enjoys life, looks after and enjoys the company of his grandchildren, does some volunteer community service, and generally leads a quiet life. At some point in this phase, however, he starts to think about his afterlife. He then gives up the ordinary way of life, and enters the fourth and the last phase of his life. He withdraws inwards and leads a contemplative life. He spends his time in yoga and meditation, and generally prepares for the day when he would leave the shackles of this earthly body and continue his journey towards liberation.

Clearly, when one is going to school, he or she should pay full attention to studies, respect one's teachers, and learn as much as possible from different teachers. Exactly how one does this would depend on the structure of the society at the time. In old days, Hindu students would go to live at an *ashram* (a sort of residential school where both the teacher and the students lived), lead a communal life, and learn from the Guru. Now we have different types of schools, but still the focus should be on education. During the school years, you do not want a student to work to earn if that is going to compromise his studies. You do not want girls to get pregnant and boys to father children. In the second phase, you want men and women to have and raise children; you want parents to earn a living, and contribute to a vibrant economy. You do not want a young married man with children just to hang out on street corners with his buddies, or to leave his family and go to a mountaintop for leading a contemplative life. Hindu thinkers, however, also recognized that some individuals might want to skip certain phases of life. There would be no problem if someone wanted to stay single, skip married and retired life, and straight go to the Himalayas to meditate there undisturbed. Men and women would have this freedom without any question.

Today we see the price individuals and the society pay when we do not respect and completely ignore the boundaries of the phases of life. Imagine a fifteen-year old girl falling in love with a forty-year-old man with three children. Clearly these two are in two different phases of life. The girl would naturally want to get married and have children; the man would probably not want to start a new family all over again. Lives get ruined when the phases of life are not respected. Once we start on a slippery slope, then babies have babies, men get women pregnant and leave, children are abused, and parents and elders are warehoused in abusive nursing homes.

Consequently, dharma recognizes the needs of the society as a whole, and recommends a specific way of life, depending on the caste and the phase of life. We have earlier examined the s-, r-, and t-type of karma. The t-type is totally contrary to the whole concept of monism, and tends to take us away from our liberation. This karma driven by anger, violence, hate, greed, and similar other emotions is undesirable and must be avoided. The desireless s-type karma is nonbinding and should be pursued. Dharma suggests that, in order to avoid t-type karma and to pursue s-type karma, one must bring some discipline into the r-type karma we predominantly pursue. It suggests that we pursue certain *scheduled* and *occasional* karma as a part of this discipline. Scheduled karma includes everything that we do on a regular basis. Dharma recommends different scheduled karma at the body-, mind-, and intellect-levels. On a physical level, we should take care of our body, perform yoga exercises, eat regularly and right, and work hard in our profession and in service to the society. On an emotional level, we should spend time in worship, prayer, spiritual music, and generally establish a personal relationship with God. On an intellectual or rational level, we should regularly spend time in meditation, read metaphysical literature, and generally attempt to experience a monist relationship with God. Dharma also recommends several rituals, ceremonies, and communal worship and prayers to be performed on an occasional basis. Dharma further suggests that we should always strive to do the scheduled and occasional karma without any desire for their fruit so that they become nonbinding s-type karma.

Dharma thus takes a holistic view of total karma — interrelations between individuals at an individual and collective levels. It establishes a structure of society based on the needs of both the individual and the society. It recommends that one should do *desirable* or the *right* karma that is appropriate for one's caste and one's phase of life. This, of course, means that one must now define a criterion for determining what karma is right and what karma is wrong.

7. The Criteria of Right Karma

Each one of us constantly faces decisions of what to do or not to do. Earlier philosophical, and probably esoteric, discussion unquestionably establishes a sound basis for Hindu metaphysics and defines a suitable structure for society. It is of little direct help for common man in making these decisions however. Hindu thinkers therefore developed a variety of guidance materials for assisting the common man in taking the necessary day to day decisions. First, they established firm criteria for the right karma. They also wrote epics of *Ramayan* and *Mahabharat,* and other extensive literature where they showed how to apply these criteria under innumerable practical situations faced by a variety of people. In Ramayan, we find examples of ideal human behavior that is probably quite unachievable by common man. It is like the North Star that always points in the right direction. In Mahabharat, we find examples of consequences of thoughtless and sometimes highly irresponsible human behavior. Some other literature, such as, for example, *Hitopadesh* and *Panchatantra,* is geared towards children, and helps them learn via simple, interesting stories.

Instead of using a primitive *textual* approach, the Hindu Thought uses a *grammarian* approach to develop criteria of right karma. In teaching a new language, for example, one could ask students to memorize hundreds or perhaps thousands of complete sentences. They would then start speaking the language with others. If everyone were taught the same set of sentences, presumably there would not be any need for anyone to learn additional vocabulary or additional sentences. This is what I call a *textual* approach. With this approach, the language would be static and extremely constraining, especially for independent thinkers and artists who would want to express new ideas. In a *grammarian* approach, however, students would be taught the grammar of the language; they would learn the rules by which sentences are formed. Unlike with a textual approach, the students would then be not limited to a prescribed set of sentences. They would be free to express themselves by forming sentences of their choice as long as they stay within the constraints of the grammar of the language. Furthermore, this grammar will be more effective and user-friendly if it is based on mathematical logic. Beginning with the early work on artificial intelligence (AI), computer scientists have attempted to analyze natural languages like English, French, and others for use with computers. They soon discovered that the sentence structures and grammars of these languages are not sufficiently logical to be useful for implementing AI on computers. Then some scientists from NASA Ames Research Center examined the old Indian language Sanskrit for this application. They quickly concluded that the sentence structures and the grammar of Sanskrit are very well suited for computer application, and that the development of an AI language was essentially reinventing the wheel that had already been invented several thousand years ago. The structure and beauty of Sanskrit are not accidental; they are the result of a logical approach used by the ancient Hindu grammarians.

The democratic republics also take such a grammarian approach in organizing their governments. The United States Constitution, for example, is a short document that enumerates only a small set of broad principles by which the nation will be governed. The United States Congress is then free to pass

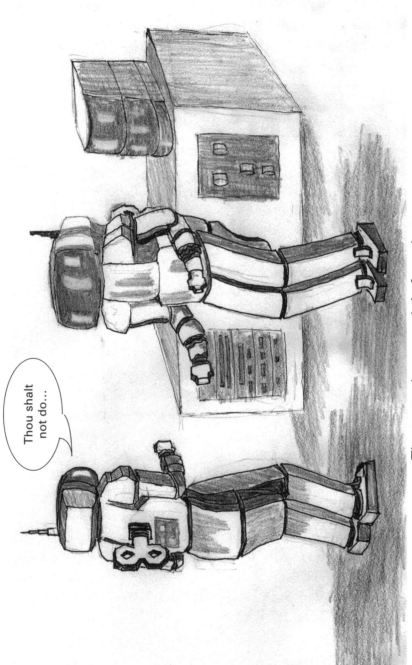

The textual approach is for robots

any law as long as it is within the confines of this Constitution. In other words, the Constitution is the grammar and the Congressional laws are the individual sentences.

Clearly, a textual approach is the easiest approach for prescribing the rules of ethical behavior, especially for those claiming to have spoken to God before prescribing these rules. For some unknown reasons, a number of followers also seem to like this textual enumeration of behavioral rules. There is no need for the followers to think or to debate, and eternally happy afterlife is guaranteed in writing. For billions of people around the world, the struggle for survival itself is so hard that one does not have enough energy or time at the end of the day to think about the mysteries of the cosmos. They find simple creature comforts beyond their reach, and are only too happy to read a verse or two from their scriptures to ensure a happy afterlife. The religious fundamentalists reduce the intricate mysteries of the ultimate reality to a book or two, and clearly this appeals to a vast majority of their followers. Only when you start analyzing individual commands you start wondering about the universal applicability of these commands. Only then you realize that, as Mahatma Gandhi had said, *an eye for an eye would make the whole world blind*. Only then you realize that a command such as *thou shalt not kill* would not work without any additional conditions. This command does not leave any discretion to the faithful. It does not say that you shall not kill a human being, or an innocent human being, or an unborn human fetus, or an animal, or a plant. It simply forbids *any killing*. Under this command, you shall not kill even in self-defense a virus, a bacterium, a tiger that is attacking you, or another human being. The textual approach of prescribing ethical behavior is thus inherently flawed or problematic. The rule itself may be unworkable, or two or more rules may sometime come in conflict. For example, *love thy neighbor* and *an eye for an eye* would be in conflict if it were your neighbor who took your eye in the first place.

Human beings should not be asked to follow some prewritten prescriptions as robots are asked to follow some computer programs written for them by a programmer. Humans are rational animals that can write appropriate sentences if they are just taught the grammar of the language. Ancient Hindu thinkers used a grammarian approach in developing the rules of ethical behavior.

To Do or Not to Do

Each one of us often faces complex situations when we agonize over selecting among different alternative courses of action. Every alternative has innumerable positive and negative elements, and it is many times difficult to decide what is the right thing to do in a given situation. Shakespeare's Hamlet, for example, faced such a complex situation. His uncle had killed the King, married the Queen (Hamlet's mother), and had declared himself to be the new King of Denmark. Hamlet was facing a choice: should he avenge the death of his father by killing his uncle, or should he make peace with his uncle as the new King and his stepfather. Hamlet found this conflict quite unbearable and asked his famous *to be or not to be* question. The legendary Roman hero Coriolanus who lived in the late 6th and early 5th century B.C. had also faced such a difficult situation. During the famine of Rome in 491 B.C., he had suggested that people should not be given grain unless they agreed to abolish the Office of Tribune. The tribunes, therefore, exiled Coriolanus, and he then joined the King of Volsci promising the king his eternal loyalty and obedience. Then when Coriolanus led the Volscian army against Rome, the Romans had his wife and mother plead with him to remember his motherland and withdraw the army from the gates of

Rome. What should Coriolanus have done — save the mother-land or keep his promise to the Volscian King? If he had proceeded with the attack, his mother and wife would have been killed and his motherland would have been destroyed, but his promise of loyalty and obedience to the Volscian King would have been kept. On the other hand, if he withdrew (which he did), his family and his motherland would be saved at the cost of braking his word to the Volscian King. Is there a *right thing* to do under this situation? If so, what are the criteria to decide what is right? If your word should be more important than your family, why, and if not, why not?

Clearly, common people do not face dramatic situations such as those faced by Hamlet and Coriolanus. Nonetheless, they face many situations where they struggle to decide what is the right thing to do in response. Is it all right to tell a white lie, give some cash to a street beggar, help someone who is evil, help some one if that makes someone else unhappy, and on and on? These questions may appear to be trivial to someone, but the fundamental problem remains — are there any criteria to determine if a certain action is right or wrong?

Truth, Non-violence, and Other Virtues

Almost all religions have said that truth, nonviolence, and respect for another's property are some of the most basic right things to do. There is no doubt that these are inherently good principles to follow. Even liars do not like it when others lie to them. The town bullies act as courageous lions when they inflict pain on the weak. When they face someone stronger than themselves however, they quickly turn into scared little lambs. Also, a society cannot be organized if every member is allowed to lie, to steal, and to commit violence against others. There is no question that these three are extremely valuable and admirable virtues, but can any of these be the ultimate criterion? For example, is it right for everyone to tell the truth at all times and under all circumstances?

In the New Testament, Paul, an apostle, has said that it is all right to lie to increase the glory of God. It is quite well known that ancient Christian evangelists routinely lied and cheated if that would help the spread of Christianity in Africa and in Asia. Even Western ethicists clearly support the notion that it is all right to tell a lie to a child and to a mentally or physically sick adult. Doctors routinely tell patients that they will get better when they know perfectly well that it is not so. Clearly, a government official or a secret agent cannot be reasonably expected to tell the truth to the enemy or to an enemy agent. Similarly, a military officer will certainly tell lies to any known enemy agent, especially during an active war. If you see a young girl running away from her attacker, and a few minutes later, if the armed attacker asks you if you had seen a girl running, should you tell the truth and give him directions? If we accept that there are certain exceptions to telling the truth, then clearly, truth cannot be the ultimate criterion. We need another criterion to decide when and where it would be all right to tell a lie.

Similarly, consider the issue of nonviolence. Every religion has commandments similar to *thou shalt not kill.* Let us at the outset stipulate that this commandment applies only to human life and not to plants and animals. Even then one can construct a number of scenarios where reasonable people would agree that it should be all right to kill a human being. If a terrorist is about to kill his hostages, or a rapist is about to rape a victim, or an arsonist is about to set fire to a house, or an armed robber is threatening to shoot someone in the house, most of us would agree that, not only would it be all right, but it would almost be our duty to kill the terrorist, or the rapist, or the arsonist, or the armed robber. The legal system clearly permits such killing as a justifiable homicide. Even when there is no loss of life involved, religions have generally recommended nonviolent behaviors. It is equally true however, that town or school bullies are not usually stopped without a credible threat of overpowering violence. Nonviolence also thus falls quite short of being the ultimate criterion of ethical behavior.

In fact, if we examine other commonly accepted virtues such as having respect for another's property, compassion, forgiveness, and others, we quickly realize that none of these can qualify to be the ultimate criterion. No jury in the world will send a mother to jail if she steals food to feed her hungry children. Preservation of life is clearly more important than someone's right of ownership of food. Also, there is a significant body of opinion that wrongly placed compassion is against the interests of the society. Many argue that helping a street beggar encourages the beggar to be lazy. It is better to teach someone catch a fish than to give him a fish to eat. One way, he knows how to feed himself for life; the other way, he only gets a meal and again gets hungry after several hours.

It must be noted here that truth, nonviolence, and other virtues are of great importance and one must strive to achieve these virtues. Also, in most situations, it takes courage of conviction to be able to exhibit these virtuous qualities. We, however, should remember that there are some inherent limitations to these, and behavior contrary to these virtues could very well be quite ethical under some difficult circumstances.

Greatest Good of the Greatest Number

In discussing the rules of ethical behavior some have even argued the very need for such rules. They have said that each individual is separately and independently on his own, and that one should pursue his happiness at any cost to anyone else. Under this scenario, there is no God, there is no afterlife, and consequently, there is no inherent need for exhibiting any virtuous behavior. If you are strong and powerful, you may torture others if that is what makes you happy. There is no accountability for your actions and you do not need to be good if you do not want to be. Under this philosophy, if it can be so called, there is no need for ethical evaluation of actions, and anything would be permissible. There would be nothing wrong with atrocities committed under Stalin, Hitler, and more recently, in South Africa, Rwanda, Combodia, and Bosnia.

If there is no need to be good, why are most people good? Some have even suggested that since everyone is seeking happiness, if we do not think about the happiness of others, they would, in turn, not let you be happy. In other words, being good to others is also a selfish act at some level. This is at least marginally better than saying that there is no need for anyone to be good to others. Under this concept of *enlightened self-interest,* we help a street beggar because seeing him hungry makes us unhappy, and we take care of our children because we want them to take care of us when we become old, and so on.

Let us now set aside this notion of pure selfishness as the basis of our actions and examine other possible criteria for judging ethics of our actions. Clearly it is not possible for us to make everyone happy with every one of our actions. In fact, our actions may even lead to consequences that we neither intended nor imagined. If we cannot make everyone happy, we can at least try to make as many people happy as possible. This is precisely why ethicists have proposed the criterion of the *greatest good of the greatest number.* Great many societies have basically accepted this notion as a reasonable one. On a battlefield or in a natural disaster, for example, when a limited number of doctors have to care for a large number of injured, they routinely limit their heroic efforts to save only a few near death so that they have a reasonable chance to save many others. When we examine it in depth however, we find that as practical and noble it may sound, *the greatest good of the greatest number* cannot be the ultimate ethical criterion.

First, we clearly believe that it is necessary to protect the fundamental rights of all even if it makes the majority unhappy. We routinely protect the rights of Ku Klux Klan members to march on the main streets of any American city even though that makes a vast majority of African Americans and Jewish Americans extremely angry. We also face another problem of deciding what is *the greatest good* because it cannot be determined as easily as *the greatest number.* Young children may like to smoke, drink alcohol, and watch some dirty movies, but most parents do not let them do that. The children may think it is good for them and will make them happy, but parents know that it is not in their children's ultimate interest. A diabetic may like to eat his favorite sweets, but that would hardly make it moral for someone to offer him such sweets. On the opposite spectrum, religious fanatics have killed some people for refusing to convert because, in the opinion of the fanatics, it is better for those people to be dead than to be following a wrong religion. Thus even the seemingly logical and sensible concept of the greatest good of the greatest number raises very fundamental issues of what is good, who is to decide, and on what basis.

Criteria of Atman's Liberation and Monism

The Hindu thinkers have consistently related everything, including the concept of right and wrong, to what is in one's ultimate interest. Clearly, happiness can be experienced at physical, emotional, and intellectual levels. Furthermore, it has been the consistent experience of innumerable people that the quality and intensity of happiness at the intellectual level are far better than those at the other two levels, and that these are far better at the emotional level than at the physical level. The Hindu thinkers have, therefore, almost totally rejected physical pleasures as the ultimate criterion for deciding right and wrong. A glass of cold water that is very pleasurable in summer is not so in winter, and a serving of meat and potatoes would hardly bring pleasure to someone with full stomach. Physical happiness is thus very relative and would not qualify to be the ultimate criterion for anything. Emotional happiness is a state of mind and consequently does not depend on anything at the physical level. If two people are equally happy, the fact that one may be much richer than the other would be quite irrelevant. Furthermore, mystics have consistently reported that the intellectual-level happiness experienced in a meditative state is far more pleasurable than that at an emotional level.

There is a story about a young and handsome Indian mystic of the seventeenth century. A daughter of a known area prostitute saw the mystic and instantly fell in love with him. She told her mother that she would not follow in the mother's footsteps and that she would like to marry the mystic. The mother told her that mystic had taken the customary vow of celibacy and that such a marriage would simply be out of the question. The daughter was devastated when she heard that; she even lost interest in living and stopped taking care of herself. She did not eat or sleep well and began to lose weight. The mother felt helpless and, as a last resort, went to the mystic and told him the story of her daughter. The mystic listened to her patiently and, to her surprise, asked the mother to bring her daughter to him. Next day, when the daughter came, the mystic just touched her on her forehead and instantly put her in a meditative state. The daughter clearly exuded serene happiness and did not wake up from that state for three days. The mother, obviously worried that her daughter was not eating anything for days, woke her up. "Why did you wake me up mom? I was in such an intense happy state," said the daughter. The mystic then asked the daughter if she still wanted to marry him. The daughter told him that she would rather learn how to be happy as that in the meditative state. That daughter grew up to be a great Indian mystic in her own right.

It is, therefore, said that it is better to be a human dissatisfied than a pig satisfied, and better to be a philosopher dissatisfied than a fool satisfied. And if the pig and the fool do not agree with this concept, it is because they do not know any better.

In addition to recognizing the above hierarchy (physical, emotional, and intellectual) in levels of happiness, we need to understand that, at each level, happiness at any particular instant is far less important than the totality of future happiness. On a mundane physical level for example, it is better to take a spoonful of nauseatingly tasteless medicine when we are sick so that we can get better quicker, and reduce the number of days we would feel lousy.

Finally, Atman's liberation, that is, its mystical awakening to the ultimate monist reality is far more important than anything else. Consequently, liberation has been accepted as the only ultimate criterion for deciding right and wrong. If any karma takes us toward our liberation, it is right; if it takes us away from our liberation, it is wrong. Since establishing a monist relationship with the universe is a gateway to liberation, clearly every right action has to be fully consistent with monism.

Based on this criterion of Atman's liberation, it is now possible to enumerate some simple notions that will help us differentiate between right and wrong karma.

1. At any level, happiness is better than unhappiness.

2. Emotional happiness is better than physical happiness; intellectual happiness is better than both physical and emotional happiness.

3. Cumulative happiness is better than the instantaneous happiness.

4. In the dualist VR world, interests of many outweigh the interests of a few or one; our own liberation outweighs everything else.

5. Any karma supporting or encouraging any wrong karma is, *ipso facto,* wrong.

With such a concept of right and wrong, it becomes quite clear that a particular action is never absolutely right or wrong irrespective of the context. The intention of the doer, the possible outcome, and other related actions must be considered before deciding if any action is right or wrong.

Revisiting earlier scenarios, now it will be clear that one should not tell the truth if it is going to assist a rapist or an arsonist in their intended mission, violent opposition to a terrorist is the right action, and so on. Furthermore, no one may hide behind *Atman's liberation* as a criterion unless it is consistent with monism. Hitler could not have justified his genocide against Jews by saying that he thought it would lead to his liberation. With monism, there is no room for any conflict of interest between a person and other elements of the universe. Hence it will be impossible to justify any action that may hurt others while benefiting yourself.

It must also be noted here that the criterion of Atman's liberation does not always lead to unique conclusions. Under exactly identical conditions, two individuals with clear consciences may act differently, and both actions may be right. Faced with one's wife and one's daughter being caught in a raging river, one person may decide to save his wife first, and that decision may cost him the life of his daughter. Under an identical situation, another person may decide to save his daughter first, and may end up losing his wife. A third person may end up saving both, and a fourth person may end up losing both. All may have the same justification for their actions, and consequently, the actions of all these persons may be perfectly all right. The end result, that is, the success or failure of one's actions, is quite irrelevant in deciding if the action is right or wrong.

8. A Path to Liberation

Liberation is essentially a mystical awakening of the Atman to the ultimate reality of monism. Atman, however, interfaces with this world of duality only via resources such as the body, the mind, and the intellect of the individual life form that it is associated with at the time. Humans have the intellect and the freedom of action necessary to understand and pursue liberation. Consequently, liberation is possible for Atman only when it is associated with a human life. Animal and plant life forms are used only to retire old karma, and liberation is not possible during these lives.

The process of liberation involves understanding the monist relationship between God and Universe that is, between the UR and the VR. Each one of us is a member of the VR universe. Atman associated with us is really a part of the UR (or Brahman or God in other words), although it has not awakened itself to that truth. Consequently, liberation is simply re-establishing the already-existing monist relationship between God, Universe, and the individual. Furthermore, since Atman uses the human BMI resources that operate on three levels, the path to liberation consists of three components — Knowledge, Devotion, and Action.

Any process of liberation must necessarily begin with a desire to liberate oneself from the shackles of the birth-and-death cycle. Such motivation is also necessary for most of our efforts in the ordinary life. If you want to loose weight, stop smoking, or save your marriage, you must really want to do it for yourself. You cannot do it for your siblings, or parents, or your spouse, or for anyone else. Then you are really not ready, and are destined to fail. Similarly, you must first truly get sick of the birth-and-death cycle, and you must want to get out. Only then you will try to find a way out of this. The other important thing is not to have a blind disbelief in anything and to be ready to try a few things out. Everyone knows that blind belief is not good, but one must realize that blind disbelief is even worse. Let us, for example, suppose that you want to look for a hidden cave in an area, and let us further suppose that five different men tell you that they have been to that cave before and can take you there. Let us also suppose that you have a blind belief that one particular person is telling the truth; you have no idea if the other four are truthful. You take with you the person you trust and start looking for the cave. If your blind belief was justified, you will find the cave; if it was mis-placed, you may not find the cave and may waste your time and effort. Even if your friend is of no help, it is also quite pos-sible that you may actually find the cave. If, however, you had a blind disbelief that none of the five is telling the truth, you would not even start looking for the cave. Surely you will not find the cave if you do not even start looking for it. Similarly, if you have a blind belief that someone is a good author, you will try to get some of his books and read them. Now if you do not like any of those books, at worst you will have wasted your time. If, however, you have a blind disbelief that someone is not a good writer, you will not even try out any of his books. Blind disbelief thus prevents any action and that cannot possibly lead to any results. Blind belief, on the other hand, may only lead to wasted effort, but does not preclude success. If you do not start your journey, you will never reach your destination. If, however, you start moving, there is at least a possibility that you may some day reach your destination.

With a desire to liberate oneself, one can then choose to concentrate on any one of the following three elements:

1. Path of Knowledge

The path of knowledge concentrates on the relationship between the universe and God, and this relationship is established on an intellectual or rational level. Once a monist relationship is established between the universe and God, a monist relationship between the self and God is automatically established.

The universe, including each one of us, is constrained by the characteristics of the 4-D reality. Our concepts, comparisons, language, similes, experiences, and other tools are limited by this reality. We deal everyday in the world of duality. Consequently, we find it difficult even to describe God as the ultimate reality. Any questions we may ask such as, is it big? is it short? is it heavy? are then necessarily answered with words such as, *not that* or *not really*. The UR has no form; has no s-, r-, or t- quality; and is not bound by spacetime. Consequently, it is very difficult to establish a monist relationship with such a *formless* and *qualityless* entity. The path of knowledge is, therefore, the most difficult of all paths to liberation.

Difficult, however, does not mean time consuming. A man, for example, may climb up a mango tree, step by step, branch by branch, carefully and slowly, and finally reach a ripe mango that he can pick. A bird, however, may see the ripe mango and simply fly there and pick it up in a few seconds. Picking a mango off a tree is difficult for a man because he is not equipped appropriately for the task. If, however, someone is tall enough or can jump high enough, he can reach the mango just as easily and quickly as the bird.

Students of difficult subjects such as thermodynamics and electromagnetics know this very well. Some students grasp the concepts quickly and understand the theory so clearly that they do not need to constantly keep solving the problems at the end of the chapters. Some students, however, keep solving the problems so that they would not forget the steps they need to take in solving similar problems. These students may not understand the theory very well, and they may find themselves helpless when faced with a problem they have not seen before. Students who clearly understand the theory can apply it to new problems without much difficulty. Similarly, if anyone can clearly understand the concept of monism, liberation can be only one step away. We all know, for example, that if we sow rice we cannot and will not get a crop of wheat. We know this so clearly, that we never try to see if, may be by chance, we will get a wheat crop from a rice field.

The difficulty of the path of knowledge is really having the required clarity of thinking and a readiness to accept the inevitable conclusion at the end of this path. On a physical level, it is not very difficult to understand that we all humans are not that different. The differences in Whites, Blacks, Chinese, Indians, and others are clearly only skin-deep. It is impossible to tell if a small piece of kidney or liver you see came from a white man or a black man. Even humans and monkeys share over 95 percent of genes. Most of our differences are at the emotional level where our minds operate. Waking up to a monist relationship with the whole cosmos would mean giving up long-held prejudices, hatreds, superiority complexes, and other emotional-level baggage. Whites will then have to accept Blacks as equals, Christians will have to permit Jews in the heaven, Arabs will have to love Israelis, Muslims will have stop issuing death sentences on those who speak against Islam, and Hindus will have to forget the present form of the caste system.

Once someone knows this monist relationship, there is no difference between the *knower* and the *subject of his knowledge.* Consequently, the very concept of knowing something simply vanishes. This is *real* knowledge. Other knowledge such as that of physics and chemistry is simply scientific knowledge in the VR. This type of knowledge is based on a duality between the *knower* and the *subject of knowledge,* and hence it does not exist in the UR. One should not confuse *scientific* knowledge with *real* knowledge; such confusion is caused by ignorance. In the UR, several truths dawn on one that are most difficult to accept. Our body, beauty, strength, IQ, and riches; our spouses, children, brothers, sisters, and parents; our pastors, priests, rabbis, and mullahs; our boyfriends, girlfriends, and our buddies from high school and college; all have been just a part of this cosmic drama in virtual reality. It forces us to forget our individual and separate identities, to leave the surface turbulence of duality, and to enter the calm and peaceful deep waters of monism in this ocean of ultimate reality. When one achieves such liberation, the state defies description. Descriptions such as *there is no returning from there, unlimited by spacetime constraints, without beginning and without end, and all encompassing,* are all based on comparative dualism and fail to do any justice to the monist reality.

2. Path of Devotion

The path of devotion concentrates on the relationship between *the individual* and *God* (Atman and Brahman in other words), and this relationship is established on an *emotional* level. This path is fundamentally easy to follow because it is both personal and emotional. Furthermore, the mind is the principal instrument of devotion because devotion is emotional. The mind, by definition and as we all know, is unsteady and wanders all over. It is then all the more difficult to focus the mind on some conceptual formless and qualityless entity. Any attempt to do so will quickly turn into the path of knowledge on the rational level, and would be again difficult. Consequently, one needs a concrete, physical, and possibly familiar entity that our mind can accept as the focus of its attention. Consider again how we define a *point* in geometry. It is an entity without any length, width, or height. We also define a *line* as an entity having length, but not width or height. We quickly draw a point or a line on a chalkboard or on a paper, but both have at least two dimensions. We, of course, try to draw as thin a line as possible so that we approach as close as possible to our definition of a line, but we know that such representations are incompatible with their basic definitions. We do that anyway however, because it is easier for us to concentrate on figures drawn on a board, and such figures help us achieve our goal of understanding theorems of geometry.

When we want to wear gold around our neck, we do not simply wrap a thick wire of gold around our neck. We spend hours of skilled labor and make necklaces of intricate designs. We know that *gold is gold,* and the *gold* in the wire is not less valuable than that in an intricately crafted necklace. But this understanding is clearly on a rational level. On an emotional level, we would, of course, prefer the intricate necklace to a plain thick wire.

We take a similar approach to the path of devotion. We first take some object — a statue or a sculpture, a picture, or a historical or a mythological character — to represent God (like we draw a line on a paper). We then focus our attention on this object, and use it as a vehicle to establish a close personal relationship with the ultimate reality of God. In doing so, however, we must remember that we draw our geometrical figures with lines that are very thin, approaching as closely as possible to ideal lines. Similarly, we must be careful when we select some mythological or other character to represent God. If the monist reality of God were to take a human form, we would expect it to act in a way that is consistent with the concept of monism. We would not expect it to exhibit any violent, hateful, uncaring, callous, deceitful, or vengeful behavior. With a rich history of thousands of years, Hindus from India have no difficulty in choosing one or more such objects of devotion. This choice is also very much individual and deeply personal. It does not matter if your choice is more popular and also has been the choice of millions of others. Equally however, just because a few millions may prefer an image of Shiva, Vishnu, or Ganesh, you do not have to accept any of them. Some may like mystics from the past such as Dnyaneshwar, Chaitanya, Raman Maharshi, or Shiradi Sai Baba. Some may prefer Ram or Krishna from the great Indian epics of Ramayan and Mahabharat. Some others may prefer Buddha or Jesus Christ. It is strictly your choice and yours alone.

Whoever we select as our object of devotion, we must clearly understand that the real goal is to establish a monist relationship with the entire universe and the ultimate reality of God. A close personal relationship with *our representation* of God is only a stepping stone to this ultimate goal. Furthermore, we can establish any kind of personal relationship of our choosing. Someone who may have lost his parents in early childhood may choose a parental relationship. A woman who may have lost a child due to a sickness or an accident may choose to shower God with her love and affection as a mother. History is full of such examples of a wide spectrum of relationships between a devotee and God.

A devotee must, however, avoid two fundamental pitfalls while following this path of devotion. First, one must not do this in the hope that God will then reward you by fulfilling some of your *worldly* desires. You do not do this because you want to get a good job or you want your son to get into some Ivy League school. It goes against the whole basic concept of a monist relationship with God. Through the path of devotion, we attempt to realize that a job or an Ivy League school is just another element of the virtual reality. Use of devotion to satisfy our dualist worldly desires is a waste of time and energy; the Law of Karma determines if our worldly desires are satisfied. We must also avoid any pride in our individual choice for the object of our devotion. Just as we are free to choose our representation of God, so is everyone else. When we think that only *our* symbol can represent God, then we ridicule other symbols. We think we are smarter than others for choosing the *right* symbol, and others are somehow lesser than us for choosing a *wrong* one. We are superior to others and they must be educated and corrected. If they do not listen to us, they should be punished, and such punishment is actually in *their* interest. Once we think that we are the only ones who understand God, we then authorize ourselves to be the prosecutor, the judge, and the jury. We then sentence to death people such as Salman Rushdie and Taslima Nasrin (a novelist from Bangladesh). It is one thing to think that we have the answers to all problems of the world, but it is altogether different to think that God gave us those answers by slipping a book or two of his word in our pockets or under our pillows. This notion of *my God is better than yours* has in the past resulted in the torture and death of millions and millions of people. Religious conflicts continue even today around the world. A basic fallacy thus leads to the untold misery for innumerable human beings.

It must be noted here that the above two problems really arise, not at an emotional level, but at the higher intellectual or rational level. It is our intellect that selects the object of our devotion, and our mind then follows the path of devotion. If our intellect is of the s-quality that understands what is in our ultimate interest, then our devotion is desireless and is devoid of pride. Such devotion then helps us over time, possibly over a number of reincarnations, to achieve our goal of liberation. If we have a t-quality intellect that takes decisions that are against our ultimate interest, our devotion is then misdirected and worthless. Fortunately, we do not have in this or other lives exclusively s-, r-, or t- quality intellect and the characteristics of our intellect vary over time. During a certain period of time, our intellect may predominantly exhibit t-quality and only occasionally exhibit s-quality. Even then, the intellect will occasionally take decisions in our ultimate interest, and we will be helped to that extent. We may momentarily experience the monist bliss. This, in turn, will suppress the t-qualities in our intellect, and will increase the proportion of s-quality. Any journey on the path of true devotion is thus never wasted. Slowly but surely, our devotion becomes increasingly desireless and devoid of pride, and eventually leads us to liberation.

Clearly devotion is a *path* and not the *destination.* The destination is still Atman's mystical awakening to its monist relationship with Brahman (God or UR in other words). Even after arriving at the destination, however, one may continue to enjoy the deeply personal relationship with God; but then you know that this is all virtual reality anyway. This is similar to an adult enjoying a game of Monopoly with a child, fully knowing that the money is not real.

3. Path of Karma

The path of karma concentrates on the relationship between the *individual* and the *universe,* and this relationship is established on a physical level. Consequently, it covers our interactions with other human beings, other animals, plants, and even the non-living matter. Our interactions with the non-living and the plant worlds are quite unidirectional and hence simple. The non-living matter does not exchange data with the outside world; it is not characterized by any BMI complex, and does not have Pran associated with it. Plants have Pran and an associated Atman, but no mind or intellect. They only react to the environment at a physical level. The quality of our interaction with the non-living and the plant world depends only on our intentions behind our actions. Our actions must be consistent with monism; it is the only criterion for judging our karma towards these two.

There are several ways in which Hindus express their special relationship with non-living matter. On the first day of the Hindu calendar, they express their gratitude towards the tools of the trade they use every day. A mechanic, for example, may decorate his tools, display them prominently in his house, and take some time to thank them for their service to him. A farmer may thank his tractor and other equipment; a homemaker may thank her washer, drier, and other household equipment; and a shopkeeper may thank his cash register. All these people are acutely aware that such a relationship with these tools is purely one-sided, and a computer, a tractor, and a drier just represent the non-living world with which they wish to establish a monist relationship. We also experience similar feelings in our day to day lives. When we sell our old house, when we sell our old car, or when our children lose their favorite toys or dolls, we all feel very sad, and sometimes we are quite disturbed for several days. These emotions are an indication of an inherent monist relationship we feel with the non-living matter.

We may grow indoor plants to enhance the beauty of our house. We may spend money on landscaping, and we may take care of those plants because they add value to our property. We may grow mango and other fruit trees in the hope of getting some fruits. This is not desire-less karma however, and although we may get some worldly benefit, it will not contribute anything towards our liberation. Depending on how hard we work, we may increase the value of our property and we may get mangos and other fruits. Long after we are gone, our children or other new owners of our property may continue to benefit from our karma for many years to come. But it is quite worthless in relation to our liberation. Sometimes, however, we do see a special plant — it may be a small plant struggling to survive in the shadow of a large plant, perhaps sick or dried out, perhaps freezing in winter, or bent or broken in a thunderstorm, and we instantly feel compassion for that plant. We take it home, or we nurse it back to health right where it is. This deed is completely desireless, expecting absolutely nothing from the plant in return. Such compassion essentially arises from our monist relationship with the plant world – a relationship based on the primeval energy Pran that we both share. This compassionate desireless karma will no doubt contribute to our journey towards liberation.

Many animals, especially those higher up on the evolution ladder, possess a mind and an intellect as we do. The qualities of the mind and the intellect are, of course, vastly inferior to those of ours, but it is still easy for us to feel some sort of unity with these animals. We become quite emotionally attached to our pets such as cats and dogs, as well as to other domesticated animals such as cows and goats that we keep for milk. We are also very fascinated with various animals in the zoo, and we are simply mesmerized with what orangutans and chimpanzees can do. In recent years, some scientists have even been successful in teaching some rudimentary language to some primates. As a result of all these factors, we experience a special monist bond with the animal world. Several organizations such as the People for Ethical Treatment of Animals (PETA), the Society for Prevention of Cruelty to Animals (SPCA), and others attest to this special bond. All our interactions with the animal world are also characterized as good or bad karma. Again, the good karma will lead to good fruit and desireless good karma will lead us to liberation.

Finally, our actions towards our human brothers and sisters are the most important elements of the path of karma. Outwardly, we have several factors that tend to separate us from one another. We have the gender separating men from women; the nationality separating Germans from French and Italians; the color of the skin separating blacks from whites; and religion separating Christians from Jews and Hindus from Muslims. If we focus on what separates us, we begin to dislike those who do not look like us and do not pray to the same god that we do. The dislike eventually turns to fear and hate. It then becomes easy for us to demonize these people. Once we turn them into demons, we have no problem killing them. It is therefore important that we focus on the fact that beneath all our differences we all belong to the human race. All our feelings of separateness can be accepted as long as they are consistent with this overarching oneness. For example, it is all right for one to feel proud to be from Hampton or Norfolk in Virginia, as long as one is equally proud to be a Virginian and to be an American. It is all right to be a proud Parisian when one is equally proud to be a Frenchman and a European.

We should all attempt to focus all our human interactions on the concept of monism. If someone says that he is going to steal some money from his wallet, we will find the whole idea quite ludicrous and lunatic. Under a monist world, stealing from someone else's wallet would appear equally ludicrous.

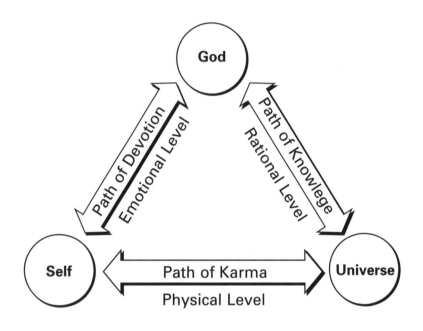

Components of the Path to Liberation

4. An Integrated Path to Liberation

Knowledge, devotion, and karma are the three elements or components of the path to liberation. One should not attempt to list them in the order of superiority or importance. They simply act on different planes, and different people have different pre-disposition or comfort level for these elements. These elements are also not mutually exclusive. We can customize our individual path to liberation to consist of varying degrees of these elements, and the combination can and often change from time to time. Furthermore, the societal environment will very much influence individual thinking and choices in this regard. For example, people from Somalia, India, Japan, and the United States may understandably choose different combination of these three elements. Consequently, this discussion presents only certain broad ideas of integrating these three elements into a single path to liberation.

We have earlier discussed the three s-, r-, and t- qualities. The t-quality in us leads us to do things that are against our ultimate interest. It also says that if I cannot have fruits of my action, I just do not want to act. The r-quality says that if I act, I must be able to enjoy the fruits of my action. We have to reject both these approaches and follow the dictates of the s-quality: act vigorously, but renounce the fruit that makes the karma binding and keeps us in this birth-and-death cycle. This is not possible until we stop identifying ourselves only with our bodies. Monism tells us, *You are God,* the ultimate reality. So we must convince ourselves that *I am God,* and start acting like one!

We should start teaching our children early that they are more than their bodies. Seeing a dirty child, when we say *how dirty you are,* we send a wrong message to the child. The disproportionate importance given to the bodies in the present societies leads to the problems of anorexia and bulimia in children, excessive use of cosmetics by young girls, obsession with the size of the breasts, and beauty contests for six-year-olds. When we hit a child and inflict pain on the *body,* the child tends to equate the bodily pain with *his or her* pain. We must understand that real freedom of action is not achieved unless we disassociate ourselves from our bodies. Tyranny is possible only when we identify ourselves exclusively with our bodies. There is a short story to illustrate this point. A demon captured a young man and enslaved him. He made the young man work endless hours, telling him, "I will eat you if you do not do what I tell you to do." The man was deathly afraid of the demon and worked for weeks without much rest or sleep. One day, he could not take it any more and stood up to the demon and told him, "Go ahead, eat me up! I am not going to be your slave anymore." The demon was not a fool. If he ate the man, who would do the backbreaking work? So he negotiated with the man and they both worked out an acceptable work schedule and a wage. Clearly it takes enormous courage to stand up to tyrants. During the years of slavery, holocaust, and apartheid, we have seen how people were so afraid to die that they simply gave in to the tyrants. We, however, also know how Mahatma Gandhi defiantly told the South African whites that they could have his body but not his obedience or respect. We all must understand that there are pleasures beyond the body. Only then we can have the necessary courage of conviction to steadfastly follow our dharma in good times as well as in adversity.

The elements of action, devotion, and intellect must also be integrated at every step of the way. Inner feelings (mind) and conviction (intellect) must accompany our outward actions (body). Only then these actions can be in service of God, that is, lead us to liberation; without this integration, everything is simply a business. Consider, for example, the nursing homes for the elderly. A doctor, a nurse, or anyone else working there could have several alternative attitudes about his work. One may say, "I know my old parents and my other old relatives. I know how much they hurt. They do not really expect a whole lot. I know how their faces light up when I come home in the evening and spend a few minutes with them. They love it when they feel they are a part of the family. So I am going to treat my patients in this nursing home as if they are my parents."With this attitude, he would do his job with inner feelings and conviction. The job would not be a burden but would be God's work to him. Another may say, "These patients are too old. All they do whole day is lie in bed or sit in a chair and moan in pain. Why do they not simply die? Why do I have to work hard for these people who do not mean anything to me? I would rather be on a golf course." With this attitude, he may go through the motions of patient care, but his mind and intellect would not be with his actions. He may also cut corners and give sub-standard care to the patients. As soon as it is time to quit, he will drop everything and run out. You cannot expect to be liberated with this kind of an attitude.

Constancy is the key to following the path of liberation. Good s-type karma then eventually becomes a second nature. It is then unattached with pride or with a desire for reward. When a baby takes her first steps, the parents are very happy. They take pictures or videos showing the baby struggling to walk. They reward the baby with hugs, kisses, and sweets. Within a week or so, however, all the celebration stops and rewards disappear. Walking now has become the baby's second nature. This is no different than other endeavors. People get awards for the first satellite launch, the first walk on the moon, the first heart transplant, and the first test-tube baby. Now NASA's shuttle launch would be lucky to get a ten-second spot on the evening news. So whatever you do, do it every day with constancy. You may choose to bow your head to Lord Ram or Lord Krishna in the morning, pray before lunch or dinner, water your house plants before your first coffee, or read a few verses from your favorite scripture every night before going to bed. What you choose to do to liberate yourself is less important than the constancy of doing it. The constancy is going to make it desireless and prideless.

We must continually remind ourselves that we are not animals who simply eat, drink, reproduce, and sleep. We have the capacity to think far ahead, not insist on immediate results, and steadfastly follow a certain course for long-term results.

Helping a stranger is a *desireless* karma

We usually come to this realization someday and start thinking about right and wrong and start exercising our power of discrimination. We then stop acting merely on selfish impulses, and discipline replaces indulgence. We see an old man cross a busy street and voluntarily step ahead to help him. We get up and offer our seat on the bus to some old man or to a pregnant woman that we have not met before, and most probably would never meet again. Then late at night when we go to bed, an inner voice tells us, "I am proud of you, you did well today." That is our Atman, our direct connection to the ultimate reality, speaking to us beyond the BMI level. We then feel proud of ourselves and keep doing these good things. Slowly but surely, it is becoming our second nature, and now there is simply no need to feel proud and no need for any reward.

Now we come to the next stage and make an effort to cleanse our minds and intellect. We start meditating everyday and spend some time alone thinking about our personal relationship with God. We may choose to sit and meditate in the early morning hours, take a long walk in the woods, listen to some devotional songs, or go to a temple. There is no fixed recipe, no rules, and no constraints. Such rules and restrictions are distracting and defeat the whole purpose of the effort towards liberation. Let me tell a classical story to illustrate this point. A man went to his guru and told him that whenever the man sat for meditation, his mind always wandered and thought about everything else but God. He asked his guru to teach him the *rules* of meditation. The guru listened to him and told him, "There is only one simple rule to follow. Do not think about a monkey during meditation." The man went home and found that during meditation his mind now thought only about a monkey. He had never before even once thought about a monkey during meditation, but now it was always a monkey. When he went back to his guru and told him this, the guru replied, "I am so happy you learned the most important lesson so early. There are no rules for establishing a relationship with God. The mind by its very nature wanders and rebels. If I had told you not to think of a dog, your mind would have thought only about a dog. So do not set any rules for this journey towards your liberation. Start slowly and do not get discouraged. The mind may, and probably will, initially wander all over the place, but you will soon see it focusing on what you are trying to do."

We must also remember that this life is just one leg of a long journey. Death is surely coming to each of us, sooner for some, later for others. We do not know what karma will bring to us in the next life. We should not waste even a minute on things that do not contribute to our liberation. There is another story about a person who went to his guru and asked him about a certain ritual that supposedly accelerated the liberation process. The guru told the man that the man had only a week more to live and suggested that he perform that ritual before that time. The guru also asked the man to come back to him after completing the preparations for the ritual. The man went home distraught and told his wife what his guru had just told him. He called his accountant and his financial manager and asked them to take care of his taxes and finances, asked his lawyer to update his will, and asked all of his distant relatives to come and visit him one last time. He talked to his sons and explained all the intricate details about his estate and prayed at his favorite temples. After a few days, his guru visited him and inquired about the preparations for the ritual. The man said to his guru, "I did not have a single minute to think about the ritual. I always thought about my impending death, and I was busy doing important things that must be done before I die." The guru then gave him the real lesson he had intended to give all along: "You are not dying next week, but fortunately you have learned an important lesson. You should always keep in mind that death could come any minute. When you face death, you do not have time for things you consider unimportant. Do not waste any more time. Follow your dharma and work on your liberation as if you were going to die tomorrow."

We also should not separate our spiritual life from our worldly life. The concept of monism must pervade all aspects of our life. People conveniently think they can isolate their spiritual lives from other aspects of their lives. A stock broker, for example, sells bad stocks to old retirees; an insurance agent sells worthless cancer insurance policies to sick people; a plumber or a home repair contractor overcharges a single mother; and they all go home in the evening and pray to their favorite gods. A terrorist kills hundreds of innocent civilians and then prays to secure his place in the heaven. Hundreds of slave owners from the United States, hundreds of Nazis from Hitler years, and hundreds of South African whites routinely went to their churches without batting an eyelash. They did not think they did anything wrong in doing so; each of them probably described himself as a god-fearing Christian. In their own minds, they separated their spiritual lives from their worldly activities. Mahatma Gandhi, however, struggled for freedom without hating his South African and British adversaries; he never made any distinction between his spiritual and other pursuits. We must always be vigilant and make sure that all our actions are consistent with monism; that is the only way we can make any progress towards our liberation.

Our idea of monism naturally extends only to the different parts of our own body. When, for example, we occasionally bite our own tongue, we do not knock our teeth out in punishment. We know that our teeth and our tongue are parts of the monist reality of our body and there is no conflict of interest between the two. Similarly, when we dislocate our left shoulder or tear our left rotator cuff, our right hand does not smell an opportunity and torture our left shoulder. It helps the left shoulder through the days of its difficulty and nurtures it back to health. Our monist relationship, however, decreases very rapidly beyond our body, and usually vanishes past our immediate family. We should try to extend the scope of this monist relationship outward and use it as a metric for monitoring our progress towards liberation.

All slave owners thought they were good Christians

Within each of us there are good and bad qualities ready to do battle with each other. The good qualities include fearlessness, compassion, truth, tenderness, forgiveness, patience, non-violence, loyalty, peacefulness, and humility. On the opposite side are the bad qualities such as vanity, ignorance, anger, hate, greed, and arrogance. Greed is never satisfied. When we do not get what we desire, anger takes over and the reasoning goes out the door. Then we forget who we are and let our bad qualities take over and destroy us. We must, therefore, constantly cultivate the above good qualities.

In short, we must individually determine our own path towards liberation. We must start with purifying our bodies because what we do with our bodies has large influence on our mind and reason. If we are always drunk, drugged, or sleepy because we overeat, there is no hope of doing anything useful with our mind and intellect. We should then commit ourselves to do good desireless karma consistent with our dharma. We naturally love our parents and children; we should now start extending our love and concern to our extended family, circle of friends, community in general and eventually to the whole universe. We should understand that everyone and everything here has a role to play in this cosmic drama and not hold anyone responsible for our misfortunes. With such an integrated effort, we will surely progress towards our liberation, and before we know it, we will escape the clutches of this birth-and-death cycle.

Part III –The Great Indian Epics (Hindu Ethics by Example)

9. Introduction to Hindu Epics

Over the past several millennia, Hindu authors have created a vast amount of literature dealing with Hindu concepts of cosmology, social structures, governance, jurisprudence, ethics, philosophy, mathematics, medicine, and other areas. This literature has been written specifically for a broad spectrum of readership covering children as well as adults of varying educational and intellectual levels. There are short animal stories for teaching certain moral lessons to children. These stories are very interesting, hold attention of the children, and teach them some lessons without they knowing that they are being taught. The adult literature also caters to a broad spectrum of people, from those with limited capability or interest in intellectual discussion to those with high intelligence and formal education.

If a professor of meteorology talks to his four-year-old child about why and how it rains, he will explain it in the most simplistic terms. If, however, he is talking to one of his doctoral students, he will talk about cumulus clouds, squall lines, microbursts, and other technical details that will sound like nonsense to those not trained in meteorology. Such a range of understanding is true also of galactic physics, cell biology, or any other science. It would be absurd to write only one book on chemistry or physics for all readers. The need to satisfy the curiosity of readers of all levels is precisely why a wide variety of Hindu literature is available. It is, of course, the reader's responsibility to find suitable literature that will challenge him at the appropriate level.

It has been said earlier that the Hindu thinkers took a grammarian approach to developing ethical concepts. Consequently, one will not find any specific list of do's and don'ts, but only broad principles on which one is expected to determine the right course of action at any time. As a supplement to these principles, the two great epics of Ramayan and Mahabharat show the common man how different characters behaved in response to various situations facing them. Several characters are portrayed as role models exhibiting the best in humans and an unparalleled courage of conviction. These characters decided to follow their dharma irrespective of how others behaved towards them, for when you only respond to others, you really let others control your behavior. They also did not let their body control their mind and intellect, but the other way around. Some other characters are portrayed exhibiting irresponsible behavior that led to unimaginable suffering to innumerable people. They let the ungodly qualities of hate, anger, jealousy, and greed dictate their behaviors. In addition to presenting these positive and negative role models, these epics also present certain themes. No human being is either fully good or fully bad. Even an apparently evil person carries the cosmic flame within him, and consequently, has some, albeit minimal, good qualities. Also, a person with apparently saintly qualities sometimes exhibits utterly irresponsible and undesirable behavior. Another common theme presented in these epics is that each one of us has choices to make, and one always has a number of good alternatives that will advance us on the path of liberation. We make wrong choices when we identify ourselves only with our bodies, we forget our essential monist identity, and succumb to the ungodly qualities of anger, greed, jealousy, and others.

Introduction to Ramayan

As a background to the story of Ramayan, the demon king
Ravan has acquired a number of divine weapons, received several boons from gods, and has become too powerful. He has
received a boon from Lord Brahma that demons or gods would
not be able to kill him. Thinking himself to be immortal, he has
become a tyrant and a serious threat to gods. The gods, therefore, go to Lord Vishnu and ask him to find a way out of this
problem. Lord Vishnu knows that Ravan was so arrogant that it
did not even occur to Ravan to ask for protection from humans
and animals. So Lord Vishnu decides to come down to the
earth in the human form, and several other gods decide to join
him, some as humans, and some even as simians. Ramayan is
the story of the eldest prince of Ayodhya, Ram, an incarnation
of Lord Vishnu. Lord Vishnu's wife, Laxmi, decides to incarnate
herself as Ram's wife Sita. Bharat, Laxman, and Shatrughna are
Ram's younger brothers. Hanuman is a simian devotee of Ram.
Vibhishan, Ravan's younger brother, knows the identity of Ram
as the Vishnu-incarnate, and is also a devotee of Ram. Each one
of these characters has a specific role in service of Ram, and
they all play these roles as their prime directive. There is no
compromise about this directive and everything else must give
if it came in conflict with this directive. Ram is an ideal that
any human can aspire to be. He is the best in everything: the
best husband, the best son, and, above all, the best king. There
is no confusion or indecision on his part. At every stage in his
life, only one dharma takes precedence: when he is the king, it
is the king's dharma that supersedes his dharma as a husband
or as a brother. Sita is the best wife there can be. She is Ram's
best friend and assists him at any cost to her in following his
dharma; everything else comes second. Laxman is the best
brother there can be. He follows Ram like his shadow and
stands beside Ram in all his trials and tribulations. Hanuman is
the best devotee, and on and on. The lives of these characters
tell us that following one's dharma is very difficult like walking
on the sharp edge of a sword. Life is full of ups and downs, and

one must always stand tall and uncompromisingly follow one's dharma. This is the only way to liberation. At every step, these characters face difficult situations and are tempted with easy ways out, but they all unfailingly make the right choices.

The story of Ram has for thousands of years been the pillar of strength, the lighthouse on the shore, and a dependable guide to millions of people in their search for truth and in their journey towards liberation.

Introduction to Mahabharat

Mahabharat is an intricate story of the Bharat clan that ultimately ends up in a civil war between cousins — the sons of Pandu and the sons of Dhrutarashtra. Dhrutarashtra, the elder of the two princes, is born blind, and is passed over as king on his father's death. Pandu assumes the throne instead. After a few years when Pandu abdicates, Dhrutarashtra assumes the throne. Among all the princes, Pandu's son, Dharmaraj, is the eldest. Dhrutarashtra, however, feels that the kingdom originally belonged to him, and that it should now go to his eldest son, Duryodhan. This family feud eventually leads to a war — a conflict between the good and the evil. There are several important lessons to be learned from the different characters from Mahabharat. Dhrutarashtra, Duryodhan, Shakuni, and Karna always let themselves be ruled by raw emotions of hate, anger, and jealousy. As a result, they consistently take irrational decisions, against the teachings of dharma. This evil behavior brings untold misery to those around them, and eventually results in the death and destruction for the people of the Kingdom of Hastinapur. Each of these characters, as evil as they are, still exhibits certain good qualities, and in spite of their ungodly behavior, the reader cannot but have certain sympathy for these characters. Bhishma, Kunti, and Dharmaraj, on the other hand, are basically good characters of conscience. Each of them, however, commits a single thoughtless and irresponsible act that leads to unimaginable unintended consequences. Bhishma, for example, swears unquestioned loyalty to the Hastinapur King of the day, and eventually fights on the wrong side of the civil war. Kunti has a son outside the bounds of marriage and abandons him at birth. That son, Karna, pays a heavy price for this indiscretion on the part of his mother Kunti, and eventually ends up fighting a war with his own brothers.

This family feud is only a small part of the entire epic of Mahabharat. The epic covers a period of several centuries, and is an exposition of dharma, the proper conduct of kings and commoners, in times of luck and calamity, of persons seeking liberation. It also addresses several social issues of births out of wedlock, abandonment and adoption of children, rape and abuse of women, and others. Consequently, this epic has always enjoyed immense popularity, especially among the people of the Far East.

The following short narrations of Ramayan and Mahabharat should be read from the above perspective. None of us is perfect, and even the apparently most evil ones have a cosmic flame within themselves. Consequently, there is hope for every one. We must also recognize that we do have choices in our behavior and that we must show courage in making the right choices.

10. Ramayan

Dasharath, the King of Kosal, is a king in the great lineage of the Sun Dynasty. He is very brave and rules his subjects like a loving father. He has three wives: Kausalya, the oldest; Sumitra; and Kaikayi, the youngest. He and his wives steadfastly follow their path of Dharma under the able guidance of the Royal Priest, Guru Vasishta.

Queen Kausalya has one son, Ram; Kaikayi has one son, Bharat; and Sumitra has two sons, Laxman and Shatrughna. The four brothers grow up in royal luxury and are very close to each other. As the oldest of the four, Ram is very protective of his younger siblings, and they, in turn, love and respect him very much. Laxman is more emotional by nature, whereas Bharat is more rational by nature. Consequently, there is quite a difference in the way these two exhibit their love for Ram. Laxman, for example, cannot bear even the thought of being physically away from Ram, whereas spiritual closeness to Ram is more important to Bharat.

In due course, they all go to Vasishta's Ashram, a kind of a residential school. In the ashrams of those days, students would give up all nominal pleasures of life and pursue knowledge in various fields. The students would sleep on the floor, walk without shoes, and seek alms from folks living in towns nearby. The princes and commoners, the rich and poor, would all be treated the same. In fact, students would be forbidden to seek alms from someone they knew. Without such a rule, rich students would always get a whole lot from their folks, compared to the poor students. This inequality, in turn, would perpetuate the differences between students and would ruin the camaraderie within the student body. Also, every student would do certain chores for the upkeep of the school facilities. The students would sleep after their guru went to bed and would wake up early before him. The guru's wife was like a surrogate mother to students and would make sure that the students missed their mothers as little as possible. It was really no wonder that the students truly learned a lot in such a wholesome and loving environment.

The guru always stressed the connection between the body and the mind, and between the mind and the intellect. Students were told that a good healthy body is necessary in achieving a focused and disciplined mind, and disciplined mind is necessary in purifying the intellect. Only pure intellect can decide what is in one's ultimate interest and lead Atman to liberation. Consequently, everything begins with taking care of the body, eating wholesome food, and exercising regularly. The teachers stressed that real knowledge leads to humility, not to arrogance. The students were told to be on constant guard not to hurt anyone, physically or mentally, by one's thoughts, words, and deeds. They were asked to make everyone happy without making any value judgment on whether anyone deserved to be happy. A tree, for example, provides shade to someone who is coming to water it, as well as to someone who may have come with an intention to cut it down. A river satisfies the thirst of a saint and of a robber equally. The students learned that each one of us must repay three debts. The debt to God is repaid by seeing God in everyone and in every part of the universe, and by loving every living being in it. The father's debt is repaid by sacrificing one's own happiness, if necessary, in service to one's parents. Finally, a guru's debt is repaid by constantly seeking knowledge and by leading one's life according to one's dharma.

Ram Returns Home and Leaves with Guru Vishwamitra

Ram, Bharat, Laxman, and Shatrughna complete their education and return home as young adults. Ram and Kaikayi always had a special bond between the two. Kaikayi thought of Ram first, and Ram, in turn, bowed to Kaikayi first, even before bowing to his own mother, Kausalya. Dasharath and the three mothers are ecstatic that the boys are back home, and they are all proud of how much the boys have learned from their guru. Ram and his brothers have mastered various areas such as philosophy, ethics, music, art, military skills, jurisprudence, and especially spiritual values.

King Dasharath and the three mothers are just getting used to the boys being home when Guru Vishwamitra comes for a visit. King welcomes Vishwamitra with utmost love and respect and assures him that he and his entire government will be honored to fulfill Vishwamitra's every command. Such promises were never given lightly in those days. Gurus like Vishwamitra and Vasishta were *liberated Atmans* with incredible spiritual powers. These gurus lived their lives only in public service and never looked for anything for themselves. Kings as well as commoners knew very well that these liberated gurus would not harm anyone and would only help everyone. If they appeared to be doing something unpleasant, they were only acting their part in the ongoing cosmic drama caused by Karmic necessity.

Vishwamitra tells Dasharath that the demon-king Ravan of Sri Lanka was fomenting trouble at the borders of Kosal. Vicious demons, using their powers of black magic, were entering Dasharath's kingdom, interfering in religious and spiritual rites, and killing innocent people. Vishwamitra then asks Dasharath to send Ram and Laxman with him for providing protection for the people of the kingdom against these vicious demons. Dasharath tells Vishwamitra that both Ram and Laxman are very young to face Ravan's mighty forces. He offers to send his army instead, and if necessary, to lead the army himself for providing the protection that Vishwamitra is seeking. The royal priest, Guru Vasishta, now intervenes and tells Dasharath, "You do not know what Vishwamitra knows via his mystical powers, and you should simply do what Vishwamitra is asking." Guru Vasishta's word was supreme, and Dasharath was not about to start disobeying his guru. He asks Ram and Laxman to go with Vishwamitra and do as he commands. Mothers Kausalya, Sumitra, and Kaikayi ask Dasharath how the father in him allowed him to send his young sons to fight mighty Ravan's folks alone without the help of his army. Dasharath tells them that a common man has the luxury of being a father or a husband, but, as the King, his King's Dharma takes priority over the father's Dharma. He reminds them that, at the time of his coronation, he had taken a solemn oath that he would put the State's affairs above his personal affairs, and that he must keep his word even at the cost of his life. In fact, *one's word above one's life* was the supreme motto of the Sun Dynasty.

Ram and Laxman now go with Guru Vishwamitra. As they travel through forest after forest, they meet a number of demons, and the two brothers fight with them with valor and kill all the demons. Along the way, many gurus give various divine weapons to Ram and tell him to use them only for the protection of the society in general, and of the weak, in particular.

Ram Weds Sita

A brave, religious, spiritual, and a very popular King Janak rules the Nation of Vishal. He is a devotee of Lord Shiva, and Shiva had given him a divine bow, which is known to be Shiva's Bow. Once while working in a field, his workers find a trunk buried in the ground. When King Janak arrives, they open the trunk and find a little baby girl in it. Janak accepts her as a gift from Mother Earth, and raises her as Princess Sita. When Sita grows to be of marriageable age, Janak is concerned about finding a suitable husband for his beautiful daughter. He wants to get someone special, with character, integrity, honesty, strength, and spirituality. Seeking divine help in his search, he arranges a wedding invitational for Sita in Mithila, the Capital of Vishal, and declares that anyone who can pick up and string Shiva's Bow will get Sita's hand in marriage. He sends invitations to a large number of kings and princes for this invitational gathering. He also invites a number of spiritual gurus to come and bless Sita at her wedding.

Guru Vishwamitra gets an invitation to this event and takes Ram and Laxman with him to Mithila. The three stay at the palace as royal guests. King Janak, the Queen, Princess Sita, and virtually everyone in the capital city are all immensely impressed when they see Ram, and wish in their hearts that he would be the one to win Sita's hand in marriage. Ram also feels instant love for Sita, and feels as if they have been together eternally as husband and wife.

Next day, King Janak opens the wedding invitational gathering and welcomes all the kings and princes to Mithila. He tells them that he sincerely hopes that one of them would be able to pick up Shiva's Bow and marry Sita. He rolls in Shiva's Bow on a platform and asks Sita to sit beside him with a big garland in her hand. The bow is deceptively small and thin. One by one, most kings and princes try their hardest to pick the bow up, but the bow stays put, and all of them return to their seats disappointed and embarrassed.

King Janak cannot believe what is happening right in front of his eyes. He is afraid that his beloved Sita may not find a suitable match and wonders if he had set an impossible task as a precondition for her wedding. Guru Vishwamitra now signals to Ram to go forward and pick the bow up. As Ram approaches the bow, the elder kings and princes derisively laugh at him for even thinking of trying to lift the bow up when everyone else had failed. With the blessing of Guru Vishwamitra behind him, however, Ram confidently goes and stands in front of the bow. With utmost respect and humility, he first bows to all the elders in the hall. He then bows to Shiva's Bow itself, and he quickly picks it up. As he then attempts to string it, the divine bow breaks into two pieces. Everyone in the hall is flabbergasted that a young prince could do what older kings and princes could not. Janak, Sita, and her mother are all ecstatic that their inner wish was fulfilled.

However, as Janak is about to congratulate Ram, an angry Guru Parashuram barges in. Parashuram was a well-known devotee of Lord Shiva. Even as a Brahmin, he was well trained in the use of various divine weapons. He also had several mystical powers including an ability to travel anywhere at the speed of mind. In spite of all his spiritual achievements, however, he still had a temper, and it was quite understandable that people got scared whenever Parashuram showed up. Some other Gurus similarly found it difficult to control their sexual desires. God Indra used to send divine dancers to lure them and interrupt their long and difficult meditations that would have given them more powers. Parashuram and other Gurus are really classic examples of how difficult it is to control anger or sensual desires even for those that are highly enlightened and have progressed very far towards liberation. These examples are always used to show that one must always be on one's guard against the ungodly qualities of anger, lust, false pride, etc.

Parashuram angrily asks to know who had broken the famous bow of his beloved Lord Shiva. He says that whoever broke the bow surely deserves to be punished by death. Ram comes forward and tells Parashuram that it was he who had broken the bow. Parashuram promptly challenges Ram to a fight. Ram respectfully responds, "As a kshatriya, I must always accept a challenge when given. However, we never attack Brahmins; on the contrary, we consider it our privilege to protect and serve them. So how can we fight?" As Parashuram was listening, he sees the face of Lord Vishnu in Ram. He is quite elated at the prospect of being in the presence of Lord Vishnu, but he wants to be doubly sure. So he gives Ram his bow that Lord Vishnu had given him in the past, and says, " If you can string this Vishnu's bow, I will be sure of what I am seeing." Ram picks up the bow, mounts an arrow, and stretches the string. He then tells Parashuram that Ram's arrow is never wasted, and asks, "What shall I now destroy with this arrow, your cumulative good karma, or your ability to travel at the speed of mind?" Parashuram replies, " My Lord, I would like to keep my ability to travel; please destroy my good karma." Ram then shoots the arrow, and Parashuram leaves. With the crisis over, Janak now invites Sita to offer a garland to Ram, and Ram tells Janak to consider him to be his son and to shower him with his love forever. Janak's royal priest now advises Janak to send a messenger to Ayodhya and propose a wedding between Ram and Sita. Janak also proposes his younger daughter Urmila for Laxman and two daughters of his brother for Bharat and Shatrughna. The four weddings are performed in royal pomp and the newlyweds return to Ayodhya.

The entire city of Ayodhya welcomes Ram and Sita with open arms and with a huge celebration. The palace is lit with thousands of lights and the royal dancers stage a big performance in honor of Ram and Sita. Kausalya, Sumitra, and especially Kaikayi are very happy because their beloved Ram is now married and they dream of having a grandchild soon. Ram promises Sita that she will be the one and the only wife he will have. He also tells her, " Please be my friend, always help me as I strive to follow my dharma, and stop me from straying away from my duty."

Dasharath Plans for Ram's Coronation

The celebrations are over in a few days and the royal family guests start returning home. Kaikayi's brother also prepares to return home, and Bharat and Shatrughna leave with him to visit their grandparents. As Vishwamitra prepares to leave, Dasharath requests that he stay a little longer because, "… it is our great fortune that we get this invaluable opportunity to spend some time with spiritual saints like yourself." Vishwamitra, however, says that he should really get back to his spiritual pursuits. He tells Dasharath that one should not postpone one's spiritual quest by getting bogged down in life's luxuries because only the spiritual pursuit will be of any help in one's ultimate liberation. Vishwamitra then returns back to his ashram.

Vishwamitra's words have a profound impact on Dasharath and he starts thinking about retiring and of living a contemplative and meditative life in a forest. He consults with his guru, Vasishta, and tells him, "I like to hand over this kingdom to Ram and live a quiet meditative life. Ram is well educated, brave, loves and is loved by the people, and is thus eminently qualified to be a king. As the eldest son, Ram would some day be the King, so why not now?" Guru Vasishta is happy that Dasharath wants to undertake spiritual pursuits. He asks Dasharath to call an assembly of people's representatives and get their agreement to his proposal saying, "Dasharath has no right to force Ram on the public if they do not want it." The concept of the *consent of the governed* is really not new and was quite a norm at the time of Ramayan.

Dasharath calls such an assembly, and asks the people how they would feel about his retiring and Ram's being coronated as their new King. The cabinet ministers and people's representatives give their unanimous approval and say that their only regret would be that they would not be seeing Dasharath any longer. Ram pleads with his father to continue being the King, but Dasharath and Vasishta eventually persuade him to accept the proposal. Ram then suggests that at least the coronation is postponed until his beloved Bharat and Shatrughna can return to Ayodhya and participate in the event. Guru Vasishta says, however, "The sooner the better," and Dasharath then makes a public announcement that Ram will be coronated next day to be the new King. Dasharath also calls Ram into his private chambers and advises him on King's dharma. This is not a father-to-son talk, but a present king-to-the next king talk.

Dasharath tells Ram in all seriousness, "A king is first the servant of the people. He cannot have privacy, family, friends, or any personal agenda ahead of service to the people. He must take a solemn oath that he will sacrifice all these things if and when they come in conflict with the public interest. If not, one has no right to be a king. A king must always listen to and respect his guru and other spiritual leaders. He should not surround himself with yes-men, and should encourage his cabinet ministers to speak out without fear. A king should also independently check on the state of his kingdom by having a competent secret service. In short, when you become the King, you must scrupulously follow the tenets of King's dharma."

Manthara hears all the commotion in the streets and goes out to find out what is going on. She sees everyone dancing in the streets because Ram is to be coronated their King the next day. Manthara is the personal maid of Queen Kaikayi. She had raised Kaikayi from her childhood, and had moved to Ayodhya with Kaikayi after Kaikayi's marriage to Dasharath. Manthara is thus kind of an outsider in Ayodhya, and her entire world is really limited to Kaikayi and Bharat. As young children, Ram, Bharat, Laxman, and Shatrughna were close to Manthara and, in fact, used to call her *Mom Manthara!* As an old lady, and because of her closeness to Kaikayi, Manthara is treated with respect by all in the palace. Unfortunately, however, her loyalties extend only to Kaikayi and Bharat.

When Manthara hears that Ram is to be the next King, all her feelings of love and loyalty towards Kaikayi and Bharat overtake her and something snaps in her. She loses her common sense and her mind starts playing tricks on her. She ignores the fact that Ram is the eldest son of the King and is loved by everyone including Bharat. She simply convinces herself that a great injustice is being done to Kaikayi and Bharat, and that the kingdom should go to Bharat. She also thinks that Kaikayi would not even notice the injustice that is about to be done to her and, consequently, she alone must do something to protect the interests of her beloved Kaikayi and Bharat. As she comes in, she sees that Kaikayi is already celebrating the good news that her Ram is going to be coronated the King the next day. Kaikayi cannot contain herself and is already distributing expensive gifts to palace workers. Manthara asks her how she could be so blind to Kausalya's machinations against her and how she could be celebrating the upcoming slavery of Bharat and Kaikayi herself. Manthara suggests that sending Bharat away to his grandfather was no accident. Once Ram is coronated, Bharat would be his personal servant, and Kaikayi would be at the beck and call of the First Queen, Kausalya. Manthara tells Kaikayi that this must be stopped at any cost. Kaikayi, of course, does not buy any of this, and says that her Ram would never be a party to this type of plot against her. When, however, Manthara asks why the coronation could not wait for Bharat to return to Ayodhya, Kaikayi could not really find a logical explanation for this urgency. She now starts to have some doubts herself, and the more she thinks more she agrees with Manthara. Eventually, she agrees with Manthara that Ram's coronation must be stopped at any cost. Ayodhya's fate is apparently going to take an ugly turn.

Dark Clouds Over Ayodhya

Manthara and Kaikayi now plan a devious scheme. Several years before, Kaikayi was driving Dasharath's chariot during one of the battles against vicious demons. During this battle, Dasharath was injured, and Kaikayi had skillfully driven the chariot away from danger and had attended to her husband's injuries. Her valiant efforts had not only saved Dasharath's life but had led to his victory in the battle. In appreciation of this, Dasharath had then given Kaikayi two boons saying, "Ask any two things you want, and this King of the Sun Dynasty will give you those with no questions asked." Kaikayi had said at the time that she would ask those two things sometime in the future. Manthara reminds Kaikayi about these promises and suggests that the time has now come to ask for those two boons that Dasharath owed her. Manthara and Kaikayi know very well that if Bharat is made the King instead of Ram, the people of Ayodhya will most certainly revolt and the army may also mutiny. They therefore think that Ram must simultaneously be removed from the scene for a long period to give Bharat sufficient time to consolidate his kingdom. All the ungodly qualities of fear, hate, suspicion, and anger within these two women were then working overtime. They settle down on two demands that Kaikayi would make on Dasharath: (1) Bharat must be made the next King of Kosal, and (2) Ram must be exiled to the forest for a period of fourteen years. Manthara also asks Kaikayi to first get Dasharath to promise on Ram's life that he will accept the demands before actually spelling out the demands to him. The evil plot is now all set! Kaikayi now sends a message to Dasharath that she would like to see him at once.

As Dasharath walks in, Kaikayi reminds him of his two boons to her and tells him that the time has now come for her to make her two demands. Dasharath says that he will be only too happy to make good on his promises to his lovely wife, and assures her that nothing is impossible for a king like him. Following her evil plan, Kaikayi makes Dasharath promise her on Ram's life that he will agree to her demands, and then tells him what her demands are: Kingdom for Bharat, and a fourteen-year exile in forest for Ram. Dasharath is sick to his stomach at this turn of events. How could he condemn Ram to a fourteen-year exile for no fault of his? He pleads with Kaikayi, "What has happened to you today? You loved Ram even more than your own son Bharat, and now you want him to go away. I have no problem and I am sure Ram will have no problem if our beloved Bharat is made the next King. Ram will very happily serve this Kingdom under Bharat's rule. But people will call me a fool, blinded by lust if I send innocent Ram to exile.

Please take back your second demand." Kaikayi is, however, quite adamant. She tells Dasharath, "You always talk about your Sun Dynasty, and how your word is important to you than your life. Now if you do not want to give what you have promised me on Ram's life, it is all right with me. But never lecture me again on how Kings of the Sun Dynasty follow Dharma. Moreover, if you break your promise, I do not want to live as a wife of someone who does not respect his own words. So either Ram goes or I commit suicide." Dasharath is speechless and almost paralyzed with just the thought of being away from Ram for such a long time. He knows that he would not survive for long.

With Dasharath so depressed and speechless, Kaikayi herself now sends for Ram. As Ram walks in, he quickly realizes that something had terribly gone wrong. He asks Kaikayi why his father appeared to be so sick. Kaikayi tells Ram that Dasharath's love for him is coming in the way of the reputation of the Sun Dynasty. Ram assures her that no king of the Sun Dynasty, and surely not his father, will let his son or anyone deter him from following his king's dharma. Ram then asks his father to tell him what he wished and promises that he would carry out his father's wish. Dasharath, still speechless, simply looks at Ram. Kaikayi now tells Ram the whole story of the two boons and the two demands she had made to Dasharath. She also says that his father does not know how to handle this conflict between his love for his son and his dharma of keeping his promise. Ram wonders why Kaikayi was so worried about his father keeping his promises to her. He says that he did not need anyone's orders to give up his claim to the kingdom in favor of his younger brother Bharat. He assures Kaikayi that he will be only too happy to live in the forest for fourteen years if that is what she wants, and if that is what it would take to keep his father's word. Ram adds that he considers it to be a son's dharma to assist his father in following his father's dharma.

Ram, Sita, and Laxman Depart for Forest

The news spreads like wild fire throughout the palace. When Ram goes to Kausalya to say "good bye," she says that she could not possibly live without Ram, and that she would simply have to go with him. Ram reminds her that Dasharath is really going to need her more and that husband's needs take precedence over her love for her son. When Sita gets ready to go with him, Ram tells her that the exile in the forest is for him and that the forest life is no cakewalk for a princess such as Sita. Sita, of course, says that as far as she is concerned, heaven is where her husband is. She also assures Ram that *Sita cannot survive without Ram* and that if he goes alone, he would surely have to come back the next day to perform her funeral rites. Ram decides to take her with him. When Laxman hears about Kaikayi's demands and about how his father had agreed to them, he simply loses his cool. He has never lived apart from Ram, and serving his beloved brother Ram has been a kind of his life-mission. He cannot imagine the injustice being done to innocent Ram. He gets ready to mutiny against his own father. He tells Ram that the people of the Kosal Kingdom will support them in this fight for justice, and that there was no one who could defeat Ram and Laxman in any conflict.

Ram scolds Laxman for even thinking about mutiny. He tells him, "Please try to understand the conflict before our beloved father. On one hand, he must protect the reputation of the Sun Dynasty by keeping his promise to Kaikayi, and on the other hand, it involves sending his beloved son, for no fault of his, into a long exile. At this time, it is our duty as his sons to assist him by honoring his word at any personal cost to us." Ram says that he has no hesitation in agreeing to the exile and that Laxman should forget about mutiny. He adds, "How can you forget all the love we received in the past from our mother Kaikayi? Now she is just being a pawn in this cosmic plan, and you cannot hold her personally responsible for what is unfolding at this time. We should simply accept our destiny without blaming anyone for it." Laxman then tells Ram that he will accompany him in the exile, and that he will, as always, serve Ram and Sita. Laxman now talks to his wife Urmila, "This is a trying time for everyone in Ayodhya. For some reason, the destiny has decided that Ram, Sita, and Laxman spend fourteen years in the forest. If, however, everyone goes with Ram, who will take care of Dasharath and the mothers? You should, therefore, stay here and take care of my parents. As my wife, take this burden off my shoulders and do my duty in my place. I know I am asking you to do a great sacrifice. However, the Sun Dynasty is going through a period when each one of us will be tested. Destiny is waiting to see how we respond to this calamity. We must now identify ourselves what we need to do, and do it with the courage of conviction. I have every confidence that you will also do your part and save this dynasty." Ram, Sita, and Laxman now put on the traditional orange colored frugal clothes like those worn by followers of contemplative life style, and leave Ayodhya.

Kevat at the River Crossing

On their way to the forest, Ram, Sita, and Laxman come to River Ganga. Kevat is waiting there with his small ferryboat for an opportunity to serve Ram. Kevat earns his living by ferrying people back and forth across the river. He had heard from some of the travelers that Ram, Sita, and Laxman were on their way to cross the river, and was hoping to be able to serve them. Ram arrives there and sees Kevat waiting for him. Kevat greets Ram with utmost love and requests his permission to ferry them across the river. Ram says that is fine, and Kevat takes them across. At the other side, Ram asks Sita to give Kevat one of her rings as a fare for the crossing. Kevat refuses to accept the ring and tells Ram that professional ethics would not allow him to take the ring. He says, " Just as one barber would not take money from another barber, or as one doctor would not take money from another doctor, I cannot take this." Ram was quite puzzled by this answer, and asks Kevat to tell

Ram, Sita, and Laxman in exile

him how they shared a profession. Kevat replies, " My Lord Ram, both you and I take people across a river. I just take them across this river. You, as the reincarnation of Lord Vishnu, take them across the *river of illusory virtual reality* to the *other bank of liberation.* We, therefore, share the same profession. Today, I am taking you across this river. So my Lord, when the time comes, take me across the river of illusion to my liberation, and we will then be even." Ram understands what Kevat means, and is overwhelmed by Kevat's pure, simple, and innocent devotion. He blesses Kevat and moves on. In a few days, they arrive at the Mandakini river and decide to live there for a while.

Dasharath's Death and Bharat's Return to Ayodhya

King Dasharath tries to cope with his separation from Ram, but not with much success. Everyone around him asks him to be strong and courageous in carrying out his royal duties. Dasharath, however, knows that the end is near; he dies in pain remembering Ram and blaming himself for what Ram, Sita, and Laxman were going through.

As fate would have it, none of Dasharath's four sons is in Ayodhya to give him his last rites. Consequently, Guru Vasishta orders that someone be dispatched at once to bring Bharat back from Kaikayi's father, and that Dasharath's body be preserved until Bharat's return. When Bharat reaches Ayodhya, he is quite puzzled by the cool reception he gets from the people; some people, in fact, turn their heads away when they see him. Unaware of his father's death, Bharat rushes to the palace to meet with his father. Manthara, however, intercepts him and brings him straight to Kaikayi's palace.

Bharat is stunned to see his mother in the traditional widow's attire — a white sari, no jewelry, and no *kumkum* (red dot) on her forehead. He instantly realizes that his father must have died while he was away. Kaikayi asks Bharat to be brave and act with courage during this difficult period. Bharat says that he is really sorry that he could not be with his father when he passed away and inquired if his father remembered him at all at the time of his death. He also adds that he was really happy that his father had at least Ram by his side. Kaikayi tells Bharat that his father never inquired about him at the time his death, but had only remembered Ram. Bharat does not quite understand this and asks his mother if Ram was not with his father when he died. Kaikayi says that Ram was not there because his father had exiled Ram to the forest for a period of fourteen years, and that Sita and Laxman had gone with him. Bharat still does not quite believe this incredible story and asks what offense had Ram committed that deserved such harsh punishment. Kaikayi tells Bharat that Ram had nothing to do with this. Dasharath had in the past given two boons to someone, and when that person asked for Ram's exile, Dasharath had to honor his promise and send Ram to the forest. Bharat tells his mother that clearly someone had conspired to bring this dark cloud on Ayodhya, and that he will surely punish with death those responsible for this deep, dark conspiracy. Kaikayi now discloses to Bharat that it was she who had asked Dasharath to send Ram in exile, and that Sita and Laxman had gone with him voluntarily. She adds that, in doing so, she was only thinking of him and had made his path clear for him. Bharat now comes to know the full story behind this — his mother and her maid had conspired to send Ram away and make Bharat the next King of the Kosal kingdom.

Bharat is disgusted to his core. He cannot believe the turn of events that brought this havoc in his absence and in such a short time. He is incredibly angry with his mother. He tells her, "How could I have been born to an evil woman such as you? I was lucky to have had a father like Dasharath, and a brother like Ram who is adored by everyone. He loved you more than his mother, and how could you send him in exile for such a long period of time. Mother Kausalya treated you like her younger sister and how could you do this to her only son and that too when he is so spotless. How did you think that I would be a party to all of this? I do not know what happened to you. I know greed is at the root of most evil, but I never thought you would succumb to it. You had everything going for you. What else could anyone want? You are not my mother anymore — I have lost my *mother* to a scheming *queen.* If you were not a woman, I would surely have killed you. But we, of the Sun dynasty, consider our dharma to protect women. Ram will not like it if I kill you, so I would not do that. However, I can tell you that I will never again set foot in your palace."

Shatrughna also cannot believe what is happening around him. He wants to punish Manthara for instigating Kaikayi in the first place and he wants to banish her. Bharat, however, reminds him that Ram is now the real king and only he can punish Manthara. They let her go.

Bharat does not know how he is going to be now able to face Kausalya. He thinks everyone will automatically assume that either he is a part of this conspiracy from the start, or at the least, he is now happy to be the next king. Kausalya, however, assures him that she never thought that for a minute. She also adds that Ram went to the forest for upholding his father's word, and that he did that without any regrets. She asks Bharat not to hold his mother Kaikayi responsible for what was happening because, "She was simply compelled by the destiny to play her part in this cosmic drama." Bharat tells her that he cannot, in good conscience, accept the kingdom, and that he will promptly go to the forest, find Ram, and bring him back to Ayodhya.

Guru Vasishta now arranges for Bharat to give final rites to his father, and asks Bharat to come to the royal assembly hall. Vasishta, the Cabinet ministers, and people's representatives then request Bharat to be their king. Bharat reminds them that, only a few days before, they had all requested Ram to be their king. He tells them that they should not let someone thrust another king on them. He says that he also feels hurt because they thought he would agree to be their king under these circumstances. He tells them, "Come with me to the forest, and let us all bring Ram back to Ayodhya. Only Ram can be the legitimate king. Please do not ask me, Guru Vasishta, to accept the thrown. If you do, I shall be compelled by my dharma to accept my Guru's command. But then we will all be doing a great injustice to Ram."

By this time, Kaikayi fully understands what she had done and repents. She apologizes to Kausalya. Kausalya, however, assures her that neither she nor Ram blames Kaikayi because, "Karmic forces are the real reason behind everyone's actions."

Ram and Bharat Meet in the Forest

Bharat, Shatrughna, Guru Vasishta, three mothers, the Cabinet ministers, a huge contingent of the army, and many folks from Ayodhya now proceed to the forest in search of Ram. Bharat also carries the Crown with him, planning to perform Ram's coronation right there in the forest. On the way, he meets several people who tell him how Ram was spending his time in the forest, how he, Sita, and Laxman walk miles barefoot, how they gather and eat fruits and nuts, and how they sleep on a bed of leaves and grass. Bharat is extremely sad to hear that, and he also gives up all royal luxuries. The royal retinue finally comes to know that Ram, Sita, and Laxman are staying on the Chitrakut Mountain, and they all proceed promptly in that direction.

Laxman is out getting fruits and nuts when he sees at a distance a huge army coming toward their camp on the mountain. He is shocked to see a number of Kosal flags of the Sun dynasty at the head of the approaching crowd. He rushes back to Ram and asks him to get ready for a battle. He tells Ram that Bharat, accompanied by a huge army, is coming towards their camp, "to clear his way by killing both of us." Laxman also assures Ram that he alone would surely be able to defeat the approaching army, and rushes to bring out his weapons. Ram tells Laxman that he probably does not know Bharat very well and that Bharat would never do anything like that. Furthermore, they both owe their allegiance to Bharat, the new Kosal King, and that they should never raise their weapons against Bharat. He adds, "If Bharat wants to raise his weapons against his brothers, let him do that. But I can assure you that my Bharat will not do that."

Bharat now approaches the camp, and seeing Ram there, he respectfully bows to him, and says, " Brothers Ram and Laxman, I have caused you all this trouble, and I am really ashamed to stand before you. Please forgive me." Bharat's pure love and devotion overwhelm Ram. Ram hugs Bharat and asks him not to blame himself. Ram also goes forward to greet his Guru and the three mothers. Seeing the mothers in white saris, he now understands that his father is no more. After receiving the blessings of Guru Vasishta, Ram, as always, bows to mother Kaikayi first. Kaikayi, in tears, hugs Ram and asks him to either forgive or punish her because, "I know I am the root cause of all this." Ram tells mother Kaikayi that he does not consider her to be responsible for or guilty of anything, and hence the problem of punishment or forgiveness does not even arise. He tells her that as far as he is concerned, she still is his loving mother as before, and that every thing happens because of karmic necessity.

Ram asks Guru Vasishta how Dasharath died so soon when he was apparently healthy before Ram left Ayodhya for the forest. Vasishta consoles him by saying, "Ram, you know very well that each one of us is on an endless journey towards our liberation. We are all like wooden logs floating in a raging river. We meet, we depart, and we may or may not meet again. Birth and death are but meaningless necessities along this journey. The Atman is beyond this birth and death cycle. So students of spiritual knowledge do not grieve over death." Ram then goes to the river and offers his last rites to his father.

Bharat does not quite know how to approach Ram with his request for Ram's return. He asks Laxman to sound Ram out. Ram tells Laxman, however, that "It is as much Bharat's duty as mine to uphold our father's word." Bharat then approaches Kausalya and asks her to command Ram to return to Ayodhya.

Kausalya, however, responds stoically, "I am sure he will never disobey my command. But how can I come between him and his dharma for my pleasure? Mother's love must be selfless. So I am simply going to watch how this cosmic drama plays out."

As they all anxiously wait, Sita's father, King Janak and his wife arrive there and join them. Guru Vasishta then tells everyone that, in absence of Dasharath, King Janak, being the elder of the family, will find a way out of this dilemma. Next day, they all gather together, and Bharat is the first one to speak: "I have always felt that Ram is the real heir to the kingdom. My mother schemed to take it away from him, and give it to me. But it is not hers to give and not mine to accept. I do not want it. Oh, Ram, please forgive me for all the troubles I have caused you, accept your kingdom, and return to Ayodhya with us."

Ram replies: "My beloved Bharat! You should not blame yourself or mother Kaikayi for any of this. I do not blame either of you. It is a very simple matter. Our father wanted me to go to the forest and you to be the king. How can we ignore his commands just because our father is now dead? It is the dharma of both of us to uphold our father's promise to mother Kaikayi."

Kaikayi then says: "My beloved Ram, please forgive me for everything. But the promises were from my husband to me. I am now acutely aware of what I have done. I repent it, and I now recall my demands. So please come back with us to Ayodhya and take your rightful place on the throne."

Ram again replies: "Mother Kaikayi, only my father had the right to release me from this obligation. It was his wish that I come to the forest and Bharat sit on the throne. I know how proud he was of us when we were ready to do anything to uphold his word. Now that he is dead, how can I forget all that and come to Ayodhya?"

Bharat says: "Let me take your place and spend fourteen years in exile and you go back to the throne. This way we will still be honoring our father's word — one in exile, and one to the throne."

Ram's reply is: "My brother, the path of dharma is very difficult. It is like walking on a sharp edge of a sword. One's duty is not a commodity that can be bartered or exchanged. One must shoulder one's responsibility himself. However, I shall accept the verdict of our respected father-in-law, King Janak."

Janak says: "My sons, Ram and Bharat, I am really proud of both of you. It is a rare opportunity indeed to witness such a battle between a son's dharma and a brother's love. This is indeed a strange fight where the winner wants the loser to take the throne. Let me, therefore, seek divine guidance from Lord Shiva on who should win this argument."

Everyone waits anxiously as King Janak prays to Lord Shiva. He then tells everyone that with the Lord's help, he has come to a decision. He says: "Bharat and Ram! This has been the most difficult decision I have had to make in my life. Ram's devotion to his dharma is rock solid and selfless. Bharat's love for Ram is pure and limitless. I have meditated for long and concluded that Bharat's love must win over Ram's dharma. I must, however, remind Bharat that pure love is selfless. It does not demand anything. It only wants to give. So, Oh Bharat, do not make any demands on Ram. Do not demand a price for your love. If you love Ram, throw your life at his service. Ask him what he would like you to do and carry out his desires."

Bharat now is overwhelmed by the responsibility of following the rules of true love. He says that, all this time, he was really thinking about how the world would blame him for Ram's exile. He confesses that King Janak really opened his eyes to true love. He goes to Ram, respectfully bows to him, and asks, "What would you want me to do now? I have no desire of my own, and I will carry out with pride whatever you ask me to do." Ram then tells Bharat, "I gladly accept the kingdom you came to give me. Please rule it on my behalf, however, until I can complete my exile of fourteen years. I shall

Bharat receives Ram's sandals

then return to Ayodhya and take it back from you." Bharat assures Ram that his wish will be carried out. He requests Ram to give him a pair of his wooden sandals — he wants to keep them on the throne as the symbol of Ram's power and presence, and wants to hold the kingdom in trust for Ram.

Bharat returns to Ayodhya with Ram's sandals. He also cannot imagine himself enjoying royal luxuries at the palace while his Lord Ram is living in the forest. Consequently, he builds a little hut on the banks of the river in Ayodhya, and decides to live there leading a meditative life and to run the affairs of the government from there. He also asks his wife, Mandavi, to continue to live in the palace and serve the three mothers. He tells her, "I understand and share your pain of separation. But during these trying times, our pain is less important than our duty. We are a team, and you should help me do what I cannot do myself — take care of my mothers."

Kaikayi succumbed only once to the ungodly qualities of attachment, greed, fear, and hate, and then even repented her actions. But one weak and thoughtless moment on her part now set in motion the wheels of life for several innocent people. Dasharath died in pain of separation from Ram. Ram, Sita, and Laxman are wandering in the forest. Bharat is living in a hut near a river outside Ayodhya. Laxman's wife, Urmila, and Bharat's wife, Mandavi, are living in the palace, away from their husbands, taking care of their mothers-in-law. Kausalya and Sumitra count the days waiting for their sons to come back. Kaikayi herself painfully carries the burden of being the cause of all these troubles. Even Manthara, who started all of this, repents and finds the pain unbearable. She locks herself into a room in the palace and lives a life of penance there.

Ram, Sita, and Laxman travel across the Dandak forest. The forest is full of demons that come from Ravan's kingdom, cross into Dandak, interfere in the rituals performed by people, and kill and eat humans. As the Kosal King, Ram is still responsible for the safety of people within the borders of his kingdom. Ram and Laxman, therefore, fight battles with these demons and rid the Dandak forest of these evil demons. They also meet a countless number of saints who give them invaluable lessons in various aspects of Hindu philosophy.

The period of exile is fast coming to an end, and now only about one year is left when they can all go back to Ayodhya.

Shurpanakha Incident

Shurpanakha is the only sister of Ravan, the King of Lanka. The people of Lanka are of demon race and are quite experts at black magic and sorcery. They can take any form at will and fly through the air. Ravan's brothers Khar and Dushan are his military commanders, stationed south of the border of Kosal Kingdom, and often attack Kosal citizens with their demon soldiers. On one of her visits to her brothers, Khar and Dushan, Shurpanakha happens to see Ram during one of her scouting flights and wants to marry him. She introduces herself to Ram as the sister of the brave demon king Ravan, and tells him that she wants to marry him. She also tells him that it was quite customary for demon women to do this and that she was simply following her dharma. Ram tells her that he must refuse her offer because he already had a wife, and that he was vowbound not to take more than one wife. Shurpanakha, as the only sister of Ravan, is used only to getting what she wants, and is quite unprepared for this response. She thinks that she could probably get Ram for herself if she would simply kill Sita. So she lunges forward towards Sita. Ram then signals to Laxman, who, in turn, intervenes and cuts Shurpanakha's nose off with his sword. Shurpanakha threatens Ram and Laxman with revenge. She adds that they have essentially signed their own death warrants because mighty Ravan and her other brothers will surely punish Ram and Laxman by death for this insult of their sister.

Death of Khar and Dushan

Shurpanakha now goes to her brothers Khar and Dushan just across the border and tells them that two mere humans had insulted her by cutting her nose off, and that she would be satisfied with nothing less than their death. Khar and Dushan assure her that they would personally punish the two men and they lead a huge army and come face to face with Ram. In their usual arrogance, they invite Ram to surrender, assuring him that their king, Ravan, will give him a fair trial, and may even pardon him for his misdeeds. Ram, however, uses his divine weapons and kills everyone including Khar and Dushan.

Ravan, Kumbhakarna, and Vibhishan

Ravan, the King of Lanka, and his brothers, Kumbhakarna and Vibhishan, are very learned individuals. They are devotees of various gods such as Brahma and Shiva, and they all had acquired a number of divine weapons from these gods. Ravan is especially brave, and, under his rule, Lanka has developed into a very prosperous city. Kumbhakarna is very large in size, probably as big as several hundred people put together. He also had performed special rituals and had been rewarded by Brahma with a boon of his choice. He had planned to ask Brahma for the throne of Indra, the king of gods. Indra had come to know about Kumbhakarna's plans and had asked the Goddess of Learning to help him keep his throne. As Kumbhakarna opened his mouth to say the words "Throne of Indra", the Goddess of Learning instead makes him say the words "Throne of Nidra". The Sanskrit word *Nidra* means sleep. Thus, instead of asking for the throne of Indra, Kumbhakarna had inadvertently asked for the throne of sleep. As a result, this brave brother of Ravan sleeps for months at a time, and wakes up only twice a year for a day or so. Ravan's other brother, Vibhishan, is a very ethical person and follows his dharma very meticulously. He is also a fervent devotee of

Lord Vishnu, and knows that Ram is actually an incarnation of Lord Vishnu.

As Ravan acquires weapon after weapon, and boon after boon, he becomes quite egoistic and arrogant, and does not think that now there is any need for him to follow his dharma. He thinks that the rules and constraints of dharma are only for the poor and the weak. According to him, whatever strong and brave people like him do, is *ipso facto* right. Ravan's sons are also equally brave and arrogant.

With Khar and Dushan dead, Shurpanakha now comes to Lanka and seeks Ravan's help against Ram and Laxman. She is a woman scorned, seething in anger, and she is not going to rest until she has her revenge. She sees Ravan in his royal chamber and speaks to the whole assembly: "I was flying through the border area when I saw Sita, the most beautiful woman in the universe. She was living in a hut with her husband Ram, and his brother, Laxman. I thought that only my brave brother Ravan should have this woman and that a woman like Sita deserved the luxuries of his palace. So I tried to take her away when Laxman attacked me and cut my nose off. Then when Khar and Dushan went to punish them, Ram killed them. In doing so, these two mere mortals have really insulted King Ravan and essentially challenged him to a fight."

Arrogant Ravan assures her that he will go himself if needed, but she will have her revenge. Ravan's Cabinet ministers, his sons, and his military chief all tell him, "We cannot have two mere mortal humans insult us like that." Ravan's younger brother, Vibhishan, is the only voice of sanity there. He tells Ravan, "My respected brother, if we attacked them first and lost, how can you blame Ram? It is not his fault. It was actually his dharma to protect the borders of his kingdom. If he killed Khar and Dushan within his borders, Ram is perfectly justified in doing that. So it would be against dharma to simply go and attack Ram and Laxman. Furthermore, if Ram alone killed our brave brothers, he does not seem to be a mere mortal. So I would surely not attack him without first finding out his strengths and weaknesses."

Ravan and his sons ridicule Vibhishan and say that the powerful do not have to worry about dharma. Whatever they do is right, because the might is right. Ravan says that with all his power, divine weapons, and various boons, why should he worry about two little humans. Ravan's military chief, however, says that there is probably a way to avoid a fight with Ram. He suggests that Ravan should simply kidnap Sita and bring her to Lanka. In the grief of separation from his wife, Ram will lose his balance and will be easy to defeat. Ravan likes the idea and several of his advisors seem to support it. Vibhishan, however, again speaks out against that idea: "Do not act like a common thief, my brother. You are brave and the leader of a prosperous nation. Your reputation will go down the drain if you kidnap a married woman. It is our dharma to protect women, not to kidnap them. You have received all your divine weapons by respecting the constraints of dharma. Now if you act contrary to the precepts of dharma, your divine weapons will not help you. Do not lose your powers by lusting after and kidnapping a married woman."

Ravan's wife, Crown Queen Mandodari, also tells Ravan that if he wants Sita, he should win her in a battle with Ram, and not steal her like a cowardly common thief. As the king of his people, he should be a role model to them by establishing standards of ethical behavior. She also suggests that Shurpanakha was not telling the truth and was manipulating the situation for her personal vengeance; consequently, Ravan should not get involved in this petty affair.

In spite of the pleadings by his wife and by his brother, Ravan decides to kidnap Sita. He therefore goes to a master sorcerer, Marich, to seek his assistance. Marich also attempts to dissuade Ravan from this behavior that is patently contrary to dharma. Ravan, however, is determined to go ahead with his plan and finally issues a royal order to Marich to help him.

Ravan Kidnaps Sita

Ravan now brings Marich to where Ram, Sita, and Laxman are living. Marich transforms himself into a golden deer. His skin is golden in color, his antlers are made of gold, and his body emits a fragrance. The deer deliberately runs around to make sure that Sita sees it. Sita is simply enchanted with this incredible deer, and wants to take it back to Ayodhya with her as a sort of a souvenir. She says that even if the deer cannot be captured alive, Ram can use its skin to sit on during his meditations. Laxman smells a rat here and suggests that the golden deer was probably a demon trick. Sita, however, brushes his concern as an overreaction and requests Ram to bring the deer to her, alive or dead. In spite of Laxman's doubts, Ram asks him to stay and protect Sita so that he could go after the deer. He also adds that if, as Laxman suggests, it is some kind of trickery, it is anyway better to go now and find out what is going on. Ram goes after the deer leaving Laxman and Sita behind.

Marich, in the form of deer, runs away from the hut with Ram in pursuit. Ram first attempts to capture it alive, but after running around for some time, decides to kill it instead. He therefore aims and shoots an arrow at the deer. The deer is hit and falls to the ground. Marich comes back to his demon form, and screams in Ram's voice, "Oh Laxman, Oh Sita, I am hurt. Come quickly and help me. Oh Laxman, do not delay. Come right away." Ram at once realizes that, as Laxman had feared, someone was playing a dirty trick on him. He is, however, not worried about Sita because he had left Laxman behind to protect her. He promptly starts running back towards their hut.

Back at the hut, Laxman and Sita hear Ram's voice calling for help. Sita asks Laxman to hurry up and go to help his brother. Laxman, however, does not move and says: "My respected sister-in-law, there is no force on the Earth that can hurt Ram. He is the incarnation of Lord Vishnu himself. Furthermore, he has asked me to stay behind and protect you. Please have faith in your husband and wait just a little while longer. Ram will very shortly return here safe and sound."

Sita, however, is an emotional wreck just thinking about the possibility of her husband being hurt. She is not thinking rationally at the time, and accuses Laxman of being a coward and adds, "It is the dharma of every woman to help her husband in time of need. This is what marriage vows mean. So if you do not want to go, give me your bow and arrow, and I will go to help my husband."

Laxman tries to convince her that Ram can never be in trouble, but Sita insists that he go to help Ram. Eventually, Laxman apologizes to Ram for disobeying him for the first time in his life and tells Sita that he will go. Before leaving, however, he first uses his arrow and draws a line on the ground in front of the hut. He then tells Sita that he had used his mystical powers to create an impenetrable and invisible barrier at that line, and that she would be safe as long as she stayed within that line. Laxman asks her not to cross that line for any reason until he and Ram return. He then goes out, leaving Sita behind.

Ravan was invisibly watching what was going on, and as soon as Laxman leaves, he arrives at the hut in the form of a brahmin. He sees Sita and tells her that he had been on a long pilgrimage, and had been walking for several days without food. He asks her for some food. Sita tells him that she would bring out some food and goes in to the kitchen. Ravan then attempts to go in after her. Laxman's barrier, however, stops him, and he backs off and sits down at the front gate. Sita comes out with a plate of food, puts it down past the Laxman Line, and asks the brahmin to come and get the food. Ravan, however, protests and says that he is very tired and she should bring the food to him. Sita tells him that she has been asked to stay behind the line and so he will have to come and get the food. The brahmin, that is, Ravan now responds loudly in anger: "Is this any way to treat a brahmin guest? Guests should always be treated with respect. I know your husband is hurt and his brother has gone out to help him. You do not know this brahmin's powers. If you do not bring me the food, I will put a curse on both of them and you will never see your husband again."

Poor Sita! She is already under stress because she thinks her husband is hurt. She now thinks that the brahmin at the door must be powerful because he even knew that Ram was hurt. She does not want to make the brahmin angrier. She falls prey to the satanic machinations of Ravan and brings the plate of food to him, crossing the Laxman Line. Now she is completely defenseless. Ravan comes back to his original form, grabs Sita, puts her on his vehicle, and flies off southward in the direction of Lanka.

Sita starts to scream for help, "Help. Help. This vicious demon is kidnapping me." She also throws some of her jewelry down, thus marking the path of her flight, so that Ram and Laxman would know she was being kidnapped against her will. Jatayu bird hears Sita's cry for help and fights a valiant battle with Ravan. Jatayu, however, is no match for Ravan. Ravan cuts one of his wings off and Jatayu falls to the ground in pain. He now struggles to keep alive so that he could give Ram a first-hand report on Sita's kidnapping.

Ram's Grief at Sita's Disappearance

As Ram is running back to his hut, he sees Laxman running towards him. He realizes that a disaster of monumental proportion is about to unfold. He asks Laxman why he had left Sita alone, and suggests that some tragedy is probably awaiting them at the hut. Laxman tells him how Sita forced him to leave her alone at the hut and hopes she will be safe at the hut. They come back to their hut, only to find it empty. They look around for Sita but do not find her anywhere. Ram, the Lord of the Universe, the incarnation of Lord Vishnu, is now grief-stricken like an ordinary mortal. He remembers Sita and cries a lot. With Laxman, he runs around in the forest looking for Sita, screaming her name out loudly. Suddenly, he sees Jatayu lying in pain on the ground. He goes there and takes Jatayu in his lap.

Jatayu tells Ram how Ravan had kidnapped Sita against her will and how he was flying southward in his vehicle. Jatayu dies shortly.

Sita in Ashok Garden in Lanka

Ravan brings Sita to Lanka. She refuses even to look at him, let alone live in his opulent palace. Ravan knows that he cannot force himself on her. Earlier in the past, Ravan had raped a married woman and was cursed by her husband. He knew that, because of this curse, if he ever tried to force himself on any woman, he would die instantly. He thinks he can win Sita over simply by offering great wealth and luxury, or by threatening to kill her. She, however, shows contempt for him and tells him:"You have been boasting all this time about your past victories over gods and how brave you are. But then what do you do? You act like a common thief and kidnap a married woman. With this unethical behavior, you are inviting your own death. I have no use for your wealth and luxuries. I am very lucky to have Ram as my husband. If you apologize and return me to him with honor, he will surely forgive you."

Ravan finally gives her one year to change her mind, and tells her:"Your husband does not even know where you are at this time, so he cannot rescue you. There is also a large sea between the island of Lanka and the mainland where Kosal is. I am sure you will eventually see the utter futility of waiting to be rescued and will come to me."

Ravan puts Sita in the Ashok Gardens in Lanka, and Sita stays under a large tree, with a large contingent of female demons watching over her. Queen Mandodari is a very ethical and spiritual woman, scrupulously following her dharma. She does not like the way her husband had changed over the years, and always counsels him to change his ways and return to the path of dharma. Clearly, she disapproves the kidnapping of Sita. She also does not like the way Sita is being treated. So Mandodari sends a set of expensive clothes and jewelry to Sita along with her personal message:"I am acutely aware that my husband has brought you here against your will. You will always be a queen however, and a guest in my eyes, and I would treat you as such. If you need anything, please do not hesitate to ask. You have a friend in me." Sita is quite overwhelmed by the sincerity of Mandodari's message. She, however, sends the gift back saying that she could not possibly wear such royal clothes and jewelry when her husband is living a frugal meditative life.

On every occasion, Mandodari warns Ravan that Sita's kidnapping is a blot on his character and that if he does not return her with honor to her husband, it will soon lead to his total destruction. She tells him that any behavior contrary to dharma would never go unpunished.

Shabari's Unparalleled Devotion to Ram

Ram and Laxman continue their tireless search for Sita. One day, a god gives Ram directions to a place where Shabari, a saintly lady, lives and asks him to meet her. The god tells Ram that Shabari would show him the way to the Pampa Lake where he would meet Sugriv, an exiled King of the Simian people. Sugriv would then help him to fight a battle against Ravan and free Sita. Ram and Laxman then proceed to meet with Shabari.

Shabari is a tribal woman and a faithful follower of her guru. Earlier as her guru was preparing to leave his physical body, he tells her that she is destined to see Lord Vishnu in the flesh when he incarnates himself as Ram. He instructs her to continue to live at his ashram after his departure and to wait for Ram. Shabari was, of course, ecstatic that she will some day get to see Lord Vishnu. So she lives at her guru's ashram, awaiting Lord Vishnu's arrival. She gets up every day, cleans the place spotless, and covers the road to her hut with fresh flowers for Ram to walk on. She also collects fresh berries and fruits, eating off a little piece of every berry and fruit to make sure that each of them is the very best available for her Lord to eat.

She has been following this routine every day of the year, year after year, waiting for Ram, never ever doubting the assurance of her guru that Ram would come. Many in her neighborhood make fun of Shabari and ridicule her by calling her a crazy woman. They ask her why she is wasting her time picking flowers and fruits for someone who has not come for years. One day, however, as Shabari is covering the path with flowers, her dream comes true. Ram and Laxman walk to her, and Ram says, " I am Ram, the eldest son of Dasharath, and this is my younger brother, Laxman." Shabari feels as if all her good karma from thousands and thousands of her past lives had suddenly come to fruition at that very instant. With tears of joy rolling down her face, she bows to Ram and invites them to walk on the flower-strewn path she had prepared for him that day, and offers them seats in her small hut. She knows that Ram had walked for miles to come to her. So she soothes his feet with warm water and massages his aching feet. Ram feels as if his mother Kausalya is taking care of him as she had done in the past. Shabari brings out the basket of berries and fruits for him. She tells Ram that, as she had done every day for the past many years, she had gone out that day and selected the sweetest berries for him. She assures him that she knew they were sweet because, "I have tasted each and every one of them myself to be sure." Laxman is not looking forward to eating these berries, half-eaten by some old lady. Ram, however, eats them with pleasure. After they all settle down, Shabari tells Ram about her guru's instruction to her and directs Ram and Laxman to the mountain retreat where exiled Sugriv is staying. Ram then blesses Shabari with liberation, and she leaves her physical body.

In today's world of instant gratification, Shabari is a classic example of faith, conviction, perseverance, love, and hard work. She shows her unquestioned trust in her guru's word and waits to meet with Lord Vishnu. Every day, she tirelessly prepares to welcome Ram to her hut. Ram does not show up for years, but she is not disappointed and she does not complain. She gets up everyday and, with enthusiasm and hope,

Shabari meets Ram and Laxman

cleans the place up, covers the road with flowers, and collects berries for Ram. She wants everything to be the best for her Lord. Ram also understands her love and devotion, and happily eats her half-eaten, already tasted berries. This story of Shabari

has been told across India for thousands of years and will continue to be told as a beacon of devotion and of the mutual bond of love between the Lord and his devotees. Lord does not care for the caste, creed, gender, education, or riches of anyone. He can be bought only with pure love.

Vali, Sugriv, and Hanuman

Vali ruled the Simian Kingdom of Kishkindha. His younger brother Sugriv was his Crown Prince. The two were brave soldiers in their own right, and were known to be righteous loving brothers. Vali had received a special boon from gods. If anyone fought with Vali face to face, Vali would get half of the opponent's strength. Consequently, he was quite undefeatable in such conflicts. One day, a very strong demon comes and challenges Vali to a fight. In response, Vali and Sugriv come out to fight with the demon. Seeing the two brothers, the demon runs away, and Vali and Sugriv go after him. The demon sees a cave just outside the city and goes in to hide. Vali asks Sugriv to stand guard at the entrance and goes in to fight with the demon. Sugriv waits outside while Vali battles with the demon inside. The fight goes on for weeks and months. After about a year or so, Sugriv sees a lot of blood flowing from inside the cave towards the entrance. He also hears the demon scream, but does not hear his brother's voice. He, therefore, thinks that his brother was probably killed by the demon. Consequently, he closes the cave shut with a huge stone so as to trap the demon inside. Sugriv then returns home and tells everyone what had just happened. The Royal Priest asks Sugriv to become the new king, and Sugriv is so coronated. Unknown to Sugriv and others, however, Vali was not killed by the demon, and the fight had continued for several more weeks after

Sugriv had shut the cave and returned home. Eventually, Vali kills the demon and comes to the entrance of the cave, only to find it shut with a huge stone. Vali removes the stone, comes out, and finds that Sugriv was gone. Vali, therefore, returns home, and is shocked to find that Sugriv was already ruling Kishkindha as the new king. Sugriv is happy to see Vali, and welcomes him with open arms. He attempts to explain to Vali how he happened to be sitting on the throne, and how he wanted to return the throne back to Vali. Vali, however, refuses to listen to Sugriv, beats him up in front of everyone in the royal assembly hall, and throws him out of the city. Some of Sugriv's trusted Cabinet Ministers accompany him to a mountain hideaway; Hanuman, the most beloved and respected devotee of Ram, is among them.

Hanuman was born with incredible powers. He was very strong, capable of lifting huge buildings or mountains off the ground, and he was also able to fly through airspace at will. As a child, he used to play tricks on people. One time, he happened to disturb a brahmin during his meditation, who, in turn, scolded him: "Oh child, you have been blessed with these powers because gods are going to need your assistance in the future. But you are just a child, and have been unknowingly misusing them. You shall now forget that you have these incredible powers and you would not be using them anymore. Only at a certain point in your life, when gods need your assistance, you will be reminded of these powers, and you will then be able to use your powers in service of Lord Ram." Hanuman, however, retains his power to take any form at will.

Ram Offers Friendship to Sugriv

With the directions from Shabari, Ram and Laxman travel to the mountain hideaway and meet Sugriv and his ministers. One of Sugriv's ministers assures Ram that Sugriv will surely help him to find and rescue Sita. He adds however, that in return, Sugriv will fully expect Ram to help him get his kingdom back from Vali. Ram responds that he cannot entertain such a political treaty with a *quid pro quo*. He tells Sugriv that such treaties are based on selfishness and are of no value to him. Ram offers him a relationship of *friendship:* "Friendship transcends caste, creed, social standing, and other factors. It is not conditional and does not keep a count of who does what for whom. Unlike political treaties, friendship can be between unequals. Even a king and a beggar, or a rich and a poor can be friends. In such a relationship, only love is exchanged, and that too, unconditionally and without being asked. I want to offer you this kind of relationship between us." Sugriv and his ministers are overwhelmed by this response. Sugriv and Ram become close friends. Ram also promises Sugriv to make him the King of Kishkindha.

Ram Kills Vali

Ram, Sugriv, and others now go to Kishkindha, and Sugriv challenges Vali to a duel. Ram, Laxman, and hide behind some trees. At an opportune moment during the fight, Ram shoots an arrow at Vali, and Vali falls to the ground. As Ram comes forward, Vali knows what had happened. He, however, cannot understand why Ram would hide behind the trees and kill him when Vali had done nothing to Ram. He accuses Ram of behavior contrary to dharma and of ruining the reputation of the Sun dynasty. Ram tells Vali in response: "You have done a great injustice to Sugriv, your younger brother. Elder brother is said to be like a father to a younger brother. Instead, you did not even listen to what he was trying to say to you when you threw him out. You became arrogant with power, and you hung your younger brother without even a trial. You deserved to be punished for this behavior contrary to dharma. Now that I am friends with Sugriv, I have every right to punish you on his behalf."

Vali then apologizes to Sugriv for the injustice done to him, and advises his own son, Angad, to follow the advice of Ram and Sugriv. Sugriv is now coronated as the new king of the Simian people of Kishkindha.

Killing of Vali is the only controversial episode directly related to Ram's behavior in the whole Ramayan. Hiding behind a tree and shooting an arrow sounds quite cowardly. Vali's boon mentioned earlier clearly made it impossible even for Vishnu-incarnate to fight him face to face. The fact remains, however, that Vali had no fight with Ram and Ram killed him without giving Vali any chance of defending himself. Volumes have been written over the past centuries by innumerable authors discussing the ethics of this action of Ram that appears to be contrary to dharma, and the possible motive of Ramayan's author to leave this singular spot on Ram's life. Possibly, the author wanted to indicate that only god can be perfect and that no human, whether god-incarnate or not, can be perfect. Each individual reader of Ramayan must eventually think for oneself and arrive at an acceptable explanation for this episode.

Hanuman Finds Sita

Sugriv sends search teams in all directions to look for Sita. A team consisting of Hanuman and others searches southward until they come to the southern tip of the present Indian sub-continent. They do not find Sita anywhere. There an eagle-bird tells them that he can, with his sharp eyesight, actually see Sita sitting under a tree in Lanka. He also estimates that Lanka was probably over hundred miles from where they all stood. This was all hardly assuring to the search party because, assuming Sita was in Lanka, they knew of no way to cross the ocean and go there. Fortunately, an old person among them knew about Hanuman's incredible powers. He asks Hanuman to look deeper inside and to try to remember the powers he used to exhibit in his younger years. Hanuman now remembers his past and is ready to serve the cause of his Lord Ram.

Hanuman shouts in a loud voice, "Victory to Ram," assumes a huge size, and flies towards Lanka. When he arrives at the city gate, he assumes a very small size and flies around the city in search of Sita. Hanuman is shocked to hear someone in a small palace there pray to Lord Ram. He wonders who in Lanka could be bold enough to pray to Ram. It is Ravan's younger brother Vibhishan. Lord Brahma had earlier promised Vibhishan that he would meet Lord Vishnu himself when Lord Vishnu incarnates himself as Ram. Vibhishan had been praying to Ram since then. Hanuman introduces himself to Vibhishan, tells him that he is also a devotee of Ram, and asks if Vibhishan knew where Ravan is holding Sita. Vibhishan directs Hanuman to the Ashok Gardens.

Hanuman quietly goes to the garden and finds Sita there, in simple clothes sitting under a large tree, surrounded by female demon guards. Hanuman hides in that tree until he gets a chance to meet with Sita at night. Sita understandably thinks that to be a trick by Ravan's demons. Hanuman, however, shows some of the identifications that he was carrying on behalf of Ram. He shows Sita the ring that she had tried to give Kevat, the boatman who had taken Ram, Sita, and Laxman across the Ganga river. He also tells her stories that only Ram and Sita would have known. Sita is now convinced that Hanuman is really a messenger from her beloved husband Ram. Hanuman tells her that they all will be coming soon to rescue her and that she should hold on a little while longer.

Hanuman then attempts to judge Ravan's military strength and preparedness by deliberately picking up a fight with his soldiers. He eats several fruits from the trees in the garden, and when the soldiers challenge him, he destroys the garden trying to defend him. As the confrontation escalates, he kills several army generals in the Ravan's army. Finally, Indrajit, Ravan's Crown Prince, comes to confront Hanuman. First he asks Hanuman why he had attacked the soldiers. Hanuman tells Indrajit that he was simply eating fruits when the soldiers attacked him first. He also reminds Indrajit that, as a part of the basic human rights, dharma acknowledges the right of a hungry person to food. In other words, Hanuman was simply defending himself. Indrajit now asks Hanuman why he could not have just asked for food instead of stealing it like a common thief. Hanuman replies, "I thought that thieves are probably rewarded in Lanka because your own king stole Sita like a common thief." Indrajit is quite taken aback at this response. He becomes very angry and shoots a divine weapon at Hanuman. Hanuman chooses to respect the weapon and allows him to be captured. He is then carried to the royal assembly to face Ravan. He tells Ravan: "I am a messenger from Ram to Sita, and I allowed myself to be captured because I wanted to talk to you. I know you have arrogantly kidnapped Sita. Because of a boon from Lord Brahma, gods and demons cannot kill you, and you think this makes you invincible. But remember that Brahma's boon does not protect you from humans and simians. If you continue to hold Sita against her will, Ram and his simian army will surely destroy you and your Lanka. Simply return Sita to her husband with full honors and surrender to Ram. He is really compassionate and will surely forgive you."

Ravan becomes extremely angry at this lecture by a mere simian, and orders that he be killed in punishment. Vibhishan, however, tells Ravan that it is against the King's dharma to kill an envoy from another king. He therefore suggests any other punishment, short of death. Ravan then orders that Hanuman's tail be set on fire and Hanuman be paraded in the streets of Lanka. Sita hears about the proposed punishment and requests the fire-god not to hurt Hanuman. With his tail on fire, Hanuman sets fires around Lanka and significantly damages the entire city before returning back to the mainland across the sea.

Ravan Kicks Vibhishan Out of Lanka

After Hanuman burns Lanka down, Ravan calls for a royal assembly for consultations. Vibhishan speaks out and tells

Ravan what he does not want to, and is not used to, hear: "My elder brother, you have done a great injustice to your kingdom by acting like a common thief and kidnapping Sita. You think that Lanka, an island far away from the mainland, is safe because it is protected from all sides. But now even a monkey came here and virtually destroyed our city. Ram did not attack our forces first. We instigated the whole episode. He has already killed Khar, Dushan, and many other demons. As a result of your reckless actions that are contrary to dharma, you will destroy yourself and your kingdom. Hundreds of thousands of innocent Lankans will suffer because of your refusal to accept responsibility and change your behavior. I know your assembly is full of *yes-men*. They will tell you only what you like to hear. But I am your brother and have only your interests in mind. I would urge you to return Sita with honor and apologize to Ram."

Ravan, of course, refuses to listen to reason. He says that if he backs off now, he will be called a coward. He calls Vibhishan a traitor and kicks him out of the royal assembly. Vibhishan reminds Ravan that whoever gods want destroyed, they destroy their intellect first, and he goes home.

Vibhishan Joins Ram

Vibhishan knows that he is not welcome in Lanka anymore, and decides to join Ram because that was the side of dharma. He is, of course, not sure if he would be accepted at Ram's camp. But he is quite confident that Lord Ram will do the right thing, and he takes his chances. Along with some of his closest confidants, he flies to the mainland to meet with Ram.

Some of Sugriv's ministers are skeptical about welcoming Vibhishan in their camp. They suspect his intentions and fear he may be a spy for Ravan. Hanuman, however tells his simian colleagues not to be skeptical of Vibhishan simply because he is a demon by birth. Ram goes one step further and says, "It is a dharma of us Sun Dynasty Kings to welcome and protect anyone who surrenders to us, and I have taken a vow to follow dharma. Furthermore, one should be judged only by one's character and actions — not by his caste, creed, national origin, beauty, and other outer characteristics. So let us welcome Vibhishan with open arms and without any reservations."

Vibhishan now comes to Ram and tells him how he was thrown out of Lanka for suggesting that Ravan follow the path of dharma. He also requests that Ram not punish the Lankan people for the arrogant behavior of their evil king. Ram assures Vibhishan that he fights only in defense of dharma and that too only with those who choose to fight with him. He says that he is not at all interested in conquering Lanka for himself. He, in fact, declares Vibhishan to be the next king of Lanka, and crowns him as such in advance.

A Bridge to Lanka

There are two architects, Nal and Neel, in Ram's party who have certain special powers. When they were young and naughty, they used to throw people's pots, pans, and other possessions into the river in their town. Once they threw a few things belonging to a visiting saint. So he told the young simian boys that, from that day on, whatever they throw in water will not sink but float in water. Ram asks Nal and Neel to build a bridge to Lanka. Thousands of simian soldiers bring whatever they can find and hand it over to Nal and Neel to throw in the ocean. Soon a sturdy bridge is constructed and Ram leads his entire army across it to Lanka. They all come on the island and camp out just outside the city limits.

Angad's Diplomacy

Ram now makes one last attempt to avoid war and give peace a chance. He tells Sugriv, Laxman and others: "A war should always be the last step in any conflict resolution. Ravan kidnapped Sita and deserves to be punished. Hundreds of thousands of innocent soldiers and civilians will however die in a war with Ravan. A war should therefore never be fought for personal reasons and I am not in this conflict to save my personal honor. I am defending womanhood and the concept of dharma itself. Even then, it would be better if the impending war could be avoided. I am therefore sending Angad as my ambassador to Ravan's court."

As Angad introduces himself to Ravan as an ambassador from Ram, Ravan does not even offer him a seat. Angad reminds Ravan that it is king's dharma to welcome any ambassador, whether from a friendly nation or not. He adds, "Political convention and reciprocity demand that I should be welcome and offered a seat at this assembly. It would actually be all right for me to go back without delivering the message I am carrying from Ram to you. This message is important however, and potentially could save thousands of lives. For the sake of those lives, I will ignore your arrogant behavior." He continues: "You have been always talking much about your strength and how you have repeatedly defeated gods in various conflicts. However, Ram has killed everyone from your side who chose to fight with him. So being afraid to face him, you acted like a cowardly common thief and kidnapped his wife. You have been acting like an arrogant fool, and your insistence on holding Sita against her will surely lead to your death and the death of innocent soldiers on both sides. So I would advice you to return Sita with honor, and Ram will surely forgive you if you surrender to him."

Ravan is in no mood to listen to this kind of reason. He gets angry and orders that Angad be arrested. Angad then simply jumps off Ravan's assembly hall and returns back to Ram. The die is now cast. There is now no other way than to fight a war with Ravan.

The War Begins

The war begins and many soldiers, generals, and some of Ravan's young nephews die in the first few confrontations. Ravan then seeks a quick end to the conflict and enters the battlefield himself. Several warriors find Ravan unstoppable. Sugriv comes to face him but soon falls down unconscious. Ravan attempts to kill fallen Sugriv. Laxman scolds Ravan for attempting to kill an unconscious warrior, saying that it is clearly against the principles of human rights as well as against the well accepted rules of engagement. Ravan says that the demon race never followed these principles of human rights and that the rules of war were *of the weak, by the weak, and for the weak*. Ravan shoots a divine weapon at Laxman, and Laxman also falls to the ground unconscious. Ram now steps out to confront Ravan.

Ram tells Ravan that clearly Ravan was very brave, but that it was quite unfortunate that he was using his powers to support unethical behavior that was contrary to dharma. During the short battle, Ravan is seriously injured and faints. His charioteer withdraws his chariot from the battlefront and brings Ravan back behind the front line. When Ravan recovers and wakes up, he scolds his charioteer for withdrawing from the front. He tells the charioteer that he would have preferred death in the battle to the humiliation of withdrawal. The charioteer, however, reminds Ravan that one of his principal missions as the charioteer is to keep Ravan alive without any consideration of Ravan's personal pride and other factors. When Ravan returns and resumes the battle, Ram burns his chariot and breaks all his weapons. Ravan is now left to stand there on the ground, unarmed and quite defenseless. Ram then tells him: "Oh Ravan, you are now unarmed and look very tired. We of the Sun Dynasty consider attacking the unarmed to be contrary to dharma. You are now safe only because I adhere to my dharma. So go back, rest well during the night, and come back tomorrow fully armed. We will then resume our battle." Ravan walks back to his palace in utter humiliation.

Death of Kumbhakarna

Ravan now orders that his sleeping brother Kumbhakarna be awakened. Kumbhakarna comes to know about the kidnapping of Sita, about Ravan throwing Vibhishan out, and about the ongoing war between Ram and Ravan. He tells Ravan that Ravan should have recognized Ram and Sita as the incarnations of Vishnu and Laxmi and should have listened to the advice of Vibhishan. "Instead," he adds, "not only did you kidnap Goddess Laxmi herself, but you now insist on holding her against her will. Now that the war has begun, however, I shall fight on your behalf. If Ram is really Lord Vishnu, I will be honored to die at his hands."

Vibhishan makes an attempt to bring Kumbhakarna on Ram's side. He tells Kumbhakarna, "I know you disapprove of what Ravan is doing, and you know that Ram's side is the side of dharma. You also know fully well that there is no way for you and Ravan to win this war. So please come join us." Kumbhakarna, however, replies, "As a younger brother of Ravan, it is my dharma to treat him like my father, and follow his commands. Both Bharat and Laxman love their elder brother Ram, and Ram also is carrying out his father's commands. It is always easy to do that when one has a brother like Ram and a father like Dasharath. My karma, however, has given me an elder brother like Ravan, but that is not a good enough reason for me to stray from my dharma as a younger brother to Ravan. I must accept the cards dealt by fate to me and go forward. I know I am going to die and eventually only you will survive of us three brothers. I can, therefore, die in peace, knowing that you will be there to give me my final rites." Kumbhakarna is killed in a long, fierce battle.

Indrajit Enters the Conflict

Ravan is devastated by the death of his brother, and for the first time, begins to have doubts about the outcome of the war. As the conflict escalates, most of his generals, and all of his sons, except Crown Prince Indrajit, are killed in the war. Now Ravan and Indrajit, the father and the son, are the only two brave leaders left on Ravan's side. Ravan's wives, especially Mandodari, keep blaming him for his intransigence and recommend return of Sita and surrender to Ram. Indrajit, however, is not yet ready to give up. He is still confident that he can defeat Ram and Laxman. He says that people should not even debate the morality of his father's actions or about how the war began. He thinks that it is now everyone's duty to circle the wagons around their king and to fight to win.

Indrajit uses his black magic to become invisible and a fierce battle goes on between Laxman and Indrajit. Finally at the end of the day, Indrajit shoots a divine serpent-weapon at both Ram and Laxman. As a result, two poisonous cobras coil themselves very tightly around Ram and Laxman, slowly but surely squeezing life out of them. Indrajit and Ravan believe that they have essentially won the war. Hanuman, however, brings from the heavens Garuda, the King of Eagles, who releases Ram and Laxman from the grip of the cobras. Ravan and Indrajit cannot believe that Ram and Laxman survived the night and were ready the next morning to face Indrajit again. Next day, Indrajit uses the feared Shakti weapon against Laxman, and Laxman falls to the ground unconscious. Hanuman quickly carries Laxman back behind the front lines, and the war ends for the day at sunset.

Hanuman and the Mountain of Medicinal Herbs

Laxman is motionless on the ground, with his eyes closed. He does not respond to anything or to anyone, his breathing is slow and heavy, and he is sinking very fast. There is no doctor or any medicine in sight, and everyone is worried that Laxman may not live through the night. Ram tells everyone that he is nobody without Laxman, and wonders how he would be able to face Laxman's mother Sumitra and Laxman's wife Urmila, and tell them that Laxman would not be coming back to them. He sits down totally dejected. Vibhishan, however, tells Ram not to give up until Laxman's last breath. He suggests that they should try to get Lanka's Royal Physician to examine Laxman. With Ram's blessings, Hanuman goes to Lanka, simply picks up the entire house of the doctor, and brings the doctor and the house back with him to Ram's camp.

The doctor tells Ram and Vibhishan that he will not help any enemy of Lanka and they should promptly return him to Lanka. Ram talks to the doctor about medical ethics: "A doctor belongs to the whole humanity, irrespective of national borders. When a doctor sees a patient needing help, the doctor's dharma compels him to treat him without question. As a result, your dharma as a doctor now supersedes your dharma as a Lankan citizen. If a doctor chooses to ignore this prime directive of dharma, his powers to cure patients would surely decline over time." The doctor is startled by the clarity of this discourse on medical ethics. He, however, inquires if Ram would trust him and let Laxman be treated by the enemy. Ram tells him that a doctor is neither a friend nor a foe. He adds, "The medical ethics that expects a doctor to treat every patient brought before him also expects the patient to completely trust the doctor. My dharma leaves me no choice but to trust you without any reservations, and that is exactly what I will do." The royal doctor agrees to examine Laxman and treat him if possible. He examines Laxman carefully, and tells Ram that the only possible remedy was one particular divine herb from one of the Himalayan Mountains, more than a thousand miles away. Ram asks Hanuman to go to that mountain and get the herb. But when Hanuman reaches the mountain, he finds it difficult to identify the specific herb, and picks up the whole mountain and brings it back to the camp. The Royal Physician

Ravan's doctor treats Laxman

uses the divine herbal medicine and Laxman wakes up instantly.

Ravan and Indrajit are simply flabbergasted to hear that the Shakti weapon was ineffective against Laxman. Indrajit now prepares for the battle next day. During the battle, Indrajit attempts to use various divine weapons against Laxman. Every weapon however, simply returns back to Indrajit without causing any harm to Laxman. It suddenly dawns on Indrajit that he has been wrong all along. He returns to the palace and

tells his father, "My respected father, I believe that Ram and Laxman are not mere mortals as we have been saying all along. All my divine weapons have been ineffective against them. It is my duty to tell you what is in your best interest. Please surrender to Ram because he is none other than Lord Vishnu." Ravan now wonders if Indrajit would withdraw from the battle. Indrajit, however, assures him, "I have started to fight and I will continue. I will follow my dharma as a son, and fight for my father. I have learned at least that much from Ram. I will be honored to die in the battle."

Indrajit comes back and resumes the battle; Laxman however, quickly kills him. Indrajit had fought very valiantly and had inflicted enormous losses on the simian army. The simian soldiers, therefore, want to assert their right on Indrajit's corpse and publicly dishonor him by parading his dead body. Ram, however, tells them that all enmity must end at death, and that a brave soldier such as Indrajit should never be dishonored. He covers Indrajit's corpse with his personal shawl and returns the corpse with honor to Lanka.

End of Ravan

Now Ravan is all alone. Mandodari continues to ask him to surrender to Ram. She pleads with him: "Now that all your brothers, nephews, sons, and other relatives are dead, what would you do even if you win. With whom would you share the fruits of this war? Even at this late stage, please follow dharma and surrender to Ram. You may think that surrender is losing the war. But you will really be the ultimate winner." Ravan, however, tells her that things are way past surrendering. Surrender would really mean an insult of all those who had died for him in the war. For Ravan, this was a point of no return.

Ravan now comes to the battleground. God Indra provides Ram with his special chariot so that Ram can fight even in the air, as Ravan is able to do. Ravan fights a fierce battle with Ram, but finally Ram uses his ultimate Brahma weapon and kills Ravan. Lankan people bring the Royal Crown of Lanka to Ram, the winner of the war, and ask him not to punish them for the evil deeds of their king. Ram tells them that he has no interest or desire to rule over Lanka, and that he had already coronated Vibhishan as their new king. He also asks Vibhishan to give final rites to Ravan.

Sita's Walk through Fire

Hanuman then goes to Sita and informs her about Ravan's death at the hands of her husband. Vibhishan, as the new king, prepares to arrange for Sita's return to Ram. Ram, however, asks Laxman to start a fire so that Sita can walk through it and come to him. Laxman thinks that his brother Ram doubts Sita's chastity and wants her to take the test of fire. He thinks that to be patently unfair. He tells Ram, "Poor Sita! She was kidnapped against her will because we failed to protect her. She spent months under arrest, under a tree. How can you doubt her purity?" Ram then tells him in all somberness, "Oh Laxman, how could you even think I would doubt Sita. The relationship between a husband and a wife is one of total, unquestioned trust. Not trusting your wife means not trusting yourself. If I cannot trust my wife, why would I trust the fire-god or others who vouch for her purity? Anyway, Ram and Sita are like two bodies but one Atman. We are one, not two. I am simply claiming my wife from the fire-god. Just before the golden deer episode, I knew that Sita was going to be kidnapped. So I had asked the fire-god to take my Sita under his protection, and create a virtual holographic Sita to play her part. Now I want the fire-god to bring me my real Sita." Laxman then starts a little fire, and in front of everyone, Sita, the virtual one, enters the fire, and Sita, the real one, comes out. Those who did not know the story of the virtual Sita are satisfied that the fire-god had verified Sita's purity.

Ram Receives Dasharath's Blessings

As Ram and Sita are united, Brahma, Indra, and several other gods show up in the sky and bless Ram. Brahma also tells Ram that he is Vishnu-incarnate and that he has now completed the main mission of killing Ravan for which he had taken birth as a human. His other mission is to establish an ideal for human behavior and act like a beacon that guides the ships. Before responding to any situation, people should first imagine what would Ram have done under the circumstances, and respond accordingly. Dasharath also shows up in the sky and blesses Ram. Ram asks his father to forgive Kaikayi and accept her back as his loving wife. Ram tells his father that Kaikayi has been very unhappy because Dasharath had forsaken her before his death, and adds, "As long as my mother Kaikayi is unhappy, I cannot be happy, and I would think I have failed in my duty to her." Dasharath is very happy that, in spite of the long exile, Ram still cared so much for Kaikayi, and agrees to accept Kaikayi back as his beloved wife. Now Ram's work in Lanka is finished and the period of exile also comes to an end.

Ram invites Vibhishan, Sugriv, Angad, Hanuman, and others who had fought for him to accompany him to Ayodhya. They happily accept the invitation, and they all board the Lankan vehicle that travels at the speed of mind and promptly return to Ayodhya.

Ram Returns to Ayodhya

Guru Vasishta, Bharat, Shatrughna, three mothers, the cabinet ministers, and almost the whole town assemble to welcome Ram, Sita, and Laxman back to Ayodhya. As always, Ram bows to Guru Vasishta and Kaikayi before going over to his mother Kausalya. Kaikayi is overwhelmed to find that Ram had not changed a bit during the fourteen years of exile. Ram, Sita, and Laxman change into their royal attire and Guru Vasishta crowns Ram as the new King of Kosal.

Ram and Sita head for the palaces they had left fourteen years before. The three mothers welcome them home with traditional garlands. Laxman, Bharat, and Shatrughna are right behind Ram. Ram says that he would go to Kaikayi's palace first. As he enters her room, Bharat stays behind. Bharat had told Kaikayi many years before that she was no more his mother and that he would never enter her palace; he had not set foot in that palace for a period of fourteen years. Ram tells Bharat that a mother should never be disrespected. Every mother should be respected and loved without qualification. God does not like a mother in tears. He tells Bharat that even their father has forgiven mother Kaikayi, and that he should come in and ask for his mother's blessings. Bharat walks in and bows to his mother and asks for her forgiveness. Ram and Sita then distribute gifts to everyone in the palace in celebration of their happy return. When he does not see Manthara there, he inquires her whereabouts. Kausalya tells him that Manthara had closeted herself in a small dark room for all these years and that she wants someone to punish her for her evil deeds. Ram takes Sita and Laxman with him, and they all go to Manthara. Manthara, in deep remorse, asks Ram to give her punishment of death and relieve her of her miseries. Ram, however, tells her that, in his younger years, she had loved him like his mother, and that she will forever be a mother to him. He tells her that he cannot forgive or punish her because he does not consider her guilty of anything to begin with.

He adds, "Each one of us is just playing our part in this cosmic karmic drama. You have suffered long enough and we should all go back to how everything was before my exile."

Ram's Promise to His Ancestors

Ram now assumes the throne and calls the royal assembly in session. He is acutely aware of the awesome responsibility he would be shouldering in wearing the Crown. He takes this opportunity and for the first time speaks to the nation as the King. He assures the Nation: "As the King of Kosal, I shall have only one mission — to serve each and every one of the Kosal citizens. From now on, I shall have no personal aspirations. I shall have no personal pleasures and no personal agenda. I shall have no wife and no family ahead of the interests of the people. If anything or anyone comes between me and my people, and becomes a hindrance to my serving the interests of the people, I shall at once discard it without hesitation, and this is my solemn promise to you. I also respectfully assure my ancestors that I shall not do anything that will make them lower their head in shame. I shall live up to the high standards established by those who have preceded me as Kosal Kings."

What a profound and open-ended commitment without any ifs, ands, and buts! A Crown is a public trust and the public interest is above everything, including the life of the king. This concept of governance was established by Hindu thinkers thousands of years ago.

Ram now begins what everyone hopes to be a long, happy, and peaceful life. Early breakfast in the family quarters, cabinet meetings, decisions on public policy, meetings with intelligence officers, open door for public, and a guarantee of fairness and justice for all. Soon Sita finds herself pregnant and everyone is excited to hear the news.

Dark Clouds on Ayodhya Again

A few people of Ayodhya are not happy that Ram had welcomed Sita after she had spent several months under Ravan's control, and made her the Queen of Ayodhya. They think that Ram had thus insulted the office of the Queen. The majority of people, however, say that Sita had even withstood the test of fire and that no one should doubt her purity. Some others claim that only Laxman and the simian people had witnessed Sita's test of fire in Lanka and that there was not a single impartial observer from Ayodhya there. The controversy thus continues to rage.

The intelligence officer now has no choice but to report the controversy to Ram. Ram is very disappointed and hurt. He wonders how the people of Ayodhya could be so cruel and heartless. Sita, the Princess of Mithila, had happily gone in exile in helping her husband to uphold the promise of their King Dasharath. She had spent fourteen years in the forest and several months under detention in Lanka. She loved the people of Ayodhya from the bottom of her heart. In return, all Ayodhya had to offer her is a doubt about her purity. Ram is very disturbed and everyone knows that something is seriously wrong. After a few days, Ram decides to abdicate and to give the kingdom to Bharat. In an effort to find out what was really going on, Sita sends her own spies in town and comes to know the real reason behind her husband's anguish. She tells Ram: "My dear husband, I know the real reason of what is bothering you. I am, however, surprised that you are not following your dharma under the circumstances. I must remind you about your solemn promise to the people of Ayodhya. If anything came between you and the people of Ayodhya, you had promised to discard that thing at once. Now I am that thing, and whether you like it or not, you must get rid of me."

Ram, of course, tells her that he could not possibly punish her when he is absolutely sure of her purity. Now that he cannot satisfy the critics from Ayodhya he would simply abdicate and the two can then go away on their own. Sita, however, is quite adamant. She reminds her husband that his promise was not to abdicate, but "to discard whatever may come between me and my people." Furthermore, he had promised his ancestors that he would not do anything that will make them hang their head in shame. Sita finally tells Ram that it is her wife's dharma to help him follow his dharma. She declares that she would take herself out of the picture. She wants to simply walk away from Ayodhya, never to return. Sita cannot idly stand by seeing Ram blamed for insulting the office of the Queen. She, therefore, asks Ram's permission to leave and to simply walk away from Ayodhya. She tells Ram, "You gave your solemn word to Ayodhya that you will not have your personal pleasures ahead of people's interest. People have spoken and you must now follow their will. If you do not allow me to go, I do not think I will live long under these circumstances."

Sita thus throws herself at the altar of King's dharma. She tells her beloved Ram:"I know you consider my character to be spotless. But at this difficult time, we both must act like a team and establish the highest standard for behavior that any human can aspire to follow. My character or purity is really not the issue here. It does not matter whether or not what people say is true. What matters is that your path of dharma remains singularly spotless and that you keep the solemn promises you have made to Ayodhya. This is not the time to seek justice for Sita. I have a husband and I must sacrifice everything to uphold my husband's reputation. Unfortunately, as the King, you do not have a wife, and you do not have the luxury of a common man to worry about your wife in any way. You simply have to serve people and uphold their will."

Ram now faces the conflict of his lifetime. His inner voice is directly in conflict with the people's will. He knows that his Atman is the ultimate judge of what is right or wrong and what his dharma is at any time. The historical precedents and guru's advice are no doubt important. The concept of one's dharma, however, is a dynamic concept. Dharma is not a recipe from a cookbook or some non-negotiable rules of behavior. Ram's Atman is telling him that Sita is innocent and should not be punished simply because a few people from Ayodhya think so. He is, however, helpless because Sita, the Rock of Gibraltar, comes down squarely on the side of people's will. Ram now reluctantly asks Laxman to take Sita away in a chariot and leave her away from Ayodhya.

Sita in Guru Valmiki's Ashram

Laxman is devastated by this development. He, however, obeys Ram's command and leaves Sita at the forest just outside Ayodhya. She meets Guru Valmiki there who invites her to come to his ashram. He tells her that he knows everything via his divine vision, and that they both should keep her identity secret from the people living in his ashram. He tells Sita that the people of Ayodhya will one-day repent what they have done to her, and that her name will shine eternally "as long as the Sun and the Moon shine in the sky." Sita decides to stay at Valmiki's ashram.

Sita tries hard to adjust to the ashram life, but finds it difficult to leave her past life behind. She constantly thinks about Ram and Ayodhya, and worries about how Ram would be coping with separation from her. Valmiki, however, reminds her that the physical and emotional health of the mother during pregnancy has a profound effect on the health and the well being of the babies she carries. He, therefore, advises her to courageously take control of herself for the sake of her unborn children. He adds, "If you could not forget Ayodhya and Ram, why did you leave them? You are carrying the future kings of Kosal, and you have a big responsibility on your shoulders. You must rise to the challenge and raise them to be like their father." Sita promises Valmiki that she would dedicate herself to carrying and raising the future royals.

Back in Ayodhya

Ram attempts to cope with the separation from Sita. First, he gives up all royal luxuries. He asks Laxman to spread a little mat on the floor for him to sleep at night. He says, "There is a strong invisible bond between a husband and a wife. A husband should not enjoy something that he cannot share with his wife. My Atman knows what kind of life she is living. I shall follow the husband's dharma and live a similar life while carrying out all of King's duties." He also remembers the last request of Sita: "Please do not blame the people of Ayodhya and continue to love them as before. Do not show your sadness, because when a king himself exhibits sadness, the people cannot be happy. You will then be an obstacle in their pursuit of happiness, one of their God-given rights." He, however, finds it very difficult to follow his dharma and radiate a positive attitude at the same time. He becomes quiet and appears to be withdrawing within himself, attempting a reserved smile when someone comes to him. Laxman becomes increasingly worried about Ram's condition. Ram is then especially vulnerable because the three mothers had gone on an extended pilgrimage and there is no elder to counsel him in these difficult days. Laxman therefore sends a message to King Janak requesting him to come to Ayodhya and help Ram.

King Janak Visits Ram

King Janak is not surprised to hear from Laxman. Sita had earlier sent him a message informing him of her decision to leave Ayodhya for good. She had also asked him not to go to Ayodhya then. Ram would have felt guilty in facing Janak, and Sita did not want her husband to accept guilt when he was not guilty of anything. Janak had simply respected her wish and stayed away from Ayodhya until he heard from Laxman.

Janak now comes to visit Ram. He is shocked, but at the same time feels proud to see the kind of life Ram is living. He would not have expected anything less from this Vishnu-incarnate. Ram tells him that Sita is not guilty of anything and that he never had any doubt about her purity. Ram adds, " I feel responsible for all the injustices done to Sita and I will gladly accept any punishment you like to impose on me." King Janak, however, consoles him: "Oh Ram! Neither Sita nor I hold you responsible for anything. I am simply watching the cosmic game being played out here. I am very proud of my daughter. She left because she wanted you to fulfill your King's dharma and your commitment to your people. Now do not let Sita's sacrifice go to waste. Please take hold of yourself and do what is called for. Also, I am sure that Sita feels your condition via the mystical link between a husband and a wife. So if you are sad all the time, you will make it much more difficult for Sita to face life during this trying period."

Ram and Laxman then go with King Janak to Mithila City to console Sita's mother. There one of Sita's maidens talks to Ram in deep pain: "All Sita got from you is pain and suffering. She was forced into an exile of fourteen years and Ravan kidnapped her against her will. After her rescue and return, all Ayodhya had to offer her was a doubt about her purity. Our beloved Sita, the Princess of Mithila and the Queen of Ayodhya, is now alone somewhere. People of Ayodhya do not respect women and they do not protect their women. I will shout loudly and tell everyone in Mithila that no one should give their daughters in marriage to boys from Ayodhya."

It has been thousands of years since Ramayan was written. It is, however, said that to this day, girls from Mithila do not marry boys from Ayodhya.

Sita and her Twin Sons: Kush and Lav

Sita now settles down in Valmiki's ashram. She works hard like others there. She picks up firewood from the forest nearby, works in the fields, stone-grinds wheat and rice, and cooks in the kitchen. At the end of nine months she delivers

Sita brings home firewood

two sons, and Guru Valmiki names them Kush and Lav. Now Sita is even busier taking care of the twins.

The boys grow year by year, and Valmiki takes them under his wings. He teaches them archery, music, philosophy, ethics, and yoga. He teaches them to respect other people, all animals, and plants, because, "As living organisms, they also have the cosmic life energy, Pran." They are taught that the essence of one's life is to make others happy. A river satisfies the thirst of saints as well as of robbers. A tree gives shade to everyone without qualification, and a cloud drops rain on everyone's land without discrimination. At an early age they become well versed in the classical Hindu concept of monism.

When Kush and Lav become teenagers, Valmiki tells them the story of King Ram and Sita, and the boys now sing the verses of Valmiki's Ramayan — the story of Ram. Both boys are much impressed with Sita's courage. They also question how Ram could let Sita go when he believed her to be so spotless. Valmiki suggests that they ask these questions to Ram himself. They also wonder how Ram could enjoy palace life when he knows that Sita's life would be so hard. Their mother — they do not know that she is none other than Sita — assures them that Ram would not do anything like that, and that Ram is, in fact, living a frugal, meditative life in the palace. Under the expert teaching of Valmiki, the boys learn how to use various divine weapons. One day, Valmiki gives them all his mystical and spiritual powers via the classical mind-melt.

Ram Initiates the Ceremonial Horse-Ritual

It is now over ten years since Sita left Ayodhya. Laxman, Bharat, Shatrughna each have two teen-age sons. Kausalya, Sumitra, and Kaikayi spend their time with their sons and grandsons. Every time the family gathers, however, there is a dark cloud of sorrow because everyone is thinking about Sita. Nothing has ever been the same without her.

Guru Vasishta suggests that Ram undertake the famous ceremonial horse-ritual. As a part of this ritual, a decorated horse would be released to roam freely, with a huge contingent of Ram's army following behind. The horse would carry a message on his forehead: "This ceremonial horse is from King Ram of the Sun Dynasty. It must be allowed to roam freely. If anyone chooses to challenge Ram's authority and captures this horse, he must at once let it go, or must be prepared to fight with Ram's army." While the horse is roaming around, Guru Vasishta and other spiritual leaders would lead other rituals in Ayodhya.

Invitations are soon dispatched to all learned Brahmins from Kosal and all neighboring kingdoms to come to Ayodhya and participate in this enormous undertaking. People of Ayodhya are all excited that they will be a major part of these festivities. In all such religious rituals, the host has his wife on his side when he sits to worship gods. People now wonder how this horse-ritual would be possible when Ram is alone and Sita has been gone for years. The people of Ayodhya vigorously debate the possible resolution of this difficulty. Some people bring up the whole issue of Ayodhya having in the past blamed innocent Sita. They suggest that Sita be found and be restored to the throne. A few die-hard male chauvinists, however, refuse to accept that they had done any injustice to Sita. They suggest that Ram now take another wife and proceed with the ritual. Some people even go as far as saying that Ram has no option but to remarry and bring a queen to the throne. Rumors now start floating around about the impending wedding of Ram.

Ram, however, is very much pained by all the rumors. He tells Vasishta and others that he is bound by his vow not to take another wife, and that there is not going to be any second wedding for him. He plans to place a golden statue of Sita next to him during the rituals and orders one of the royal sculptors

Ram and the golden statue of Sita

to make such a statue. The sculptor makes a beautiful statue of Sita in a sitting posture. Everyone thinks for a moment that Sita is back in Ayodhya. Ram proceeds with the rituals with Sita's statue sitting next to him. The people of Ayodhya could not have expected anything less from Ram.

The ritual horse is now readied and released. A huge contingent of army headed by Shatrughna follows the horse everywhere. No one, of course, dares to pick up a fight with Ram's army. Everyone greets the horse and respectfully offers gifts to Ram. In Ayodhya, the rituals continue during the day and various gurus present religious discourses during the evening hours.

At Valmiki's Ashram

One day, Ram's ceremonial horse wanders in Valmiki's ashram, and Lav and Kush happen to see it. They wonder about the meticulously decorated horse and bring it in. Lav reads the challenge written on the gold plate on the horse's forehead, and is amused: "... if anyone catches this horse, he must at once let it go, or must be prepared to fight with Ram's army." Lav tells Kush that it is their kshatriya dharma to accept any challenge offered to them. They also notice a touch of arrogance in their King Ram issuing such a challenge. Lav decides to hold the horse. He thinks that Ram would then be forced to come and fight with them to get his horse released. It would also offer them the opportunity to ask Ram something that has been troubling them for long — why did Ram let Sita leave when he knew she was pure and faultless?

Ram's soldiers now catch up with the horse and see two young boys in typical ashram clothing holding the horse. The soldiers explain to Lav and Kush that the horse is a ceremonial horse and that they should let it go. They add that Ram's ritual could not be completed unless the horse returns to Ayodhya. Lav tells the soldiers that he is going to keep the horse, and if Ram wants to get his horse back, he must come and fight for it. The soldiers simply laugh at him. They tell him that he will have to fight with many brave warriors before Ram would enter the picture. Lav adamantly refuses to release the horse and the soldiers now have no option but to fight for the horse. They are, of course, no match for Lav, and Lav puts the whole contingent in a deep sleep with the help of a divine weapon. A messenger now goes back to the camp and tells Shatrughna what had just happened. Shatrughna cannot even comprehend that two young boys had captured the horse and had defeated the entire army contingent accompanying the horse. He now comes forward and sees Lav and Kush, the two radiant young boys. He again attempts to reason with them, and says that he really does not feel like attacking them over this matter. Lav, however, tells Shatrughna that it is a matter of principle, and, as kshatriyas, they are dharma-bound to accept Ram's challenge written on the golden plate on the horse's forehead. Lav adds that he has no desire to fight with anyone else and Shatrughna should simply go back and get Ram. Shatrughna tells him that he is equally bound by Ram's command to protect the horse, and he will not go back without the horse. There is now a short battle between the two and Lav also places Shatrughna in a state of deep sleep.

Lav and Kush Meet Ram

A messenger rushes back to Ayodhya to alert Ram about the unfolding tragedy at the ashram. One by one, Laxman, Bharat, and others come to the ashram, first plead and then argue with the boys, and eventually fight with them; Lav and Kush promptly put all of them in a state of sleep.

Ram now comes to the ashram to rescue the horse. He sees the boys and instantly feels fatherly love for them. He tells them that he really does not want to fight them. He goes through the same arguments with them but fails to convince them to release the horse. Finally, Ram pulls out an arrow, and as he is about to mount it, Guru Valmiki arrives at the scene.

He asks Ram why he was mounting his arrow against the two young boys. Ram tells him the whole story and adds that the boys are obstinately refusing to listen to reason. Guru reminds Ram that a King is supposed to protect women and children and that a king's anger is not a proper response to juvenile behavior. Valmiki also asks Lav and Kush why they are holding their King's ceremonial horse. Lav tells him that he felt compelled by his kshatriya dharma to accept the challenge given on the horse's head-plate. He also saw an opportunity to meet Ram and ask him the one question they had always wanted to ask. Ram then asks Kush what that question is. Kush says: "My respected King Ram, our Guru Valmiki is teaching us the story of your life. He always tells us that you are establishing the ultimate standard for human behavior and you are the singular embodiment of dharma. But what kind of dharma were you following when you sent innocent Sita to forest exile?"

Ram answers: "I never for a second doubted the innocence of Sita. My King's dharma however compelled me to do what I did. An ordinary man must take care of his wife, family, and friends. That is his primary dharma. When the same man becomes a king, however, he does not have that luxury. He must sacrifice his individual happiness in service of his subjects. There is then no right or wrong and no just or unjust. King's only dharma is to serve the people and abide by their wishes."

Lav and Kush then realize that it was really the people of Ayodhya and not Ram who had done great injustice to Sita, and that Ram was as much a victim as Sita was in this regard. Guru Valmiki suggests that Lav and Kush try to get justice for Sita from the people of Ayodhya. Lav and Kush apologize to Ram, and Ram says he is proud that they are the citizens of his Kosal kingdom. Lav and Kush then release the horse, withdraw their divine weapons, and wake everyone up from their deep sleep. Ram, Laxman, Bharat, and others return to Ayodhya with the horse.

Lav and Kush Know Their Identity

Sita comes to know about the confrontation between Ram, Laxman, and others and Lav and Kush. She scolds her sons and tells them that they were about to commit the greatest sin — of taking up arms against their father! Now it becomes at once clear to Lav and Kush that Ram is their father, and their mother is none other than the most respected Sita. Ram, of course, still does not know any of this.

Sita's Ultimate Test

Guru Valmiki asks Lav and Kush to go to Ayodhya and attempt to change people's minds about Sita. They go around the town and sing the story of Ram and Sita — Ramayan. Through their lyrics, they ask: "Oh people of Ayodhya! How could you have been so cruel to your queen Sita? She came as a young princess from Mithila and spent fourteen years in exile in the forest. She went through the test of fire for you. She only loved you, treated you like her children, and sacrificed her all to uphold the spotless reputation of her husband, your King Ram. How could you send her to the forest?"

As they go from one town square to the next, people of Ayodhya begin to realize the terrible injustice they had done to Sita. The public opinion begins to move in her favor. Finally, this news reaches Ram and he sends for the boys and welcomes them in his palace. Lav and Kush meet with Ram, as their father for the first time. They still do not reveal their identity to Ram.

Ram invites the boys to come and sing at the royal assembly. For several evenings, the boys sing to the assembly and present the story of Ram and Sita. They win the crowd over including the royal family. They disclose at the end that they are the twin sons of Ram and Sita, seeking justice for their mother from the people of Ayodhya. Ram asks them if they could provide some proof of their identity. Lav and Kush boldly say that they have never told a lie in their whole life and that their word should be proof enough. Moreover, they say that their Guru Valmiki would also attest that they are Ram's sons. Ram says that he has no problem accepting their word or their Guru's word. But he adds that the people of Ayodhya must ultimately accept Sita to be their queen and Lav and Kush to be their princes. Ram suggests that Sita appear in front of the royal assembly and give her word that she has been pure and faithful, and that Lav and Kush are his sons. Lav and Kush go back to Valmiki's ashram with that message.

Next day, Valmiki, Sita, and Lav and Kush appear before the royal assembly. Valmiki speaks to the assembly first, and assures them with all his spiritual force that Sita is pure and has been faithful to Ram, and that Lav and Kush are Ram's sons. Some people in Ayodhya are willing to accept Valmiki's word, but there are some holdouts that want Sita to personally give her word in this regard. Ram says that he had never had any doubt about Sita, and he does not need a test of fire or to hear from her that she is pure. As a king, however, he must keep his personal convictions to himself. Sita should, therefore, end the controversy once for all by assuring the assembly about her purity.

Sita now comes forward and speaks to the assembly: "I have been, by words, thoughts, and deeds, totally faithful to my beloved husband Ram. I have spent my every waking moment in support of my husband. I have happily suffered exiles to uphold my husband's reputation. I was kidnapped against my will and spent several months under a tree in Lanka. After the war, I went through a test of fire. In the male-dominated society, however, none of this appears to be enough. I am now tired of proving my innocence over and over again. This is an insult to womanhood, and I am sorry that a woman is not respected in the society. I am now going to end this controversy once and for all. If I am as pure as I say, I invite my mother Earth to take me home with her. Oh mother Earth, please take

Sita goes home with Mother Earth

me home where no one will ever again question me about my purity. I cannot bear this injustice to womanhood anymore. I have suffered long enough. With whatever I do, there will always be some that will not be satisfied. So mother Earth, please take me home."

As Sita speaks, the Earth splits like in a severe earthquake, and mother Earth appears there in flesh. She invites Sita to join her and Sita goes to her mother. Sita bids farewell to everyone including Ram. She requests Ram not to punish Ayodhya's people, but to continue as before to love them like a father. She tells him that her incarnation is now over, and it is time for her to go back to their heavenly abode and wait for him there. She and mother Earth quickly go down, and the spilt in the earth closes. The incarnation of Laxmi, the wife of Lord Vishnu, thus comes to an end.

Ram, Lav, Kush, and the entire assembly are shocked to see Sita disappear in the ground. Ram is very angry and asks mother Earth to return his dear Sita to him. Lord Brahma, however, appears and tells Ram that his mission as Lord Vishnu's incarnation is still not finished, and that he should let Sita return to their abode in the heavens. He assures Ram that Sita will be waiting for him in the heavens.

The story of Ram is now essentially over. Ram stays in Ayodhya as the King for many more years. When all the princes grow up, he distributes the Kosal kingdom among them, ends his incarnation, and returns to the heavens to join Sita there.

11. Mahabharat

King Bharat of Hastinapur has nine children, but selects someone outside the royal family to be the Crown Prince. Bharat's mother complains that he had essentially deceived his sons and denied them their birthright. King Bharat, however, maintains that the kingdom is not anyone's property and no king or the royal family is greater than the kingdom. The king must first be loyal to his subjects and act in their interest. He says that he does not consider any of his sons to be qualified to be the next king, and appointing an undeserving son to be the Crown Prince would have been a grave injustice to his subjects. He adds that the King's Office is a position of service to the people, and it is the ultimate responsibility of the king to make sure that each of his acts is in the interest of his subjects. With such idealism and a concept of public service, is it any wonder that this epic is called the Great Epic of the Bharat Dynasty — Mahabharat, and that the Nation of India came to be known as the land of Bharat?

The idealism of Bharat, however, slowly erodes by the time Shantanu becomes the King of Hastinapur. When he asks river goddess Ganga to marry him, she says that she would agree only on one condition — he should not question any of her actions and that she would simply walk away if he so does. Shantanu agrees and marries her. In spite of Ganga's constant reminders, he totally ignores his kingly duties and spends all his time with her. When their first son is born, Ganga takes him to the river and drowns him there. Shantanu, bound by his promise, keeps quiet. One by one, Ganga similarly drowns six more sons and Shantanu keeps quiet. Unable to find a way out of this, he consults the royal priest. The priest says that if a king cannot even protect his sons, how can he protect his subjects or save the country? He admonishes Shantanu for giving such an open-ended promise to Ganga. Clearly, one must think very hard before throwing a stone, shooting an arrow, pulling the trigger of a gun, or pushing a rock off a hilltop. Once you do any of these things, you then have no control over the stone, the bullet, or the arrow, although you are fully responsible for both intended as well as unintended consequences. Similarly, King Shantanu must now pay the price of his promise foolishly given to Ganga. On the birth of their eighth son, he could not keep silent anymore and objects when Ganga prepares to drown the newborn. She then walks away with her son as promised and Shantanu is now alone. Ganga raises her son, Bhishma, and trains him in various disciplines such as art, history, philosophy, and warfare. When Bhishma is about sixteen years old, Ganga returns him to his father. Bhishma tells his father different things he had learned from his teachers. He says that knowledge, only when accompanied by humility, makes a person learned. Bhishma also describes the utmost significance Hindu Thought attaches to one's parents. He says that a family priest is ten times more important than one's teacher, the father is hundred times more important than the family priest, and ultimately, one's mother is thousand times more important than one's father. King Shantanu is very impressed by what he hears from Bhishma. Bhishma is always respectful towards his father and is willing to sacrifice anything to make him happy. In course of time, Shantanu proudly presents Bhishma as the Crown Prince and the future King of Hastinapur. The King's court and the people of Hastinapur are very pleased with the announcement.

Several years later, while on one of his hunting trips,

Shantanu meets Satyavati, the daughter of a boat owner. She operates a small ferry across a river. Shantanu instantly falls in love with her and extends his stay in the forest to be with her. He approaches Satyavati's father and asks his permission to marry her. The father wants Shantanu to promise him that Satyavati's son, and not Crown Prince Bhishma, would inherit the kingdom. Shantanu tells Satyavati's father that he could not possibly do that because it would be a grave injustice to Bhishma. Shantanu, however, cannot bear to be away from Satyavati, and is depressed and silent all the time. He keeps to himself and continues to stay in the forest camp, completely ignoring his royal duties. Back in the palace, Bhishma wonders why his father is not returning from the hunt and goes there himself to investigate. He soon finds out about Satyavati, although he still does not know about her father's demand and Shantanu's response to it.

Bhishma believes that both as the Crown Prince and as a son, he has a duty to the Hastinapur nation and to his father respectively to take care of any problem facing Shantanu. He goes to Satyavati and comes to know about the demand of her father that separates his father from his love. Then and there, he renounces his claim to the throne. Also, since he cannot promise anything on behalf of his yet unborn sons, he vows not to marry so that there would be no claim to the throne in the future. Satyavati's father is now satisfied, and Bhishma brings Satyavati to his father. Shantanu does not like what Bhishma had done without consulting him. He argues that a Crown Prince is to be chosen by qualifications and not by birth. Consequently, a great injustice has now been done to Hastinapur by promising *a priori* that Satyavati's yet unborn son will become the Crown Prince and the future King of Hastinapur. Satyavati also realizes the great injustice done to Bhishma and feels very guilty. Shantanu, on the other hand, blames himself for putting Hastinapur's future in danger for his personal happiness. He is, however, very proud of Bhishma for his willingness to sacrifice everything in service to Hastinapur. As a reward, he gives Bhishma a boon that Bhishma can live as

Bhishma vows to be celibate

long as he wishes and can himself choose the moment of his death. Bhishma also swears loyalty to future kings of Hastinapur and thereby assures his father about the safety of the kingdom.

Bhishma thus makes three promises to his parents: he renounces his claim to the kingdom, he takes a vow of celibacy, and he swears his loyalty to all future kings of Hastinapur. These actions of Bhishma are at the center of all Mahabharat. Over the next several generations, the Bharat dynasty and the City of Hastinapur go through a series of calamitous events that lead to a bloody civil war. At every step of the way, Bhishma's promises come in the way of common sense solutions to the problems at hand. Clearly, one must think hard before making such open ended commitments. Such commitments can have unacceptable unintended consequences, and lead to situations where *the remedy is worse than the disease.*

Shantanu and Satyavati have two sons. Shantanu continues to feel guilty and soon dies in grief. His son becomes the King and marries two sisters, Ambika and Ambalika. Before he could have any children, however, he becomes seriously ill and dies. The throne is now empty and there is no heir to be declared the Crown Prince.

Satyavati now approaches Vyas, her ascetic son she had received in the past via mystical powers of a priest. She asks Vyas to similarly use his mystical powers and give Amba and Ambalika sons. She also tells her two daughters-in-law that they must now finish the duty to the country that their husband could not do. Vyas wonders if the two queens would be bold enough to receive his mystical powers, but agrees to follow his mother's orders anyway.

Ambika is afraid of Vyas's ascetic look and his mystical powers, and closes her eyes during the mystical ritual. So Vyas tells his mother that Ambika will give birth to a blind son. Ambalika is also equally scared, and trembles and becomes pale during the ritual. So Vyas tells her that her son will not be healthy. Satyavati is terribly disappointed and asks Vyas for one more chance. Both queens refuse to go to Vyas and send in one of their maids instead. She is not afraid and successfully goes through the ritual. Vyas assures Satyavati that the third son will be great and will serve the nation admirably. In due course, the three sons are born —Dhrutarashtra, the eldest one, is blind; Pandu, the second son, is unhealthy; and Vidur, the healthy son of the maid.

All the three sons attend royal school and come home after graduation. The tradition demanded that the eldest son, Dhrutarashtra, be installed on the throne. Vidur, however, suggests that a blind king could not possibly be able to perform his royal duties and it would be a great injustice to Hastinapur to install blind Dhrutarashtra as its King. The stage is now being slowly set for the main story of Mahabharat to unfold. Dhrutarashtra, the elder brother is denied kingdom that traditionally belonged to him, and his unhealthy younger brother, Pandu, is installed as the King.

At the request of his mother, Bhishma goes to the King of Gandhar and proposes that Princess Gandhari marry Dhrutarashtra. Gandhari's brother, Shakuni, is furious that his sister was invited to marry blind Dhrutarashtra and not his brother King Pandu. He recommends that his father should unceremoniously reject this offer and send Bhishma back to Hastinapur. Gandhari, however, tells her father and her brother that it is not for them, but for her, to either accept or reject the proposal. She declares that she wants very much to marry Dhrutarashtra and she vows blindness by putting a tape around her eyes then and there. She says that if her husband cannot *see,* she does not want to *see* either. When Gandhari comes to Hastinapur however, even Dhrutarashtra says that he had hoped to see the world through the eyes of his wife, and now even that would not be possible. He tells Gandhari that he keeps wondering why he is blind and why, as the elder brother, he is not the king. He says that even if he cannot be the king, he hopes that some day his son would become the king. If Pandu gets a son first, however, the kingdom would go out of his reach forever.

Soon thereafter, Pandu marries Princess Kunti, and what Dhrutarashtra fears now becomes a distinct possibility. Kunti, however, has been keeping an incredible secret of her short young life. A high priest satisfied by her sense of service and hospitality during one his visits with her father had given her a *mantra*. By chanting that mantra, she would be able to summon at any time any god of her choice, who would then give her a gift. As a young girl, she always wondered if such a thing was at all possible. Once while offering her daily prayers to the Sun god, she tries out the power of that mantra by summoning the Sun god himself. The Sun god immediately appears before her and says that he must give her something before returning. Using his mystical powers, he gives her a son, Karna, born with an impenetrable body armor. With a newborn in her arms, Kunti trembles with fear, and quickly realizes the enormity of the situation. As a young princess, how would she convince the world that she is still a virgin and that the son was given to her by the Sun god using his mystical powers? How could she now face the society? In fear, she wraps the infant in a blanket, puts him in a box, and sends the box floating down the river behind her palace. She asks for forgiveness from her son as she bids him a tearful goodbye. She must now live with this painful decision for the rest of her life.

This story clearly reflects the views of the society of those days regarding births out of wedlock. Premarital sex was totally unacceptable, and whether we like it or not, Kunti's choices were very limited. This clearly shows that biology has placed an undue burden on women, and the society has continued to hold women alone responsible for out-of-wedlock births. Furthermore, social scientists have only recently begun to ask questions as to why a child born outside the bounds of marriage should bear the stigma of illegality.

Kunti abandons Karna at birth

While on a campaign to expand the borders of Hastinapur, King Pandu takes on a second wife, Madri, and Kunti openly welcomes her as a younger sister. After the long campaign, Pandu decides to take a well-deserved vacation. He temporarily designates Dhrutarashtra as the King, and heads with Kunti and Madri towards a mountain retreat in a forest.

With the crown on his head, old feelings keep coming back to Dhrutarashtra, and he says that the crown belonged to him to begin with. Shakuni, Gandhari's brother, who hates Bhishma for proposing blind Dhrutarashtra to Gandhari, is in Hastinapur, and seeks every opportunity to pour oil on the fire. He keeps inciting Dhrutarashtra and tells him that he will never forgive Vidur for suggesting in the past that Hastinapur did not deserve a blind king and that the crown should be given to Pandu. Gandhari, the voice of sanity, however, keeps reminding her husband that the crown really belonged to his brother Pandu and he should not get used to wearing it. She suggests that, after a reasonable time period, Dhrutarashtra should on his own send messengers to the mountain camp, invite Pandu back to the city from vacation, and hand over the crown to him.

As Pandu, Kunti, and Madri, are enjoying their free time, something terribly goes wrong. While running after a tiger during a hunt, Pandu shoots an arrow *at a sound,* and hits a mystic. Pandu feels very guilty for causing such an accident. For crossing the line of responsible behavior, the mystic puts a curse on Pandu that Pandu would die if he ever embraced his wife with passion.

Pandu tells both of his wives all that had happened, and they all return to Hastinapur crestfallen. Pandu meets with Dhrutarashtra, Vidur, Bhishma and other elders, and all state ministers in the royal chambers. He reports to them on what had happened in the forest and seeks their advice. Vidur, the respected voice of reason, tells Pandu that no one, even the King, is above the law, and that there should be some punishment because an innocent person had been killed. He says that if it were a premeditated murder, he would have no hesitation in recommending the death penalty. However, since it was an accidental homicide, Vidur recommends that Pandu do some penance in the forest. Everyone in the chamber agrees with Vidur, and Pandu prepares to go back to the forest, this time for penance. Kunti and Madri insist on going with him, and the three soon head back to the forest. Dhrutarashtra continues to carry the crown on his head.

Pandu remembers the curse very well and keeps away from his wives. Kunti, however, now tells him about her boon and suggests that she use her mantra to invoke gods and ask them to give her some children. Pandu and Madri agree to this. Using her mantra Kunti invokes three gods who then use their mystical powers and give Kunti three sons: Dharmaraj, Bheem, and Arjun. She also invokes two more gods, and asks them to give Madri two sons. So gods give Madri two sons: Nakul and Sahadev. These five sons are collectively called the Pandav — meaning Pandu's children. Pandu and his two wives now begin the difficult task of raising their five sons in the frugal forest environment. As the sons are growing into young boys, however, one day Pandu sees a bathing half-clad Madri and is irresistibly attracted to her beauty. In spite of her protestations, he passionately embraces her, and instantly dies as cursed. Madri holds herself responsible for this mishap and jumps into Pandu's funeral pyre. Kunti is now alone with five young sons and heads back to Hastinapur.

In the meantime, back in Hastinapur, Dhrutarashtra and Gandhari have one hundred sons (Duryodhan, Duhshasan, and others) and one daughter named Duhshala. Dhrutarashtra's sons are known as Kaurav (of Kuru dynasty) princes. Dharmaraj is the oldest among all the sons of Pandu and Dhrutarashtra. Whatever Dhrutarashtra had feared had happened after all! It is, of course, important to note at this time that Kunti's first son Karna is really the oldest, although no one except Kunti knows this fact.

Almost all the elements now seem to be falling into place for the story of Mahabharat to unfold. Dhrutarashtra was born blind, was denied the kingdom, and his younger brother Pandu was coronated the King. Pandu is dead and Dhrutarashtra now carries the crown. Pandu's son Dharmaraj is the oldest of the royal princes. Dhrutarashtra, however, is convinced that the crown belonged to him in the first place and that it should be passed on to his first son Duryodhan. Revengeful Shakuni is ever present to add fuel to the fire. Bhishma, the great grand father of Dharmaraj, Duryodhan, and other siblings, is oath-bound to serve the King, no matter what. There are only two voices of common sense and reason — Gandhari and Vidur. Gandhari, the Queen, is blind by choice and consequently quite helpless; and Vidur, the son of a royal maid, is only the Chief Minister, and must obey the throne.

Bhishma enrolls the five Pandav and one hundred Kaurav princes in the royal school run by Guru Drona. Drona begins to teach them different disciplines such as warfare, politics, religion, and ethics. He stresses that as potential kings, they should understand that a king must always put the interests of his subjects ahead of everything else including his own self-interest. A king should never think in terms of *my friend, my child,* etc.

Birth and Childhood of Lord Krishna

Kunti's brother Vasudev is married to Devaki, the princess of Mathura. Devaki's brother, Kansa, is an arrogant bully who deposes and throws in jail his own father, and declares himself to be the King of Mathura. Once Kansa hears a voice from the sky prophecy that he will be killed by the eighth son of his sister Devaki. Kansa, in response, decides to kill both his sister and her husband, but Vasudev tells him that his problem is really with the yet unborn eighth son. Therefore Kansa should simply put Devaki and Vasudev in jail and kill the eighth son when he is born. Kansa also thinks that he would become

immortal if he could kill his potential killer. In a way, his arrogance forces him to attempt to defeat the prophecy.
Consequently, he throws Vasudev and Devaki in jail, and to be
absolutely sure, decides to kill all Devaki's children as they are
born. Devaki has six sons in a row, and Kansa kills all of them
right after their birth. When Devaki becomes pregnant again,
she gives her seventh pregnancy to Vasudev's second wife,
Rohini. Both Kansa and the royal doctor are puzzled and do
not understand what happened to the fetus that seemed to
have simply vanished. Rohini carries the pregnancy to term
and delivers a baby boy named Balram.

When Devaki delivers her eighth son, Krishna, a voice from
the sky tells Vasudev and Devaki that the child will be the
future of the mankind, and that Vasudev should take the child
to his friend Nanda of Gokul, a village across the river Jamuna.
Miraculously the jailers fall asleep and the heavy doors of the
jail fling open allowing Vasudev to do just that. Nanda takes
Vasudev's son in his care. Nanda's wife, Yashoda, had also deliv-
ered a daughter during the same night and was lying unconscious in her bed before she knew if it was a boy or a girl.
Nanda gives his newborn daughter to Vasudev and asks him to
take her back to jail. Vasudev, of course, does not want to take
the girl to a certain death. Nanda, however, tells Vasudev that
Kansa will not kill a girl because he is afraid of only the eighth
son. Vasudev then returns to jail with the baby girl. The jailers
wake up to the cries of the baby and inform Kansa of the birth
of a child in the jail. Kansa rushes to the jail and is surprised to
find a girl instead of a boy. He decides to kill her anyway, just
in case! As he swings the child, the girl slips out of his hands
and ascends to the heavens in front of everyone. A voice from
the sky then declares that the *Lord of the Universe* has taken
birth as the eighth son of Devaki and is quite safe outside the
prison. The voice also assures Kansa that this son would surely
kill him when the time is right.

In Gokul, Nanda and Yashoda, his second parents raise
Krishna, the son of Vasudev and Devaki. The story of Krishna's

childhood is a combination of his joining his friends in eating butter from homes in the neighborhood, a number of miracles, flute playing by Krishna, and the legendary devotion to him by a young girl named Radha. Dairy farmers essentially inhabit Gokul, and cows, milk, and butter are central to the life and the economy of the area. As a child, therefore, Krishna would tend to cows and play with young cowherds. Krishna and his young friends would sneak into neighborhood homes and eat home-made butter. This is, in fact, an open secret in Gokul, but the women loved Krishna so much that they would get offended if Krishna did not come and steal butter from their homes. The women also play games with him by hiding the butter in a pot and hanging it high from the ceiling. The boys then would make a human pyramid so Krishna could reach high up and bring the pot of butter down. This concept of God playing pranks as a child has been so popular over these years that this scene is enacted throughout India on Krishna's birthday every year. As a part of the birthday celebrations, people hang a pot of butter high up at street corners, and teams of young boys go from place to place, make human pyramids, and attempt to bring the pot down. Other people hose the boys down with water, throw slippery butter on the ground, and generally try to prevent the boys from reaching the pot.

Radha, a young girl from Gokul, is also a unique character in the early life of Krishna. Her love for Krishna is both mystical and legendary. She loses herself when Krishna plays melodious tunes on his flute. With the unparalleled devotion to Krishna, her position is so unique among his devotees that Hindu temples usually carry idols of Radha and Krishna together, and Krishna is lovingly known as Radhakrishna. Radha signifies pure and unconditional love that demands absolutely nothing in return. Radha and her love for Krishna are the subjects of lyrical poetry of many Indian languages. It is quite unfortunate, however, that the Western society identifies love only at the physical level, and in an exhibition of corruption and bank-ruptcy of mind, recognizes Radha as the *mistress* of god Krishna.

Krishna plays flute for Radha

Krishna now decides to go to Mathura, kill uncle Kansa, and release from Kansa's prison his parents, Vasudev and Devaki, and his grandfather. Mother Yashoda and people of Gokul are, however, not yet ready to face separation from Krishna. They still want him to be a child and to steal their butter forever. They all ask Radha to beg him to stay. Radha, however, says that she is only his worshipping devotee and that, as the Lord of the Universe, he really belongs to the whole world. She asks the townsfolk to learn to share Krishna with the world. She herself bids him a tearful farewell. She tells Krishna, "You know everything I know, and we both know that. What is then left to say? Just go and do what you think is the best for the world." Krishna tells her about his love for her and tells her that he would now give up playing flute because he cannot imagine playing flute for anyone but his Radha. With such a powerful story of devotion, it is no wonder that Radha is the yardstick by which Hindus measure their love of God and their spiritual progress towards liberation. Krishna now goes to Mathura, kills his uncle Kansa, and restores his grandfather to the throne.

Karna, the Son of a Charioteer

The royal charioteer had found Karna when Kunti had abandoned him at birth. The charioteer and his wife had decided to keep the child and are now raising him as their own son. Karna, really a son of a princess and the Sun god, is thus raised in a lower caste. His father wants to enroll him in Drona's school where Pandav and Kaurav are studying. Drona refuses to accept him as a student because he was neither a prince nor did he belong to the martial caste of Kshatriya. Karna, however, sees that Drona, a Brahmin by caste, has enrolled in the school his own son who is *neither a prince nor a Kshatriya.* This form of blatant elitism and nepotism does not escape Karna's attention, and he has to constantly fight against this denial of opportunity based on his background. He vows to himself that he will spare no effort to become the best archer of the world, surpassing any student Drona may have to offer.

All the upcoming main characters of Mahabharat — five Pandav brothers, one hundred Kaurav brothers, Krishna and Balram, and Karna are now in school. Dhrutarashtra is still blaming his stars and dreaming of his son Duryodhan as the next King of Hastinapur. Evil Shakuni is scheming his best to take the ultimate revenge on the royal family for the injustice he thinks was done to his sister Gandhari. Bhishma, Vidur, Kunti, and Gandhari are all wondering what the future holds for Hastinapur. They know that unless this family feud is settled fairly and amicably, the innocent people of Hastinapur will have to pay a terrible price. They also find themselves helpless and see no option but to wait patiently and accept the course of history, whatever it may be.

As the princes come close to finishing school, Vidur arranges for a special arena for holding the convocation ceremony. He invites the local population to see for themselves how their princes have been educated. He is sure that Pandav brothers will win the hearts of the people, and wants Bhishma to take this opportunity to declare Dharmaraj to be the Crown Prince. The exhibition games and the demonstration of weapons skills are planned at the gathering.

Every prince comes to the front, introduces himself to the crowd, and shows his skill with various weapons. Most of the princes introduce themselves as the *son of so-and-so* and the *student of so-and-so,* etc. Arjun, however, introduces himself only as Drona's student. Dhrutarashtra is quite puzzled and asks him if that was all. Arjun says that one should have only one identity so that there is never a conflict of interest between different identities. What a profound statement coming out of a young adult! In addition to marksmanship, Arjun demonstrates his skill in archery by shooting arrows to invoke rain, lightning, and storms. Drona, very pleased with Arjun's performance, proudly tells the assembly that Arjun is by far the best archer in the world. Young Karna now comes forward and says that Drona should not say Arjun is the best without any test, and openly invites Arjun for a competition. Drona then asks Karna to introduce himself, reminding him that only a prince could challenge another prince. Karna cannot introduce himself because he does not even know who his real parents are. He stands there in front of the entire assembly quite embarrassed. Duryodhan, however, comes forward, gives Karna the Ang territory, and declares Karna to be the King of Ang. Duryodhan, consumed with jealousy and hatred of Pandav brothers, wants Karna, now that he is a king, to fight Arjun. Arjun, however, says that Karna cannot become Kshatriya by caste by accepting a gift of kingdom and that Karna will continue to be the son of a mere charioteer. Karna feels insulted, but before he could say anything, the Sun sets and the sports event comes to an end. Unaware of Duryodhan's motives, however, Karna is quite moved by Duryodhan's generosity. He tells Duryodhan that he will be eternally indebted to Duryodhan and that he will live for and die for Duryodhan. This loyalty of Karna towards Duryodhan and his anger towards Arjun are two important elements of Mahabharat and play a vital role in the events of this great epic.

Krishna Moves from Mathura to Dwarka

King Jarasandh, the father-in-law of Kansa, holds Krishna responsible for Kansa's death and repeatedly attacks Mathura. Krishna suggests that wicked Jarasandh will keep on attacking Mathura and that it may be better to relocate the capital city elsewhere. Mathura cabinet ministers do not like this idea because they think they will be called cowards. Krishna, however, says that during a war between kings, it is always the innocent soldiers on both sides who lose their lives. Consequently, it is better to walk away from a fight, and a war should be considered to be the absolutely last resort in settling disputes. The leaders of a nation have a tremendous responsibility on their shoulders. Millions of innocent lives, both military and civilian, are lost in a war, and too often, political leaders start wars for political reasons and for supporting their personal agendas. Krishna, however, suggests that leaders, even at the risk of being called cowards, should, if at all possible, walk away from a fight in order to save innocent lives. Clearly, if one party is intent on fighting, walking away may not be enough, and there may come a time when one must stand up and fight. Krishna eventually convinces the people of Mathura, and the entire capital city moves to a newly constructed city of Dwarka.

Back in Hastinapur

Pressure is building on Dhrutarashtra to declare a Crown Prince. The people of Hastinapur and elders such as Bhishma, Drona, and Vidur want Dharmaraj. Shakuni wants Duryodhan to be the Crown Prince. Vidur firmly tells Dhrutarashtra, "A son has rights only over his father's wealth. A kingdom is not King's personal wealth. If Dharmaraj is also not qualified, he cannot claim it simply because he is Pandu's first son." People also threaten revolt if Dharmaraj is not declared to be the Crown Prince. Dhrutarashtra finally presents Dharmaraj as the Crown Prince and the next King of Hastinapur.

Shakuni continues to incite Duryodhan. He however warns him to keep his grief and thoughts to himself and think how he could destroy Pandav brothers one by one. Together, they concoct a scheme to kill Dharmaraj. A state fair is coming up in the town of Varnavrat, and they ask Dhrutarashtra to send Dharmaraj to the fair as the royal representative. They also hire a builder to construct a special house for Dharmaraj — a house built entirely of highly flammable material, and plan to set it on fire with Crown Prince Dharmaraj in it. As always, Karna, the brave warrior, does not support this idea at all. He tells Duryodhan that he cannot run away from his conscience. Karna says that he could not be a coward, and would rather fight Pandav brothers face to face. Duryodhan tells Karna that he really could not care less for the kingdom, and that he would not mind making Karna the King of Hastinapur. He cannot see that crown on any son of Pandu, however, because Pandu had unfairly taken the crown away from his father Dhrutarashtra. Karna assures Duryodhan that he is eternally indebted to Duryodhan and would follow him anywhere. Shakuni and Duryodhan are pleasantly surprised to learn that all five Pandav brothers and their mother Kunti had decided to attend the Varnavrat fair; now they can solve that problem once and for all.

Vidur suspects something is going on because Shakuni and Duryodhan are outwardly so happy to see Pandav brothers planning to go to the fair. Consequently, he sends a spy to Varnavrat, and comes to know that the builder for the new house for Dharmaraj had bought enormous amounts of highly flammable building materials. Vidur immediately sends an expert tunnel digger to Varnavrat, instructing him to dig a tunnel under the house for Kunti and her sons to escape. With the escape tunnel in place, the Pandav brothers burn the Varnavrat house ahead of Shakuni's schedule, and they all escape to safety through the tunnel. Unknown to them, however, five traveling drunkards and their mother had taken shelter that night in that house, and the entire family dies in that fire. Duryodhan and Shakuni think their plan had succeeded and they both are elated that Kunti and Pandav brothers are all dead.

Everyone in Hastinapur is shocked to hear the news of the fire and of the death of beloved Kunti and her sons. Dhrutarashtra suspects a murder plot behind these deaths. He tells Gandhari that Shakuni is capable of anything. Bhishma, Drona, and others also suspect that Shakuni and Duryodhan were somehow involved in this mishap. Only Vidur knows the truth. He keeps it to himself, however, because he wants to know the scope of Shakuni's conspiracy. Conspiracies have always played a major role in politics. This episode of the house of flammable materials showed thousands of years ago that when politics ignores the common good and concerns itself with personal profit, it leads to disastrous consequences.

Draupadi Weds Five Pandav Brothers

After escaping the fire, Pandav brothers decide to spend some time incognito so that they can find out the depth of Shakuni's conspiracy; they move from village to village. King Drupad had a long-standing feud with Drona. He performs a special religious ceremony so that he could get a heavenly son who can then kill Drona. He gets one son and one daughter from heavenly gods; both appear before King Drupad as grown up children. This daughter is Princess Draupadi. When she becomes of marriageable age, Drupad arranges a wedding invitational for her. The candidate husbands, however, must first qualify by exhibiting their archery skills in a specific test. He places a rotating toy fish at the ceiling of the assembly hall. Right under it, there is a small pot of water. Next to the pot, there is a table with a large bow and arrow on it. Anyone seeking marriage to Draupadi must pick up the bow, string it, mount an arrow, look into the water in the pot, and shoot the arrow through an eye of the rotating toy fish. Many kings and princes including Duryodhan and Karna come to this event. Pandav brothers are also there in disguise. Lord Krishna, who always considered Draupadi as his sister, is also present there, and he is the only one who knows the identity of the Pandav brothers.

An arrogant Duryodhan comes forward but is utterly humiliated in front of the whole gathering when he could not even budge the bow in an effort to pick it up. A proud and confident Karna now comes forward to demonstrate his skill. Draupadi, however, tells him that she was not about to marry a son of a charioteer and forbids him from participating in the proceedings. Duryodhan protests that this should have been made clear to the assembly at the beginning so that Karna's humiliation could have been avoided. A woman's right to choose her mate was supreme, however, and Karna backs off. He never for-gives Draupadi for this insult, and this episode will come back to haunt Draupadi in the future. Arjun, disguised as a brahmin, now comes forward to try his skill. He easily picks up the bow, mounts an arrow, looks into the water in the pot on the floor, and shoots the arrow right through the eye of the fish at the ceiling.

Arjun takes Draupadi back where Kunti and his brothers are staying incognito in the forest. He just calls out for Kunti from outside and asks her to look at what he had brought home. Kunti thinks that he is talking about the daily alms he and his brothers bring home everyday. Without even looking at what he had brought, she tells Arjun, as she had told them everyday, to share it with his brothers. Everyone now quickly recognizes the gravity of the situation. Mother's word must prevail, and the Pandav brothers must now take Draupadi as their common wife. But does not Draupadi have any rights? She had accepted Arjun as her partner at the wedding invitational and no one had told her then that it was going to be a package deal! Everyone now wonders why fate had dealt this card to them and how anyone could make any sense out of all this. Krishna, who happens to be there, questions Arjun and Kunti why they both were so casual about potentially serious matters. Arjun should not have insulted Draupadi by equating her with alms, and Kunti should not have asked him to share something with his brothers without even looking at what he was referring to. Krishna, however, also offers an explanation for what had just happened. In her earlier life, as a part of a boon, Draupadi had asked God Shiva to give her a husband who was an embodi-ment of truth, super strong, a master of archery, the most hand-some, and the ultimate in tolerance. Shiva had then told her that all these five qualities were not possible in one person. According to Krishna, Arjun and Kunti were simply unknowing participants in a cosmic scheme to make good on Shiva's boon to Draupadi, and that Draupadi had taken a chance in asking seemingly an impossible boon from God Shiva.

Arjun brings Draupadi to Kunti

King Dhrutarashtra Splits the Kingdom

Vidur, who knew all along the whereabouts and the activities of Pandav brothers, now tells Dhrutarashtra that Pandav brothers are alive and well, and that Arjun had in fact won Draupadi's wedding invitational. He also suggests that Dhrutarashtra send for Kunti and her sons and welcome his daughter-in-law to Hastinapur. He tells Dhrutarashtra that he knew that Dhrutarashtra did not have any hand in the attempt on Dharmaraj's life, and that it was all Shakuni's plot.

Now Hastinapur is put in an untenable situation. It has two Crown Princes — the original one Dharmaraj, and Duryodhan, who was appointed when everyone thought Dharmaraj had died in a fire at Varnavrat. Except for a handful including Shakuni, almost everyone including Queen Gandhari now expects King Dhrutarashtra to ask Duryodhan to vacate the position of Crown Prince for Dharmaraj. Duryodhan, however, tells his father that he would commit suicide if he were asked to vacate his position as the Crown Prince.

Hastinapur elders such as Bhishma and the Royal Priest Kripa think that it would be an injustice to ask anyone to give up the position of the Crown Prince. Duryodhan, they say, was installed as the Crown Prince quite legitimately, and Dharmaraj was the Crown Prince to begin with. They suggest that Hastinapur be divided into two parts, and the two sitting Crown Princes be each given half the Kingdom. Dharmaraj tells Dhrutarashtra not to divide the Kingdom and rather to give the whole Kingdom to Duryodhan. The King, however, knows very well that such a step would not be acceptable to his subjects and that they all would rebel against such a move. He, therefore, divides the Kingdom and gives the region of Khandav forest, the area west of the River Jamuna, to the Pandav brothers. This piece of land is essentially worthless, but Pandav brothers accept it simply to avoid a conflict within the family.

Dharmaraj is now coronated the King of Indraprastha, the kingdom built by Pandav brothers out of the Khandav forest. The elders give him precious advice on governing — a Kshatriya King must protect civil rights and human values within his kingdom, and he should fight a war only as the last resort. These two themes have been stressed throughout Mahabharat over and over again at every opportunity.

Arjun Weds Subhadra

Krishna knows that his sister Subhadra wants to marry Arjun. So he arranges for this wedding and personally works hard to take care of the guests at the wedding. The Lord of the Universe doing physical labor at a wedding is a clear signal in Mahabharat to establish the dignity of labor. Draupadi welcomes Subhadra with open arms. Pandav brothers now get busy consolidating their Indraprastha kingdom and extending its borders. They build a beautiful palace that includes a spectacular hall of magic and illusions. All visitors to this palace are simply awestruck both by the general opulence and especially by the illusions. One would run into walls of mirrors, step into small ponds of water thinking it to be a regular floor, be afraid to step onto a floor thinking it to be a pond of water, and so on.

The Pandav brothers are happy that their Indraprastha kingdom is finally established with extended borders and that the people are quite prosperous and happy. They arrange for a huge celebration and invite various kings and princes to Indraprastha. They declare Lord Krishna to be the Chief Guest at the event. During this celebration, Krishna cuts one of his fingers and bleeds a little. Draupadi quickly tears a little piece from her very expensive sari and wraps it around Krishna's finger. Krishna says that he is indebted to Draupadi and would someday repay her thousand folds.

During these celebrations Duryodhan happens to enter the hall of illusions. He sees a door, but in an attempt to go through it, he runs into the wall. In another room, he sees water and is

Son of a blind is also blind

afraid to step in it, but then sees a servant walk across a normal floor. The door and the water are pure illusions. Next time when he sees water, he is sure it is a regular floor. He steps on it with confidence, but falls into a pool of water. He is quite embarrassed and looks around to see if anyone had seen him fall in the water. He sees Draupadi laugh at him and say that apparently the *son of a blind is also blind.* Duryodhan feels insulted and disgraced, and vows to someday avenge this insult by Draupadi.

Duryodhan always feels that the destiny has dealt him a bad card. His father is blind and was denied the throne because of that disability. His mother is also blind, albeit by her choice. He is the first son of Dhrutarashtra, but then Pandu's first son Dharmaraj is older than he is. He believes that the throne was taken away from him twice. He had received very little parenting, if any, from his blind parents. On the contrary, he had his uncle Shakuni constantly fanning his fires of jealousy. He had seen Draupadi insult his friend Karna. He was embarrassed at Draupadi's wedding invitational when he could not even lift the bow, let alone shoot an arrow at the rotating mechanical fish. And now this insult — the son of a blind is also blind.

Duryodhan's anger now knows no bounds and Shakuni takes this opportunity to play his trump card. He asks Duryodhan to invite Pandav brothers to Hastinapur for a game of dice. As usual, Karna does not like this conspiracy and tells Duryodhan so. He says that he would rather fight Pandav brothers and punish them for their misdeeds towards Duryodhan. Duryodhan doubts if Pandav brothers would accept such an invitation to a game of dice. He is also not sure if his father, King Dhrutarashtra, would agree to such a game anyway.

Shakuni is confident that Dharmaraj, a Kshatriya, will never decline such an invitation. When challenged in war or in a game of dice, a Kshatriya is duty-bound to accept such a challenge. He is also sure that King Dhrutarashtra will never say no to his beloved son Duryodhan. Shakuni, therefore, sends

Duryodhan to seek his father's concurrence and permission for such a game.

Vidur advises King Dhrutarashtra not to extend such an invitation to Pandu's son. He says that brothers should not play such a game because it can destroy the family. Furthermore, once started, it is difficult to end a game of dice. It is probably the only game where both the winner and the loser do not want to stop. A winner thinks he can win more, and the loser hopes to recover his losses.

The Game of Dice

All are now assembled in the game hall in Dhrutarashtra's palace in Hastinapur. King Dhrutarashtra is in his royal seat. Bhishma, the most senior of the Bharat clan and King's grandfather, the family priest Kripa and Guru Drona are all in their usual seats. The Chief Minister Vidur is there too. On a raised platform in the center of the hall, the Pandav brothers — King of Indraprastha Dharmaraj and his four brave brothers — are seated on one side. Prince of Hastinapur, Duryodhan, his brother Duhshasan, his friend Karna, and his evil uncle Shakuni are seated on the other side. The entire scene is quite somber. Except for Dhrutarashtra, Duryodhan, Duhshasan, and Shakuni, no one wants this game to proceed and no one believes that any good could come out of this game.

The board is spread out and there is a little box holding the dice to be used. The King directs the game to begin and the rules are set. Dharmaraj suggests that his younger brother Duryodhan go first, and Duryodhan declares that Shakuni will play on his behalf. Shakuni is known to be an expert at the game and is also quite capable of playing a dishonest game. Even then Dharmaraj agrees to let Shakuni play for Duryodhan. Shakuni's evil plan is succeeding beyond his wildest dreams and he is finally getting his revenge against the Bharat clan for inviting his sister Gandhari to wed blind Dhrutarashtra.

Shakuni throws the dice and the game begins. Dharmaraj bets and loses first few throws. Bhishma then suggests that the game be ended there. He says now that Dharmaraj has respected the invitation of his uncle, King Dhrutarashtra, and that Duryodhan has won at least a symbolic victory, there is no need to continue. Duryodhan, of course, wants to continue the game and says that he wants to give Dharmaraj a chance to regain his losses and asks his father not to listen to Bhishma. The game continues and, step by step, Dharmaraj loses all his wealth and his kingdom. Bhishma and Vidur plead with Dhrutarashtra to end the game then. Duryodhan, however, protests that Bhishma and Vidur would not have asked to stop the game if he was the one who was losing.

The game now turns more vicious. Shakuni, Karna, Duryodhan, and Duhshasan are ecstatic that the Pandav brothers are now penniless. They want to continue and Dharmaraj wants to continue as well; he wants to regain his losses. Dharmaraj now bets the freedom of his brothers, and one by one, all his four brothers become personal slaves of Duryodhan. Dharmaraj now bets his own freedom and loses. He then tells that the game cannot continue because he now has nothing to bet. Karna reminds him that Dharmaraj still has his *arrogant Draupadi,* and Duryodhan says that he should bet her freedom as well. Vidur cannot stand it anymore. He tells Dhrutarashtra that Draupadi is the most honorable daughter-in-law of Hastinapur. He says that Duryodhan has crossed the line of decency and Dhrutarashtra should part company with his son; he suggests that Duryodhan should be disowned and be thrown out. Duryodhan asks Vidur to shut up and says that if Vidur had not been his uncle, he would have had him killed that instant. He tells Vidur that he should know his place in front of the Crown Prince and should keep quiet like Bhishma and Drona or get out of the game hall.

The game continues, Dharmaraj bets his wife's freedom, and loses. Duryodhan wins Draupadi as his personal maid and sends for her. She refuses to come and asks the messenger to

The game of dice

go back to the game hall and ask the elders on her behalf if Dharmaraj had lost his freedom before betting her freedom in the game. Duryodhan, seeing everything go beyond his wildest imagination, is not in any mood to entertain any questions from Draupadi, now his maid. Vidur makes a feeble attempt in getting Dhrutarashtra and other elders to answer this valid question from Draupadi. Unfortunately, King Dhrutarashtra is completely blinded by his love for his son and he does not interfere. Duryodhan reminds both Bhishma and Drona that the State treasury is supporting them and that they better quietly watch what is happening.

By now, Duryodhan, encouraged by Shakuni, Karna, and Duhshasan, has taken leave of his common sense and decency. He wants total disgrace of Draupadi in public for all the insults he thinks he has suffered at the hands of Pandav brothers. He asks his younger brother Duhshasan to go to Draupadi and, if necessary, drag her into the hall. Duhshasan goes and asks Draupadi to come with him. She repeats her question and asks him to find the answer to her question. He tells her that she is now in no position to ask any question and that if she does not cooperate, he will drag her into the hall. Draupadi tries to argue with him that he must respect his sister-in-law but to no effect. He simply grabs her by her long and beautiful hair and drags her across the floor into the game hall.

Everyone is stunned to see Draupadi, the Queen of Indraprastha, the wife of five brave Pandav brothers, being dragged into the hall. Her five husbands also quietly watch the spectacle. Draupadi now repeats her question to King Dhrutarashtra, "Tell me if Dharmaraj had lost his freedom before he bet mine. If so, he had no right to do that. Also, personal freedom of his brothers and of his wife was not Dharmaraj's *property* that he can bet." Vidur appeals to all elders to look Draupadi right in the eye and answer her question. Duryodhan again protests that it was not he that made Dharmaraj do what he did and that all these questions are being asked only because he is on the winning side. Why, he asks, did anyone not stop Dharmaraj from betting all that he lost. He tells Draupadi that she is now his personal maid and invites her to come and sit in his lap. He tells her that all her five husbands are also his servants and would not lift a finger without his command. Karna also tells Draupadi that she, with her five husbands, is nothing but a prostitute and that Duryodhan could even ask her to sit naked in his lap.

Duryodhan then asks Duhshasan to strip Draupadi naked in front of everybody. Draupadi tells Dhrutarashtra that he is lucky to be blind so that he does not have to watch his son disrobe the King's daughter-in-law. She scolds all Pandav brothers for sitting there shamelessly while she is being violated. Draupadi is now completely helpless. Her brave husbands, her father-in-law, and Hastinapur elders are of no help to her. She now has only one person to turn for help. She closes her eyes and calls for Lord Krishna and tells him that he is her only refuge and prays for his help. Duhshasan starts to pull her sari off her. Shakuni, Duryodhan, and Karna watch with pleasure. Everyone else has his head down in shame.

Lord Krishna does not let Draupadi down. As Duhshasan keeps pulling Draupadi's sari, miraculously, Draupadi is continuously clad with new material. First, this miracle escapes everyone's attention. After Duhshasan makes a heap of saris, however, everyone realizes that this is really a miracle beyond their understanding. Duhshasan keeps pulling the sari off, but is eventually tired and gives up. Now it is Shakuni, Duryodhan, and Karna's turn to put their heads down in shame. Bheem gets up and makes two personal vows. He declares that one-day he will break Duryodhan's thighs for inviting Draupadi to sit on them, and will pull Duhshasan's arms off his body for attempting to disrobe Draupadi.

Draupadi begins to speak in rage. She first scolds her husbands for not coming to her help and then scolds the elders in the hall for allowing Duryodhan to take things this far. She then begins to curse the entire Bharat dynasty, when Gandhari enters the hall and begs her not to curse the entire dynasty for

Duhshasan attempts to disrobe Draupadi

the crimes of a few. Gandhari tells Duryodhan that any insult of Draupadi is an insult to all womanhood and that if he had enough courage, he should order Duhshasan to disrobe her too! She scolds her husband, King Dhrutarashtra, for being blinded by his fatherly love for his son to the extent that he allowed Duryodhan to cross the line of human decency. She tells Dhrutarashtra to go ask for Draupadi's forgiveness, although Draupadi may possibly not forgive him.

Dhrutarashtra now takes matters into his own hands. He declares all the results of the game of dice null and void, and orders Pandav brothers and Draupadi to go back to Indraprastha. Shakuni and Duryodhan are now devastated. But Shakuni is not about to give up! He tells Duryodhan to go back to his father and ask for one last throw of dice. The loser should spend twelve years in the forest followed by one year incognito; if during that thirteenth year, he is discovered, he should start the thirteen-year cycle all over again. Duryodhan goes to his father and gives him an ultimatum: "Permit me to play one more game or I shall commit suicide." Dhrutarashtra reluctantly gives his permission. Dharmaraj, against the advice of his brothers and others, accepts, saying, "As a Kshatriya, I cannot say no to an invitation to a war or to a game of dice." He must uphold his kshatriya dharma!

Dharmaraj again lets his younger brother Duryodhan go first, and Shakuni again throws the dice on behalf of Duryodhan. Dharmaraj loses this game as well, and Pandav brothers prepare to go to the forest. Draupadi insists that she must go with them; Kunti agrees to stay behind. She tells Dhrutarashtra that she could not possibly stay in the palace where he had allowed his sons to publicly humiliate her daughter-in-law. She chooses to live with Vidur and his wife. Draupadi and the five Pandav brothers leave for the forest. They now have a long difficult period ahead of them.

Pandav Brothers begin their Forest Life

The Pandav brothers build a modest hut and start their life in the forest. The brothers fetch firewood and food everyday and Draupadi cooks their meals on open fire. Duryodhan, Duhshasan, and Karna deliberately set up a royal camp close by and flaunt their wealth and luxury in front of the Pandav brothers. Once Duryodhan runs into a beautiful local tribal girl from the Nag tribe and attempts to entice her into his camp. He tells her that he is the Crown Prince of Hastinapur and she should visit him in his bedroom that evening. The girl feels insulted at this unwanted sexual attention and complains to her village council. The Nag tribesmen are furious at the arrogance of Duryodhan and attack his camp at night when Duryodhan, Karna, and others were drinking excessively while watching the performance of the royal dance troupe. Heavily inebriated Karna runs away and the Nag warriors easily capture Duryodhan and put him on trial on the spot. The chief personal bodyguard of Duryodhan then runs to the nearby Pandav camp for help in rescuing Duryodhan. Arjun and Bheem are very happy that arrogant Duryodhan is being taught a lesson that he should have received long time before. Dharmaraj, however, tells them that Duryodhan is their first cousin and it is their duty to help him. He tells them, " ... during our family disputes, it may be that we are five against our hundred Kaurav cousins. When it comes to a third party dispute, however, we all are one hundred and five." So Bheem and Arjun rescue Duryodhan from the Nag tribe and he returns to Hastinapur in humiliation.

Arjun Acquires Divine Weapons in the Heaven

Lord Krishna knows fully well that Dhrutarashtra's dreams and Duryodhan's evil nature have now made war inevitable. Consequently, he advises Pandav brothers to start preparing for the upcoming war. He tells Dharmaraj that Arjun should go to the heavens and acquire various types of divine weapons from Indra, Shiva, and other Gods.

Arjun then undertakes severe penance, wins over Gods, and enters heaven. There he acquires several weapons and gets trained in their use. At the suggestion of his father God Indra, he also gets training in music and dance. Arjun actually questions Indra about the usefulness of this training in the upcoming war. Indra assures him that the training was very vital and that Arjun would soon know its purpose.

. While in the heavens, a royal dancer named Urvashi falls in love with Arjun. These heavenly dancers are blessed with endless youth and beauty, and their primary function is to entertain Gods and other heavenly visitors. Arjun knew that Urvashi had stayed as a wife with one of his ancestors. He, therefore, tells Urvashi that she is like a mother to him and that he could never be romantically involved with her. Urvashi explains to Arjun that normal rules of relationship do not apply to heavenly dancers who live forever, and that she does not need to abide by human ethics based on the life-and-death cycles. Arjun, however, assures her that he could see her only as a mother and what she had in mind was forever impossible. Urvashi is enraged at this rebuff and curses Arjun to be impotent forever. Later at the behest of Indra, she relents and limits her curse to be valid for one year of Arjun's choosing. Indra tells Arjun that this curse and his training in music and dance would be useful to him during the year he and his brothers must spend incognito.

During one of the very important episodes in the forest life, Dharmaraj answers the questions posed to him by Yaksha, a divine character. Mahabharat uses such episodes to espouse certain philosophy and to give lessons in Hindu Thought. The details of the episode itself such as how Yaksha happened to ask Dharmaraj these questions are not of any significance. In fact, the meeting between the two appears to be quite contrived. Some of the questions and the answers are, however, as follows:

What is heavier than the Earth?	Mother
Who is taller than the sky?	Father
What travels faster than wind?	Mind
What has fully covered the universe?	Ignorance
What is laziness?	Not doing one's duty
Who is a happy person?	One who is free of obligations
What is really a sacred bath?	One that cleans up one's mind
What is blacker than the black ink?	A spot on one's character
What is modesty?	Staying away from things one should not do
What is compassion?	Wishing happiness for everyone
What is the best marvel of the world?	Everyone knows that death is certain but thinks that it would not happen to him

A Year Incognito

As the twelve-year period of forest life comes to an end, the Pandav brothers arrive in the court of the King of the Matsya Nation and take up jobs there. Dharmaraj works as the King's courtier and Bheem works as the royal cook. Arjun chooses to go through Urvashi's curse now and becomes a eunuch, working as a music and dance teacher to Princess Uttara. Nakul and Sahadev take care of horses and cows respectively, and Draupadi becomes the personal maid of Matsya Queen. The royal family of Indraprastha is now working as commoners in the Matsya Kingdom. Several months go by quite uneventfully.

As the year comes to an end, Queen's brother Keechak, who is also the Commander-in-Chief of Matsya army, happens to see Draupadi in the royal hall. He is struck by her incredible beauty and lusts after her, and invites her to his chamber. Draupadi tells him that she is happily married, and that it is his duty to protect every woman's honor as his mother's. Keechak, however, tells her that he is the Commander-in-Chief, and no one including the King himself, has any power to stop him. Draupadi then consults with Arjun and Bheem and arranges to meet one night with Keechak in the royal dance hall. Keechak comes there as planned and is killed there by Bheem.

Back in Hastinapur

Duryodhan is furious that his spies lose track of Pandav brothers and that their identities have not yet been exposed. All this time, Shakuni, Duryodhan, Duhshasan, and Karna have been hoping that Pandav brothers would be identified and would proceed to stay in the forest for another twelve years. The news of Keechak's death reaches Hastinapur. The circumstance of his death is, however, quite puzzling and its importance is not lost on Karna. Keechak was a very reputed warrior, and only six people were considered to be capable of killing him in combat: Balram (Krishna's brother), Bhishma, Drona, Duryodhan, Karna, and Bheem. Karna quickly concludes that it must have been Bheem that killed Keechak and that Pandav brothers are hiding in the royal palace of Matsya King.

Duryodhan wants to attack Matsya Kingdom and expose the identity of Pandav brothers. He knows that, if Pandav brothers choose to remain in hiding and not to come to the help of Matsya King, Hastinapur army would easily defeat

Matsya army. He is, however, equally sure that after accepting for almost a year the hospitality of Matsya King, Pandav brothers will find themselves duty bound to come to his help. He is sure that Pandav brothers will find forest life for another twelve years far more acceptable than running away from a guest's dharma to help the host. Without telling his father the real reason, Duryodhan somehow gets his permission to attack Matsya Kingdom.

Bhishma, Drona, Kripa, Karna, Duryodhan, and the Hastinapur army now march toward Matsya borders. As expected Pandav brothers take up arms in defense of Matsya. As a form of respectful greeting, Arjun first shoots arrows at the feet of his great-grand-father Bhishma and his guru Drona. They all now recognize Arjun, and Duryodhan declares that there is no need to continue the war because Pandav brothers have now been exposed. He tells Pandav brothers to go back to the forest right away. Everyone now comes to know that Duryodhan had undertaken this action simply to expose Pandav identity. Bhishma and others tell him that by some mathematical calculations the period of incognito life for Pandav brothers had ended one day before that encounter. The war then begins and Arjun single-handedly fights with all the brave warriors of Hastinapur and sends them back in defeat.

King Matsya thanks all the Pandav brothers profusely and asks for their forgiveness for treating them as servants of the royal family. Dharmaraj, however, thanks him instead for giving them shelter in their hour of need. Arjun also asks Princess Uttara if she would marry his son Abhimanyu. She consents and the wedding takes place in a big ceremony.

Winds of War

Everyone in the Pandav camp debates how Pandav brothers should get their Indraprastha Kingdom back. They all know that Duryodhan would not easily give it back and that war is inevitable. Lord Krishna, however, says that Pandav brothers should simply ask Dhrutarashtra to give them their Indraprastha back and see what happens. He reminds everyone that soldiers in Duryodhan's army had not personally done any injustice to Draupadi or to Pandav brothers, and it is they who would lose their lives by the thousands in any war. War should never be started for any personal vendetta or for fulfilling anyone's vows. It should only be fought in defense of *right against wrong.* He recommends that Dharmaraj send an ambassador to Hastinapur and make an attempt to get Indraprastha back without initiating a war.

In Hastinapur as well, everyone is debating what should be done next. Vidur advises Dhrutarashtra not to wait to hear from Dharmaraj, but to send for Pandav brothers and to simply give them their Indraprastha back. He tells Dhrutarashtra that his duty to Hastinapur as its King far outweighed his duty to Duryodhan as a father. Vidur also tells Bhishma and Drona that by blindly supporting Dhrutarashtra, they are really not defending Hastinapur. Their silence would be interpreted as their tacit approval of Duryodhan's agenda, Shakuni's duplicity, and the uncivilized behavior of Karna and Duhshasan. Queen Gandhari also tells Dhrutarashtra that she would like the history to show that he and his sons are as respectable as their ancestors, and that he should take a decision befitting a Kuru king.

Dharmaraj's ambassador arrives in Hastinapur and meets with Dhrutarashtra and his ministers in the royal chambers. He tells them that Pandav brothers have fulfilled their obligations under the game of dice and that they now wish to return to Indraprastha and resume their rule. Dhrutarashtra tells the ambassador that he would consider Dharmaraj's message and would soon get back to him. The next day, Dhrutarashtra sends Sanjay, his charioteer, to Dharmaraj as his personal ambassador. He confides in Sanjay that he cannot ask Pandav brothers to *forget and forgive,* and he cannot also let his son fight a losing war. He asks Sanjay to give Pandav brothers blessings on his behalf and ask them to stay happy in Matsya where they are.

When Sanjay meets Pandav brothers, Arjun asks him if he was sent by the *King of Hastinapur*, or by the *father of Duryodhan*, or by *their uncle*. Sanjay says that he does not understand the question because all these three are the same. Lord Krishna, however, explains to Sanjay that the division of Hastinapur was not done by Dhrutarashtra the King, but by Dhrutarashtra the father. The person who kept quiet at the uncivilized behavior of Duhshasan was Dhrutarashtra the father, not the King or the uncle. Sanjay says he would not know how to answer Arjun's question and repeats Dhrutarashtra's message that Pandav brothers should stay happy where they now are.

Dharmaraj gives his response to Dhrutarashtra's message: "If Duryodhan had asked, as my younger brother, for Indraprastha, I would have gladly given him that. But we cannot accept any injustice done to us. We respect all the elders of Hastinapur. If they choose to side with injustice, however, we are not afraid to fight them. We prefer peace with justice, but we are ready for war as well. It is your choice."

Both Arjun and Duryodhan Seek Krishna's Help

As the two sides take steps towards war, various kings and princes start choosing sides in the upcoming conflict. Shakuni tells Duryodhan that he should try to get Krishna's help so that his large well-trained Dwarka army would fight on his side. Duryodhan, therefore, goes to Dwarka to talk to Krishna. Arjun also wants Lord Krishna on his side. He is not even thinking about Krishna's army however when he comes to Dwarka.

Duryodhan enters Krishna's chamber first and finds him taking a nap. He sits on a chair near the headboard of Krishna's bed and waits. In a matter of minutes, Arjun walks in, sees Krishna napping, and sits on a chair at his feet. Naturally, when Krishna wakes up, he sees Arjun first and asks him why he is there. Duryodhan interjects that he was there first. Both Arjun and Duryodhan tell Krishna that they are there to seek his help in the upcoming war. Krishna tells both of them that since he is related to both, he will not help one against the other. He adds that he will not take up arms in any potential war and that he will separate himself from his army. There is thus a choice of help from Dwarka: unarmed Krishna on one side and his huge well-equipped army on the other. Furthermore, Krishna says that Arjun should have the first choice because he is younger than Duryodhan and that Krishna saw him first.

The stage is now set! Duryodhan is really interested in the army; Arjun is only interested in Krishna. Arjun has the first choice and Duryodhan is worried that Arjun will choose the army. To Duryodhan's surprise and relief, Arjun says that he is not there to ask for the army to begin with, and that he just wants Lord Krishna on his side, even if he is unarmed. Arjun asks the Lord to be his charioteer and he agrees. Duryodhan says that he is happy to oblige Arjun and take Krishna's army to fight on the side of Hastinapur.

This story of Arjun and Duryodhan visiting Lord Krishna is highly symbolic in nature and is filled with mystical message. In ancient Hindu cultures, students attended residential schools run by specific teachers, known as gurus. The guru and his wife were the surrogate parents of these students. The guru sat on a small platform, and the students sat at his feet on the floor. Consequently, sitting at someone's feet has long been identified as a form of high respect for and willingness to receive knowledge from that person. Both Duryodhan sitting near the headboard and Arjun sitting at Lord's feet, therefore, are filled with the hidden message about Duryodhan's arrogance and of Arjun's humility. There is also another important message that Lord's direction and guidance are far more valuable than help from any army.

Arjun and Duryodhan seek Krishna's help

Lord Krishna's Peace Mission

Lord Krishna wants to make one last attempt at peace with Hastinapur. He tells Draupadi that in spite of all that had happened to her and Pandav brothers, peace would still be preferable to war because of the terrible price the innocent civilians and soldiers would pay in any armed conflict. When two adults decide to fight, it really signifies a defeat of reason. In a conflict between two parties, both cannot be on the side of dharma. One should fight a war only when it is necessary to protect dharma. Hastinapur now prepares for a peace mission by Lord Krishna. Vidur again recommends that Indraprastha should be unconditionally returned to Dharmaraj. Bhishma also asks Dhrutarashtra to remember that Krishna was coming to Dhrutarashtra — the King of Hastinapur, and not to Dhrutarashtra — the father of Duryodhan.

Bhishma clearly faces a conflict between his vows and his conscience. His vows compel him to fight on the side of Hastinapur, but his conscience wants Pandav brothers to win. He tells Karna that they would never win the war because they are defending injustice, and even advises Karna to get out of Duryodhan's shadow. Karna, of course, reiterates that he is eternally indebted to Duryodhan and could not now abandon him at the time of his greatest need.

The next day, Krishna meets Dhrutarashtra and his cabinet in the royal assembly hall. He tells everyone that he has not brought any formal proposal from Dharmaraj but that Pandav brothers would agree to anything he agrees to. Krishna gives an eloquent speech to the assembly: "Oh Dhrutarashtra! There can only be one winner in a war although both sides will certainly lose a lot. Millions of innocent soldiers and civilians will die. Ultimately, history will hold you responsible for this unnecessary disaster. History will not question Shakuni about his cheating at the game of dice, it will not ask Duryodhan and Karna about their uncivilized behavior towards Draupadi, and it will certainly not question Duhshasan for dragging Draupadi by her hair into this assembly hall. It will, however, question you about these things because you — the King — are the ultimate authority here, and you have allowed these things to happen in this chamber. This is a dispute within the family. Even if you win the war, would you be happy to see your nephews dead? So avoid this war by returning Indraprastha to Pandav brothers."

Duryodhan tells Krishna that he would not give an inch of any territory to Pandav brothers. So Krishna should go back if he does not have any other proposal. Krishna then tells Dhrutarashtra that Pandav brothers will be happy with just five small villages. Duryodhan rejects even this demand, and attempts to have Krishna arrested. Lord Krishna, however, then shows his divine form and leaves the assembly hall.

Karna Comes to Know His True Identity

With the failure of his peace mission, Krishna heads back to Dharmaraj. Before leaving, however, he makes an attempt to bring Karna to the side of Pandav brothers. He first tells Karna that there is something fundamentally wrong in siding with injustice, and that this should outweigh any gratitude Karna may feel to Duryodhan. "Sometimes," Krishna adds, "it is better to stay indebted than to do something immoral to pay off the debt."

Karna, however, responds that he should have thought about all this before accepting his debts, and now he must act irrespective of the consequences. Krishna finally tells Karna that he really is the first son of Kunti. Krishna adds, "Pandav brothers will accept you as their elder brother and will follow you to the ends of the earth. You will be the King of Indraprastha and eventually of Hastinapur, and Dharmaraj will be too glad to be your Crown Prince. So please come with me and join your brothers."

Karna is devastated to hear this. He feels that now he would not be able to fight his younger brothers and that he has essentially lost the war before its beginning. He tells Lord Krishna," I know that with you on the Pandav side, Duryodhan can never win the war; nevertheless, I am indebted to Duryodhan and now must fight on his side. Please do not tell Pandav brothers about my identity before my death. If they know this now, Dharmaraj will surely hand over his Indraprastha to me, and I will feel obliged to give it to Duryodhan. This way, Pandav brothers would not be able to fight for justice."

Karna Gives up His Divine Armor

The character of Karna is a special one in Mahabharat. He is born as a kshatriya to Kunti and Sun God. He is, however, raised as a charioteer's son. Pandav brothers and Draupadi constantly put him down. He is a great warrior but everyone accepts Arjun to be the greatest. Fate has really dealt him a lousy deck of cards. He, however, is known for one thing. At the end of his daily prayers to Sun God, if anyone asked him for anything, Karna never says no. This is his single-most identity: *the greatest giver of the universe.*

Now that the war is approaching, Indra God is understand-ably worried. His son Arjun cannot win the war without defeating Karna and Karna is born with eternal, impenetrable armor given to him by his father, Sun God. Indra plans to go to Karna during his daily prayers and ask for his armor. Sun God comes to know about this and warns Karna about Indra's impending visit. He asks Karna to *just say no* and send Indra back. Karna, however, very stoically replies, "I have been cheated by fate out of my mother's love and of my identity. Everyone constantly insults me as being a charioteer's son. I have nothing to fall back on other than what I have achieved myself. Now I only have my reputation as the greatest giver, and I will not compromise it even if it costs me my life." Sun God would not have expected anything less from his brave son. He then tells Karna that Indra God would feel sorry for the injustice he would do to Karna in asking for his armor, and would want to give him something in return. At the time, Karna should, Sun God adds, ask for a powerful divine weapon for use against Arjun.

One day Indra comes to Karna at his daily prayers and asks for his armor. As expected Karna gives it to him and gets the divine weapon from Indra. Except for that weapon, Karna is now defenseless against Arjun.

Karna's Promise to Kunti

Kunti visits Karna during one of his morning prayers. She tells him that she is his real mother and that he should come and join his brothers. Karna is overwhelmed by this meeting and comes to tears. He, however, tells her that she should not call herself his mother. He says, " When I was insulted over all these years as being a charioteer's son, you kept quiet. Why didn't you come forward and scream to the world that I was your son? When everyone shunned me, Duryodhan became my friend and gave me everything. I shall forever be indebted to Duryodhan and I cannot leave him now. Indra God took my armor and now both you and Krishna have completely disarmed me by revealing to me my true identity. So simply ask me what you came to ask for. You know I will not say no."

Kunti tells Karna that he should come with her and she would proudly tell the whole world that he is her son. She does not ask him for anything. Karna, however, tells her that he will give her something anyway. He says, "I promise that I shall fight only with Arjun because only that would be a fight between equals. This means that at the end of the war, only one of us will survive. This way, you will still have your five sons at the end of the war."

It is quite unbelievable how the author of Mahabharat has described the inner feelings of Karna, his doubts about his identity while growing up, his fight for respect for his achievements, his search for his biological mother, and his feelings of being abandoned at birth. All the psychological conflicts faced by Karna completely mirror those faced by adoptees today.

Pre-War Days

Everyone is sure that the war between Pandav brothers and Hastinapur is imminent. Vidur goes to Dhrutarashtra and resigns as Hastinapur's Chief Minister. Vidur tells him that a King deserves to have a Chief Minister who is fully behind this war, and since he does not support this war, it is his moral obligation to resign. The concept of a government official resigning because of policy differences is not new and is at least several thousand years old. Vidur resigns and goes home.

Bhishma is bound by his vows to fight in Duryodhan's camp. Drona is on the Hastinapur payroll and must now fight on Duryodhan's side as well. These two great warriors end up on the side of injustice! Duryodhan appoints Bhishma as his Commander-in-Chief.

Sanjay, the Royal Charioteer, Gets Divine Vision

Sage Vyas visits Hastinapur and offers Dhrutarashtra divine vision so that he could see what happens on the battlefield. Dhrutarashtra, however, tells Vyas that such a vision would be useless for him because he would not be able to recognize anyone. He, therefore, requests Vyas to give that divine vision to his charioteer Sanjay who can then describe to him what happens in the war. Vyas gives the divine vision to Sanjay and leaves.

Duryodhan prepares to leave for the battlefield. He goes to his mother, Gandhari, and seeks her blessing for victory. She, however, tells him that where there is justice, there will be Lord Krishna, and where there is Krishna, there will be victory.

Consequently, she says she cannot give him such a blessing. Duryodhan leaves without his mother's blessing.

Prior to the start of hostilities, Pandav brothers and Lord Krishna meet with Bhishma and seek his blessings. He gives his blessings for their victory. It must have been really a great sight to see the Commander-in-Chief wishing for his enemy's victory because justice was on the enemy's side. As one of the most respected elders of Hastinapur, they all ask Bhishma to lay down the rules of engagement by which the war should be fought. He enumerates the following rules:

1. Man should fight only with a man and not with a woman.

2. If anyone is unarmed, or fallen down with injuries, or running away, he should not be attacked.

3. Medical rescue teams should have a right of free passage and should not be attacked.

4. One warrior should be engaged by only one warrior and not by many at a time.

5. Daily hostilities should end at sunset.

6. Anyone surrendering to the enemy should be protected.

7. Soldiers from both sides should be free to visit each other after sunset.

Clearly, these rules support the notion that the war is to be fought in defense of justice and not for any personal reasons. Pandav brothers assure Bhishma, Duryodhan, Shakuni, and others that no one from the Pandav side will be the first one to break these rules. They make it clear, however, that if anyone on Duryodhan's side broke any rule first, Pandav side will not unilaterally abide by these rules.

First Day of War and Bhagwat Gita

The two armies stand face to face on the battleground. The five Pandav brothers and many kings and princes are on one side. Bhishma, Drona, Kripa, Duryodhan, Duhshasan, Shakuni, Karna,Ashwatthama (Drona's son), and several other kings and princes are on the opposite side.Arjun asks Krishna to take his chariot to the center stage and Krishna does so. Arjun now takes a look at all the warriors facing him. He sees his uncles and cousins, his guru Drona, his beloved great-grand-uncle Bhishma, his friends, and other close relatives poised for war. All these years,Arjun had thought about avenging the insult of Draupadi and had prepared for just this war. The fact that all these relatives are poised for war was fully expected and should hardly have been a surprise for Arjun.At the last minute, however, he could not bear to see that sight. He is now completely disillusioned and depressed and loses his nerve to fight. He tells Krishna that he really does not want to fight this war and that the victory would not mean much if he has to kill all these folks that are so dear to him. He simply throws his bow and arrows down and sits down all confused.

Lord Krishna now gives him a long discourse on Hindu metaphysics to convince him that it is his duty to fight in defense of dharma against anyone, who, for one reason or the other, chooses to fight on the other side.This discourse is the famous *Bhagwat Gita* and forms one of the most valuable elements of Hindu Thought. The metaphysical concepts presented in this book are no different than those of the Bhagwat Gita.A detailed discussion on Gita would be simply a repetition of everything discussed earlier in this book. Consequently, a very short synopsis is presented here for continuity.

Lord Krishna tells Arjun: "You are worrying about something that is really not worth worrying about.You are identifying Bhishma, Drona, and others you love with their physical bodies. Their essence is, however, their Atman — the indestructible and everlasting entity — and their bodies are simply like the clothes we wear. When a piece of clothing becomes old, we throw it away and wear a new one. Similarly, the Atman, on his unending journey towards awakening to reality, takes on different bodies. Consequently, the death of a body does not

Lord Krishna enlightens Arjun with the sublime message of Bhagwat Gita

mean the death of a person. You are not the one who caused them to be born, and you certainly are not the one who would cause them to die. Their life and death cycle is controlled by their karma. They were here before and will be here in the future. The ocean waves come and go. Neither do we celebrate their birth, nor do we lament their death. Childhood, youth, and old age are natural and inevitable for everyone who is born. Consequently, these things should not bother one who has awakened to reality. You should only do your duty and leave the rest to the cosmic forces. Your duty now is to fight this war for justice, and so get up and fight. You really have no control over winning and losing, so do your duty without paying any attention to the outcome of your actions. Any karma done without any desire for its fruit is non-binding and would not add to your sum-total of karma."

"All desires are based in duality and there is no place for them in the monist reality. Do not be affected by the duality of win-loss, success-failure, and happiness-sorrow. Give up the ungodly qualities of fear, anger, false pride, arrogance, lack of compassion, and ignorance. Strive to inculcate godly qualities of fearlessness, charity, non-violence, truth, desire-less action, peace, broad-mindedness, compassion, forgiveness, character, integrity, and honesty. Let your every waking moment be a pursuit of awakening."

"Give up all your desires and be happy within yourself. Do not be depressed with sorrow or be overjoyed with happiness. Just as a tortoise withdraws its legs and head under its shell, you withdraw all your senses inwards. Once you awaken to the ultimate reality and enter the world of monism, the sensual desires will automatically disappear. Control your behavior on the physical level, and that will surely purify your mind at the emotional level. Let the mind control your senses, and not the other way around."

"Whenever one thinks about various sense-objects, it creates a desire for these objects. When these desires are unfulfilled, it leads to anger. Anger leads to irrational behavior and it makes one forget about the need to follow the path of awakening. This ultimately leads to a wasted opportunity presented by being born a human being. Consequently, do not get distracted from your present duty to fight a war for justice. Get up and fight like a true kshatriya."

"Both you and I have been born innumerable times before. You do not remember any of your past lives, but I remember them all. I am the god-incarnate, and whenever the society is filled with evil, I arrange myself to be born here to restore the order. I am not bound by karma because all of my actions are without personal desire. Just listen to me and uphold dharma by fighting against everyone including your relatives and friends who have chosen to support injustice."

During this discussion, Krishna also gives Arjun divine vision and shows him his divine form. Arjun finally gets up and tells Krishna that all his doubts are gone and he is now ready to fight in defense of dharma.

The War Begins

Dharmaraj goes and bows before Bhishma, Drona, and Kripa, and seeks their permission to start the war. He also asks for their blessings; they all readily give him their blessing for victory. Dharmaraj declares to all that the impending war is in defense of dharma, and that it is not being fought for any personal gains. He invites anyone from either side to switch sides if they think justice is on the other side. One of Duryodhan's brothers actually comes over to Pandav side in response to this invitation.

Bhishma and Bed of Arrows

The war begins and there is death and destruction all over. One by one, Dhrutarashtra's sons are killed in combat. Even after nine days of fierce fighting, however, the end of war is no where in sight. Pandav brothers realize that unless something is done, this war may never end. Bhishma is an insurmountable obstacle, and has received a boon from his father that he can choose the time of his death. He has taken a vow that he will not go until he sees Hastinapur safe and sound from all directions. Furthermore, he has told Duryodhan that he would not kill Pandav brothers. In short, the Pandav brothers cannot kill Bhishma and Bhishma would not kill Pandav brothers. How is then this war going to end? Pandav brothers consult Lord Krishna for a way out of this dilemma. Krishna asks Dharmaraj to go to Bhishma and return the blessing of victory that Bhishma had given him earlier. Krishna says: "Bhishma knew very well that this situation was inevitable and he still chose to bless you with victory. So ask him how it would be possible. If not, let him take his blessing back."

Dharmaraj and Arjun now visit Bhishma in his camp. As usual, Bhishma comes forward to greet them and bless them. Dharmaraj tells him that he should not be giving such a blessing of victory because, "You know very well that only you are standing between us and our victory." Arjun adds that this is precisely why Lord Krishna has asked us to return your earlier blessing of victory. Bhishma smiles because he now knows that it is really Lord Krishna who is behind this scheme. He tells Arjun that Krishna knows that I cannot take back what I once gave. However, "Tell him that as a kshatriya, I cannot fight against a woman." Arjun tells Bhishma that he does not understand him because no one from the Pandav side also would fight a woman. Bhishma, however, brushes Arjun aside and assures him that Krishna would understand his message and would tell you what to do next.

This brings us back to the story of Amba, Ambika, and Ambalika, the three princesses that Bhishma had brought to Hastinapur to be married to his half-brother, the son of his father and Satyavati. When they all arrived in Hastinapur, Amba had told Bhishma that she was in love with someone else and could not marry Bhishma's half-brother. Bhishma, therefore, had sent Amba back to her father. There, Amba's fiancé had refused to marry her. Consequently, she had then returned back to Hastinapur and had insisted that Bhishma take her as his wife. Bhishma, of course, is bound by his vow to be celibate. Amba was then helpless because no one was powerful enough to force Bhishma to break his vow and marry her. She had then accused Bhishma of starting a chain of events on which he had no control and had told him that she was the real victim in all this. She had then vowed that she would somehow be the cause of Bhishma's death even if it took her several incarnations. Shikhandi, Draupadi's brother, is that Amba reincarnated. Only Lord Krishna, Bhishma, and Shikhandi know this, and as expected, Krishna understands the implication of Bhishma's message.

Krishna asks Arjun next day to take Shikhandi with him on his chariot. Duryodhan and Shakuni smell a rat when they see Arjun and Shikhandi coming towards Bhishma. Their attempts to shield Bhishma, however, fail and Shikhandi starts shooting arrows at Bhishma. As soon as Bhishma sees Shikhandi, he lays down his arms. Now taking Shikhandi as his shield, Arjun shoots arrows at Bhishma. One by one, dozens of arrows pierce through Bhishma's body and he collapses. With arrows halfway through his body, he lies down on a bed of arrows. He does not die however because only he can choose the time of his death, and he must wait until his beloved Hastinapur is safe and sound from all sides. He is, however, essentially taken out of war. Different warriors from both camps visit him regularly during the evening hours.

Death of Abhimanyu – Son of Arjun

Duryodhan appoints Drona as his next Commander-in-Chief. Drona develops a strategic plan to capture Dharmaraj so that the war would automatically end. He, however, knows that it would be impossible to capture Dharmaraj as long as Arjun was there to protect his brother. So Duryodhan promises

Bhishma on the bed of arrows

Drona that he would somehow take Arjun away from his brother, and Drona plans to use the famous Maze formation of his forces. Only Arjun and Krishna from the Pandav side knew how to successfully enter this formation, fight a battle, and back out to safety. Drona, therefore, thinks that with Arjun and Krishna away from the scene, Dharmaraj will have no option but to surrender. The trap is thus set for the next day, and Duryodhan goes to bed confident that war would soon end in his victory. King Dhrutarashtra, being continuously briefed by Sanjay, also rejoices at this possibility.

It is, however, partly true that only Arjun and Krishna knew how to penetrate Drona's Maze formation. Several years before, when Arjun's wife Subhadra was pregnant with Abhimanyu, one evening Arjun was describing to Subhadra the intricacies of the Maze formation. Abhimanyu in utero was listening to this conversation. Unfortunately, after Arjun described the entry procedure, Subhadra fell asleep before Arjun could talk about the exit procedure. As a result, Abhimanyu knew only how to get in but not how to back out of the Maze formation.

Next day, when Arjun is taken away from the center stage of the battlefield, Drona arranges the Maze formation as planned. Dharmaraj now has a dilemma on his hands. Abhimanyu tells his uncle Dharmaraj that he knows how to get in but not how to come out. Bheem suggests that the remaining four Pandav brothers should follow behind Abhimanyu and help him fight his way out. Dharmaraj is understandably reluctant to let young Abhimanyu shoulder this great burden. He also knows that Arjun would never forgive him if something happens to Abhimanyu. As Abhimanyu's eldest uncle, Dharmaraj considered himself responsible for the safety of his nephew. Everyone, however, quickly recognizes that there are really no good options to choose from. It is either sending Abhimanyu in or surrendering to Drona and ending the war that day. Dharmaraj finally agrees to let Abhimanyu lead the charge with his three uncles and several other warriors following closely behind.

Abhimanyu enters the Maze, but unfortunately, his uncles are held off and are unable to follow behind him. Abhimanyu is now all alone fighting his way into the Maze. At the end of the Maze, Abhimanyu finds Duryodhan, Duhshasan, Karna, Shakuni, Drona, Kripa, and Drona's son Ashwatthama, seven warriors in all, standing side by side, ready to fight him. All the seven seasoned warriors together fight with young Abhimanyu. Abhimanyu even protests to Drona that it is against the rules of war agreed upon by both sides before the beginning of the hostilities. Duryodhan, however, asks him to shut up and fight. After a fierce battle, Abhimanyu falls to the ground, injured and unarmed. Clearly, he thought, it would be highly irregular and against all rules for these elder warriors to continue attacking an unarmed and injured person. But Duryodhan and his friends have long thrown their decency away! The seven so-called Kshatriyas go ahead and kill unarmed and injured Abhimanyu anyway.

Death of Drona

Drona is the Guru of all Pandav brothers as well as of Duryodhan and other sons of Dhrutarashtra. He is well versed in the use of divine weapons and is known as a brave warrior. Lord Krishna tells Pandav brothers that it would not be easy to kill Drona. He says that only if Drona thinks his son Ashwatthama is dead, Drona will be overwhelmed with grief, and will lose interest in fighting. It would then be possible to kill him. Krishna asks Dharmaraj if he would be willing to tell a white lie in order to accomplish this. Dharmaraj is known for not telling a lie, and he would have to commit sin and ruin his reputation if he agreed to lie. Lord Krishna tells him that no price is large enough to defend dharma. Dharmaraj agrees and Krishna then comes up with a plan. As a part of this plan, Bheem kills an elephant named Ashwatthama, and starts screaming that Ashwatthama has died. Drona hears the commotion and hears people scream that Ashwatthama is dead. He, however, does not believe it and says that he would believe it only if Dharmaraj would confirm the news. So he goes towards Dharmaraj and asks him if Ashwatthama has just died. Dharmaraj says that it is true that Ashwatthama is dead; he, however, adds in a whispering tone so that Drona would not hear him, "But I do not know if it is an elephant or a human." Drona cannot bear to hear that his son is dead. He drops his weapons, closes his eyes, and sits down in the middle of the battlefield. Draupadi's brother, King Drupad's son, now quickly comes and beheads Drona with a sword.

End of Duhshasan, Karna, and Shakuni

Next day, Duryodhan appoints his friend Karna to be the next Commander-in-Chief. The day opens with a fierce fight between Duhshasan and Bheem. Bheem remembers fully well how Duhshasan had dragged Draupadi by her hair and had attempted to disrobe her in front of everyone; how Bheem had vowed to pull Duhshasan's arms off; and how he had vowed to let Draupadi avenge her insults by washing her hair with Duhshasan's blood. He knows that Draupadi would not braid her hair again until that happened. With this fire of revenge, Bheem is invincible and Duhshasan is no match for him that day. After a long and tiring battle, Bheem pulls Duhshasan's arms off his body and breaks open his chest. Bheem then drinks some of his blood as he had vowed to do, and brings some blood back to the camp for Draupadi. She now considers Duhshasan to be sufficiently punished for his ungodly uncivilized behavior towards her, and braids her hair for the first time since that day of the dice game in Hastinapur. Duryodhan is devastated to hear about the death of his closest and the only surviving brother, Duhshasan. Gandhari is now acutely aware that out of all her hundred sons, only Duryodhan is still living.

Everyone fully expects Arjun and Karna to fight a decisive battle the next day. Kunti visits Karna in his chambers. When Karna bows before her, she gives him a blessing for long life. Karna reminds her that Arjun, as his younger brother, had more right to that blessing than him. Karna also tells her that Gandhari has lost ninety-nine of her sons in the war and Kunti has not lost any yet. He says that if Hastinapur asks her what sacrifices she has made for the nation, he does not want her to be embarrassed because she has not made any. He adds that she should be ready to give at least one of her sons in service to the nation.

Karna now prepares for the battle next day. He is quite restless because he knew that he had two skeletons in his closet. Several years before, he had shot an arrow at sound and had accidentally killed a cow. The brahmin owner of the cow earned his living by selling her milk. He scolds Karna for his arrogance of shooting an arrow that he cannot control and curses him that his chariot would get stuck in the mud during the greatest battle of his life. Karna also had a second curse hanging on his head. When he was young, several famous gurus refuse to accept him as a student because he was *neither a prince nor a kshatriya.* He, therefore, had enrolled in a school by pretending to be a brahmin. When his guru comes to know this, he curses Karna that Karna would not remember the invocation of divine weapons at the time of his greatest need. Karna is sure that his end is now near, but does not really know how this is all going to play out. He is also acutely aware that he had earlier used the divine weapon given to him by Indra against another warrior. He now has no sure weapon against Arjun.

Next day, Arjun and Karna engage themselves in a battle. It is really a fight between equals and no one shows any sign of slowing down. Towards the end of the day, however, one of the wheels of Karna's chariot suddenly sinks into the ground, and the chariot tilts to a side. Karna is unable to stand and fight because the floor of the chariot is not level. He also has difficulty in remembering the invocations for activating different divine weapons. He knows that his karma is coming to haunt him. He gets down from his chariot and tries to free the wheel up. He asks Arjun to suspend his attack until he could free up the wheel. Arjun shows some hesitation when Krishna reminds him that Karna himself had not followed any rules of war and that he is a full partner in all the evil things perpetrated by Duryodhan and Shakuni. Krishna also reminds him that Karna is one of the seven who had killed his injured and unarmed son Abhimanyu. He asks Arjun to shoot the arrow without any hesitation. Karna dies in an instant. Sahadev kills Shakuni on the same day.

The news of Karna's death quickly spreads over both the camps. Duryodhan who had responded earlier very stoically to the death of all his brothers cries like a baby over the death of his beloved friend Karna. When hostilities are suspended at sunset, Kunti goes to the battleground, takes Karna's head in her lap and quietly weeps in grief. Pandav brothers are shocked to see the sight and ask her why she is crying over the death of their enemy. She finally reveals the truth that Karna was really her first son, eldest of the six Pandav brothers. Dharmaraj and his brothers are all devastated that they had killed their own eldest brother. Dharmaraj gets very angry with Kunti for keeping this secret for all these years; this terrible secret had caused the war, and Pandav brothers would never be able to get over this. He curses the entire womanhood that women would never be able to keep any secret.

Duryodhan goes to Bhishma who is still lying on his bed of arrows and informs him of Karna's death. Bhishma reveals the real identity of Karna to him and tells him that Karna had known that he was Kunti's son, and still had chosen to fight on Duryodhan's side. Duryodhan is overwhelmed by Karna's unquestioned loyalty to him. That night, Duryodhan gives Karna his last rites and bids him farewell. Duryodhan is now the only one left to continue the war.

End of the War

Duryodhan visits his mother Gandhari and again seeks her blessing for victory. She says that she still cannot do that and that he should go to Dharmaraj and seek some compromise. Duryodhan tells her that he does not want to insult all those who had died for him by seeking such a compromise at this time. He, however, also confesses that the Kingdom of Hastinapur has no use for him now if he cannot enjoy it with his brothers, Karna, and his friends. He adds that even if he wins the war the next day, he would give Hastinapur to Dharmaraj. He tells his mother that he would now go and get ready for the war next day.

The mother in Gandhari cannot face the prospect of death of her last surviving son, Duryodhan, wicked or not. She tells Duryodhan to take a bath in the river nearby and come to her absolutely naked. Duryodhan questions the propriety of such an action, but Gandhari assures him that there is nothing wrong for a mother to see her children naked. Duryodhan goes to the river, takes a bath, and walks back naked as instructed. On his way back to Gandhari, he meets Krishna. Krishna laughs and ridicules the idea of an adult male child standing naked in front of his mother. So Duryodhan wraps a little towel around his waist and goes to Gandhari. Gandhari prays to Lord Shiva, removes the strip of cloth tied over her eyes, and opens her eyes for the first time in decades. She puts the power of all her godly karma into her vision and looks at Duryodhan. She is shocked to see the little towel around his waist, and tells Duryodhan what terrible mistake he had made in not coming to her naked as she had ordered. She tells him that she had put a lot of moral force behind her vision and that all the parts of his skin that she saw would become an impenetrable armor. The parts covered by the towel would now be left vulnerable and unprotected. Duryodhan pleads with his mother that he would take the towel off and that she should take another look. Gandhari tells him that she would not have that power again in her vision.

Next day, Bheem and Duryodhan fight a duel. Both are experts at wielding the mace weapon. Bheem, however, quickly realizes that Duryodhan's skin had turned into an impenetrable armor, and that Duryodhan is able to withstand any amount of pounding. Lord Krishna then signals to Bheem that he should hit Duryodhan on his thighs. It is, however, against the rules of mace to hit anyone below the belt. When Bheem hesitates, Krishna reminds him that, during the game of dice, Duryodhan had insulted Draupadi by asking her to sit on his thighs, and that Bheem had vowed to break his thighs in punishment. Bheem then quickly follows Krishna's advice and kills Duryodhan by breaking both of his thighs.

With the death of Duryodhan, the war is over. The Pandav brothers win a decisive victory. The good wins over the evil. Hastinapur's uncounted millions paid the ultimate price for their King's blind ambition. Duryodhan, Duhshasan, Karna, and Shakuni paid for their ungodly arrogant behavior. Dharmaraj now ascends the throne of Hastinapur. Dhrutarashtra, Gandhari, and Kunti go to the forest to start a contemplative life. Seeing his Hastinapur safe and secure in good hands, Bhishma ends his life and goes back to his mother Ganga. After a few more years, Lord Krishna also decides to end his mission on the Earth and returns back to his heavenly abode as Lord Vishnu.

Pronunciation Key

a	act, bat, marry	oi	oil, joy, boil
å	age, paid, say	õõ	ooze, fool, too
ä	palm, balm, part	t	quattro (spanish)
e	edge, set, merry	th	that, either, smooth
ê	equal, seat, bee	u	pull, book, push
i	if, big, mirror	ü	rule, youth, mule
o	over, boat, no	û(r)	urge, burn, purge
ô	order, ball, raw	w	witch

Pronunciation of Sanskrit Words

Ashram	äshrûm	Atman	ätmûn
Bhagawat Gita	bhûgwût gêtä	Brahman	brûhmûn
Brahmin	brähmûn	Dharma	dhûrmû
Guru	gurü	Hindu	hindü
Karma	kûrmû	Kshatriya	kshûtriyû
Mahabharat	mûhäbhärût	Mahatma	mûhätmä
Mantra	mûntrû	Pran	prän
Ramayan	rämäyûn	Sanskrit	sûnskrut
Shudra	shõõdrû	Vaishya	vûishyû

Pronunciation of Proper Names

Abhimanyu	ûbhimûnyü	Amba	ûmbä
Ambalika	ûmbälikä	Ang	ûng
Angad	ûngûd	Arjun	ûrjun
Ashok	ûshok	Ayodhya	ûyodhyä
Baba	bäbä	Balaram	bûlräm
Bheem	bhêm	Bhishma	bhêshmû
Chaitanya	Chûitûnyû	Chitrakut	chitrûkõõt
Dandak	dûndûk	Dasharath	dûshûrûth
Devaki	dåwûkê	Dharmaraj	dhûrmûräj
Dhrutarashtra	dhrutûräshtrû	Dnyaneshwar	dnyänåshwûr
Draupadi	drûüpûdê	Drona	dronû

Drupad	drupûd	Duhshasa	duhshäsûn
Duryodhan	duryodhûn	Dushan	düshûn
Dwarka	dwärkä		

Gandhar	gändhär	Gandhari	gändhärê
Ganesh	gûnåsh	Ganga	gûngä
Gokul	gokul	Gujar	gujûr

Hanuman	hûnumän	Hastinapur	hûstinäpür

Indra	indrû	Indrajit	indrûjêt
Indraprastha	indrûprûsthû		

Jamuna	jûmunä	Janak	jûnûk
Jarasandh	jûräsûndh		

Kaikayi	kûikûyê	Kansa	kûns
Karna	kûrnû	Kaurav	kûurûv
Kausalya	kûusûlyä	Keechak	kêchûk
Kevat	kåvût	Khar	khûr
Kishkindha	kishkindhä	Kosal	kosûl
Kripa	krupû	Kumbhakarna	kumbhûkûrnû
Kunti	kuntê	Kuru	kuru
Kush	kush		

Lav	lûv	Laxmi	lûxmê

Madri	mädrê	Maharashtra	mûhäräshtrû
Maharshi	mûhûrshê	Mandakini	mûndäkinê
Manthara	mûnthûrä	Marich	märêch
Mathura	mûthurä	Matsya	mûtsyû
Menaka	månûkä	Mithila	mithilä

Nal	nûl	Nakul	nûkul
Nanda	nûndû	Neel	nêl
Nidra	nidrä		

Pandav	pändûv	Pandu	pûndu
Parashuram	pûrûshuräm	Pratap	prûtäp

Radha	rädhä	Radhakrishna	rädhäkrushnû
Raman	rûmûn	Ravan	rävûn
Rohini	rohinê		

Sahadev	sûhûdåw	Sai	säê
Sanjay	sûnjûy	Satyavati	sûtyûwûtê
Shabari	shûbûrê	Shakuni	shûkunê
Shantanu	shäntûnu	Shikhandi	shikhûndê
Shiradi	shirûdê	Shivaji	shiväjê
Shurpanakha	shõõrpûnûkhä	Sita	sêtä
Subhadra	subhûdrä	Sugriv	sugrêw
Sumitra	sumiträ		

Urmila	õõrmilä	Urvashi	õõrwûshê
Uttara	uttûrä		

Vali	wälê	Valmiki	wälmikê
Varnavrat	wärnäwrût	Vasishta	wasishtû
Vasudev	wûsudåw	Vibhishan	wibhêshûn
Vidur	widur	Vishal	wishäl
Vishnu	wishnõõ	Vishwamitra	wishwämitrû
Vyas	wyäs		

Yaksha	yûkshû	Yashoda	yûshodä